PLANTATION LIFE ON THE MISSISSIPPI

ST. LOUIS PLANTATION MANSION

The beautiful old home stands today on the original "Home plantation," land acquired over 150 years ago by Joseph Erwin. It was built by Edward J. Gay, just prior to the Civil War. Facing the Mississippi River a short distance below Plaquemine, it is a fine example of the architecture of the old days, one of the loveliest of the remaining plantation homes. The building is in a grove of oaks surrounded by lawn gardens. (Photograph by the author)

Plantation Life

on the Mississippi

by

WILLIAM EDWARDS CLEMENT
in collaboration with
STUART OMER LANDRY

A FIREBIRD PRESS BOOK

Gretna 2000

Manufactured in the United States of America

Published by Pelican Publishing Company, Inc.
1000 Burmaster Street, Gretna, Louisiana 70053

To
My Wife, Laura McCloskey Clement.

—W. E. C.

CONTENTS

LIST OF ILLUSTRATIONS

(Art work and maps by Hereford Studios)

PREFACE

This book is an effort to record a mode of living which was gracious and happy, a pattern of life that is long since "gone with the wind."

In Chapter One I give my personal reminiscences of plantation life in the old South after the Civil War. When I was a boy slavery had been abolished some twenty years, but except that the planter aristocracy were poorer and many had lost their plantations and moved away, the way of life was much the same as in ante-bellum days.

Since I am from Iberville Parish and since this Parish is historically important, I have included sketches of some of the early citizens who helped to create plantation life before the War Between the States. I have told about some of the founding fathers of Iberville, and related their private histories which were often replete with action, romance and achievement.

I must ask the reader's indulgence for having emphasized the careers of members of my own family. This preponderance of family history is due to the fact, that, in the first place, they were interesting personalities and their stories are worth telling, and in the second place, the facts about them are more accessible.

Joseph Erwin, my great-great-grandfather, who was not only one of Iberville Parish's earliest settlers and, at one time, one of Louisiana's wealthiest and most progressive men, but he was the progenitor of hundreds of descendants now scattered all over the United States, many of whom have achieved fame and fortune. Emphasis has been placed on "Captain" Erwin's background, because it is that of the ancestors of millions of Americans and interesting to read about.

I have reprinted from Parton, details of the duel with Charles H. Dickinson, the son-in-law of Joseph Erwin, not only because this is a celebrated "affair of honor" and an interesting description of a duel, but because it had a direct bearing upon Iberville Parish, in that many of its families who later became prominent moved to that locality as a result of the tragic encounter between Gen. Andrew Jackson and Charles Dickinson. Among these were the members of Erwin's own family, his sons Isaac and John; his sons-in-law, Nicholas Wilson, John B. Craighead and Col. Andrew Hynes; his grandson and ward, Charles Dickinson; his grandson Wm. Blount Robertson, Jr., his wife's nephew Wm. Thompson, a large land-owner; his friend Dr. Charles Clement, and later the Gays, Edwards and others.

In my search for facts and details I was fortunate in uncovering two documents of great interest—from a human relationship standpoint as well as from a literary and historical point of view. One of these is a pamphlet, TRUTH IS NO SLANDER by Samuel Clement, now in the Library of Congress at Washington, and the other the diary of Michael Schlatre describing the Last Island storm, the original manuscript of which is in the Louisiana State Library at Baton Rouge. The Diary was published in the Louisiana Historical Quarterly for July 1937, with an introduction by Dr. Walter Prichard, after having been carefully edited by Dr. Orr. Because of the limited circulation of the Quarterly most people have never read or heard of Schlatre's Diary. It is worthy of wider recognition and I hope that my small effort here will help to bring this about.

Samuel Clement's brochure is an attack and criticism of General Andrew Jackson. It is particularly pertinent now, as there is a growing interest in Jackson and his times. Marquis

James wrote his BORDER CAPTAIN, and not so long ago the AGE OF JACKSON by Schlessinger was published, and then only recently Irving Stone's THE PRESIDENT'S LADY, the story of Mrs. Jackson. Above all Clement's TRUTH IS NO SLANDER gives many details and caustic comments about the Battle of New Orleans, and should be of great interest to all Louisianians. I have not reprinted these two documents in full, but have used excerpts from them liberally.

As I have said this book while centering much attention on plantation life in the Iberville section, is not intended as a history of this particular Parish. A well written chronicle of the old and newer days has already been done by the late Albert L. Grace of Plaquemine in his book THE HEART OF THE SUGAR BOWL, the Story of Iberville Parish. In the years following my departure from Iberville it was always a great pleasure to visit Plaquemine and discuss Parish matters with the well-informed "gentleman of the old school," Mr. A. L. Grace.

The well-edited LOUISIANA HISTORICAL QUARTERLY, has been of particular assistance. From the "Quarterly" I took material for the Gov. Hebert chapter and from it have copied a considerable part from Michael Schlatre's Diary. From this journal I have taken excerpts about the leading character of this book, using Alice Pemble White's "Plantation Experiences of Joseph and Lavinia Erwin, 1807-1836." Miss White's thesis covers 135 pages and goes into remarkable detail, indicating much research. In her "Introduction," written in 1944, she said, very interestingly:

With the uncovering of many mildewed, blurred, and faded records that have reposed in their sheath of dust for years in remote attics and cellars, a consciousness of plantation significance has entered the latest histories and the present-day historian takes a more critical and accurate view of the history, romance, and tradition of the "Land of Dixie" than those of the previously prevailing literature.

I have illustrated my book with pictures—not only of these outstanding personages but of a number of Iberville's fine old ante-bellum homes. Unfortunately a very considerable number of these have disappeared as a result of either the river's encroachment or by reason of fire.

In recording these histories, incidents and anecdotes about some of Iberville's past leaders, I have gotten such information as I could from the records that were available, many from private sources.

I would like to thank Alfred H. Clement of Mentone, Alabama; Edward J. Gay of St. Louis Plantation, Iberville Parish (ex-United States Senator from Louisiana); Ashley Wilson of Buffalo, New York; Mrs. Charles J. McClung of Knoxville, Tennessee (the former Miss Anna Gay of St. Louis Plantation, Iberville Parish); Mrs. Oric Bates of Groton, Massachusetts (the former Miss Natica Yznaga Inches); Mr. Edward Desobry of New Orleans; Mrs. W. B. Middleton of Plaquemine, Louisiana (the former Miss Maria Schwing); Paul E. Marioneaux, Principal of Shady Grove School, Rosedale, Louisiana; Mrs. Harry M. Row of Sunny Side Plantation, Maringouin, Louisiana (the former Miss Lenora Barrow); Dr. Pierce Butler of Natchez, Mississippi; Miss Eleanora G. Semmes of Frederick, Maryland; A. E. Becnel, Jr. of Plaquemine, Louisiana; Mrs. V. C. Folse of Plaquemine, Louisiana; Mrs. George M. Murrell; Mrs. George Pigman; Miss Vera Morel; Mrs. John E. Morrill; and Raymond J. Martinez, all of New Orleans, for their interest in my undertaking and their valuable aid.

I particularly want to thank Charles H. Dickinson of Pacoima, California, a great-grandson of the Dickinson killed in the duel, for his invaluable help. From him I obtained old letters, newspaper clippings, family genealogies and the miniature of Charles Dickinson, his great-grandfather.

Included in an appendix are the genealogies of several of the families about whom I have written. These genealogies have been authenticated as to dates, and printed, they will record permanently the correct information about these ancestors which will be of interest to their thousands of descendants of the present and future generations.

In justice to my able collaborator, Stuart O. Landry, I must say this book would never have been attempted if it were not for his availability in editing and helping gather together the great mass of needed information. I was especially fortunate as the Landry files already included interesting data on the pioneering geniuses of Iberville Parish, due to the fact that like myself he is a direct descendant of Joseph Erwin.

WILLIAM EDWARDS CLEMENT

INTRODUCTION

By HARNETT T. KANE

(Nationally known New Orleans writer, author of twenty-three best sellers, which have reached several million copies, including "Plantation Parade," "Natchez," "Gone Are the Days," "Bride of Fortune," "Lady of Arlington," "Gallant Mrs. Stonewall," "Queen New Orleans," "Louisiana Hayride" and others.)

Some years ago, I was fortunate in that William E. Clement permitted me to see in manuscript form his lively and authoritative "Plantation Life on the Mississippi." Since then, on a number of occasions, I have reread this volume and consulted it for verification of many details in the writing of a number of my books, magazine and other writings.

Mr. Clement understands, out of intimate experience and long, full observation, the scene and the people of whom he writes. He has had a unique opportunity to study the rich subject, and he has taken happy advantage of his opportunity. We, his readers, are the beneficiaries of that situation.

He does not over-elaborate, over-tell, or over-burden the meaningful story that he gives. In the simplicity of his volume there is perhaps its greatest conviction, its strongest effect.

William E. Clement describes the Roosevelt family's pioneering Mississippi River steamboat and its epochal arrival in New Orleans in the 1812 period. He tells of one of his forebears, Samuel Clement, captain of the third steam vessel on the great stream; of Samuel Clement's role in the dramatic fighting at the Battle of New Orleans. The author also offers vivid details of the tragic duel between Andrew Jackson and Charles Dickinson — one of the harshest of all American meetings on the so-called "field of honor." And Mr. Clement contributes an impressive account of the "Last Island" storm, which Lafcadio Hearn gave to the world in his "Chita."

But above all this volume offers a fascinating portrayal of daily life in the Louisiana Sugar Bowl of the Reconstruction era. As Mr. Clement portrays it, the tempestuous period also had hours of quiet and simple plantation existence. For several years I have retained a vivid memory of Mr. Clement's loving recreation of those days in the sugar area of Iberville parish and its environs. Rereading the book in recent weeks, I have been newly impressed with it. It has a flavor that is very much *sui generis*, unlike that of any other that has been written on Louisiana.

CHAPTER I

MY YOUTH ON A SUGAR PLANTATION

The days of my childhood were indeed happy. I lived on "Retreat Plantation," near Plaquemine and our little family comprised Grandmother Clement, her daughter, Henrietta, known to us as Aunt Yetta, my widowed mother and my brother Alfred. We were well supplied with good servants and they were a part of the family life. There was an excellent faithful and happily endowed colored cook, "Aunt" Josephine. "Aunt" to us younger fry, by plantation courtesy of the old days, was a mark of respect due those older and long-service people of the dark-skinned race who guarded and served us well. Then there was the yard man, "Uncle" Anthony, an ex-slave of truly patriarchal appearance. The milk-maid was "Aunt" Tilda, who not only milked the four or five cows, but looked after the little dairy under the big, cool cistern, churned the butter and made our delicious brand of cream cheese.

The slightly garrulous "Uncle" Ike was our coachman. He took care of the family horses, carriages and buggies and the stable. Ike, in stately array, was driver of the big family barouche on Sundays or special occasions. Ordinarily, however, we youngsters and my mother, did our own driving. I must not fail to mention a grand old white-haired ex-slave, the carpenter, "Uncle" Aaron who lived nearby in a little cottage, readily available when his services were required. Two of his daughters still live—or did up until very recently—in this same little old cottage on the plantation. "Uncle" Aaron was a terrible stutterer, but a splendid worker. One of his daughters usually served as personal maid to Grandma Clement. Brother Alfred had a small colored boy, George, who acted as his faithful bodyguard. I had "Little Ike," who, likewise, was detailed to play with me and act as my helper when needed.

This colored boy "helper" arrangement was an old southern custom. The white boy who has not had a colored playmate, as Will Percy that well known Mississippian wrote, has not really lived. But it was a plantation custom and the colored boy was usually slightly older than his white companion. The idea seemed to be that he would thus help train the master's son. Many southerners, who later gained distinction have testified as to the devotion of the two playmates to each other.

In our home it was a part of the duty of these two little colored boys to take turns in pulling the cord which operated the large "punkah" fan over the big dining room table, at meal time. One of these youngsters would seat himself high up on the stairway leading to the attic at the end of the dining room. From that vantage point he would pull the cord which caused the big wooden fan to swing backwards and forwards, keeping the flies off, and helping to cool the diners, often eight or ten people at the table. In those days there were of course no electric fans, yet only a few families seemed to have made even the progress we had in the art of cooling by installing a punkah. The only trouble with this arrangement was that the monotonous pulling of the rope and the swish of the fan induced drowsiness and the little colored boy would—at times— go to sleep. The fan would gradually slow down to nothing. A call from somebody would wake him up and we would be favored with a furious pulling of the cord for a while. Then if the soporific tendency asserted itself again, there would be another slow down and another harsh return from dreamland. Even so, the arrangement worked out nicely and visitors always seemed to remember our punkah and would congratulate the family on this idea.

Our rambling old Retreat Plantation* house with its many log-fire chimneys and outer "galleries" centered around a main building with a most comfortable, old-fashioned large living room into which visitors walked after being received hospitably at the main entrance. Two ells reached out from the two rear corners in opposite direction, one contained large extra bedrooms, the other kitchen, store-rooms and laundry. There was ample room for the family, and accommodations for the flow of guests from New Orleans—dear ones, friends and relatives who were almost constantly coming and going— much to the enlivenment and interest of all, especially for my brother and myself. It was quite usual for guests to bring with them when they came from New Orleans, candy, cakes, pate de foie gras and all kinds of delicacies—those special confections and importations quite unobtainable in our plantation section. Our "big house" was a one-story affair and small compared to the more palatial two-story Gay home not far away. It was whispered around among the youngsters that, while our cousin Edward J. Gay of about our age was domiciled in a room on the ground floor, his colored nurse used to take him upstairs occasionally, so as to "make him high-minded."

The Clement house fronted on a plantation road, which ran to the main riverside highway—the road running alongside the levee and Mississippi River. In the other direction the plantation road passed through the "quarters" where the little houses of the colored workers stood, then on to the sugar house mill, and back to the woods. Our house was about a half mile back from the river. A white-washed picket fence enclosed the big front yard, which included a number of lovely trees, rose bushes, old fashioned camellias and sweet magnolias. Branching off from the house was a side yard containing a large

*Retreat Plantation was so named at time of the Civil War when grandfather Clement, apprehending danger from Federal gun boats stationed in front of Plaquemine, thought it best to move his family to the safety of his plantation home. Hence the name "Retreat".

number of fruit-bearing orange trees. In the rear was an extensive vegetable garden, and an orchard of fruit trees, such as peach, pear, a grape arbor—all in good bearing condition. There was a large group of fig trees of the delectable "Celeste" variety. Each year we had a big time gathering the figs during a period of several weeks. The excess crop was made into preserves, to be kept for later consumption or shipped to favored relatives and friends.

On the other side of the plantation house was the carriage house and other small out-buildings. In the back yard was the great oak which many visitors have written about. A central point for the grouping of vehicles, a shade place for animals in the heat of the day, this big tree unfortunately—in my early youth—had already met death's withering hand. I can remember its great dead branches reaching up starkly to the sky. It was quite a while however, before it was cut down for use in the woodpile. The woodpile, by the way, was no mean affair. Not only was it the entire source of heat for the winter, big log fires kept going all day long, but all the cooking and water heating the year round was done with wood fuel. Up in "town" some people were commencing to use coal in smaller grates and in stoves. We scorned anything like that as being dirty and smelly. Many country folk to this day, notwithstanding efficient central heating systems in their city or country homes, must still have their log fires—or else winter loses one of its chief joys.

That great dead tree, before it was cut down commenced to attract occasional groups of turkey buzzards. Those keen visioned but horrible looking vultures, scavengers of the neighborhood, liked the vantage point of the high-up bare limbs. These big birds, as everyone knew, were protected by law, but that did not prevent us from casting a baleful eye on the intruders.

One morning, in fun and in a boyish spirit of adventure I turned my little "twenty two" rifle on a buzzard up in the old tree. I did not think my rifle could reach that high, or bring down such a big tough bird. To my horror the big buzzard did not fly away, but turned over without a struggle, the ghastly looking thing falling dead at my feet. My aim had been far better than I thought it would be. Immediately I destroyed "the evidence" by dropping the ugly corpse down a nearby abandoned well. Even so my guilty conscience had me in a funk whenever I saw strangers coming down the road to our place. I would think, "the jig's up, here's the sheriff to put me in jail." Probably my tender years plus the prestige of the family would have saved me, but I suffered nevertheless, no one gave aid or any comfort whatever.

But the big dead tree was later to furnish birds of another kind. A pigeon house was built in the lower section of this old tree. Grandmother was fond of succulent and tender squabs, and, by keeping the pigeons well fed, we had an almost continuous supply of this delectable addition to the menu. In the backyard we had, as is usual on farms, a number of chicken and turkey roosts or houses.

Our plantation food production was largely a self-supporting or self-contained affair. Sugar and molasses were in abundance, as that of course, was our main business. Very little food was bought on the outside except coffee, tea, ice, and a few other table delicacies. In our garden were grown in profusion many vegetables including the artichoke, loved by gourmets. In season we always had plenty. It seems a little unusual, but at our place we had tobacco plants growing in the fence corners of our yard. The big leaves were put up in the attic of the barn to dry and cure. Well do I remember shredding the leaves after they had dried into a sort of crimp-cut condition and then packing them in small bags for use.

When short of pocket money we boys would have the cook make a big freezer full of ice cream, packed with plenty of ice. We would load it in a spring wagon and go over to a neighboring plantation where the "hands" were being paid off. A quick "sell out" of our ice cream and little tobacco bags—all at low prices—no taxes included—was generally effected.

Fitting in with the plantation economy of producing whatever goods could be made by local handicraftsmen and thus keeping the money at home, my aunt, at the proper time of the year, would send us boys to the woods to cut strips from the palmetto shrubs growing in profusion there. These strips were dried, sliced into proper sizes, plaited into long sections and then sewn together and shaped into hats and bonnets. Lined with cheap cotton and of light-weight, both the broad-brimmed hats for men and sunbonnets for the women were effective in protecting the wearers from the actinic rays of an almost tropical sun.

Palmetto leaves were also used to make fans. We thought it much fun to cut palmettos and never objected to the chore. Probably today in Louisiana not many know how to make hats, and not many bonnets are worn. But whether the palmetto is plentiful or not I do not know.

ANNUAL PECAN HARVEST

Each year in the fall, Aunt Yetta would marshal together a crew of youthful helpers, white and black, to get in our big crop of pecans. Dozens and dozens of barrels would be filled, many finding their way to the waiting New Orleans market— usually with a good cash return.

A picturesque feature of this annual pecan event was "thrashing" of the branches of the pecan trees with a long pole. This required the services of an expert "thrasher". Tom Cowan, a local colored man, made a sort of specialty of this kind of work. Climbing a tree he would venture far out on a limb and with his pole bring the nuts raining to the ground into the hands of us children engaged as "pickers". Tom after successfully doing our thrashing work for years, climbing around the big trees, once foolishly and surreptitiously took a bottle of whiskey up with him, hiding it somewhere in a crotch of the tree. Frequent reference to this cache of intoxicating treasure eventually proved Tom's undoing. His fatal misadventure entailed also a narrow escape for the writer of this page, then ten years old. I was working under the colored climber at that time. Well do I remember the awful thud as his huge body hurtling down from above hit the ground. It fell within a few feet of me, as I blanched with fear. The unconscious and partly intoxicated exthrasher was carried off the field with broken legs, arms and serious internal injuries. Tom died from that terrible fall, a dire warning to all secret drinkers, one which did not go unnoticed.

Aunt Yetta was an excellent business woman, and after the death of my father, Alfred H. Clement, Sr., it was she who managed plantation jobs such as pecan gathering, kept the books, and "bossed" things generally. The job she liked best was the management and direction of our big pecan harvest. At times we had an "over-seer" or manager who lived on the place, but more often "Retreat" was run by my dear, semi-invalid aunt. I can see her now almost overcome by asthma and at times afflicted with other serious disabilities—bravely struggling to keep going. "Miss Henretta", as the colored folk called her, the tall slender maiden lady, was a tower of strength. In her kindly, quiet, but determined and able way she was the one who made possible the continued operation of the plantation.

In a pasture adjoining the main house, we raised a large number of sheep, providing fresh mutton for the table. Mother would never allow us youngsters to see the killing of sheep or hogs. She thought the effect bad on children and that it tended to make them hard-hearted and cruel. They must not become inured to death and like the Vestal Virgins point their thumbs down to signal for the slaughter of living things, nor see the despair in the frightened eyes of the poor sheep or hogs that met death the plantation way—by having their throats cut.

We had sheep-shearing times at Retreat also. When the wool was gathered it was treated for cleanliness. Some of it was used on the plantation. We boys used to help Aunt Yetta in the processing called "carding" wool. Later these "cards" of fluffy wool were sewn into "comforters," or made into rough garments. Much of the wool production was sent to the New Orleans market.

The shrimping season brought each year a pleasant variety in our table menu and some excitement for us. Beginning in the late spring it lasted four or five months. We caught the shrimp by placing shrimp-boxes in the Mississippi River, out in front of our place. These boxes were kept filled with table refuse, ham-bones, or cantaloupe rinds together with a little cornmeal, which attracted quantities of shrimp into these home-made traps. Once in, the shrimp were unable to get out. We youngsters always welcomed the opportunity to go swimming in the river, while bringing these moored boxes to shore. Often the boxes would be emptied of enough shrimp to fill several tubs and washpans. These delicious crustaceans would be made into a savory shrimp "gumbo" Aunt Josephine was noted for, or boiled and served on an immense platter—enough for everyone. Boiled river shrimp eaten cold with salt and pepper was a standard dinner entree nearly every day in the summer. There is no greater delicacy than Mississippi River shrimp. They are smaller but the flavor is more subtle than the larger gulf shrimp—truly a dish for an epicure.

It was during the shrimping season that we developed as swimmers. Especially was this true when our Cousin Edwin Schlater visited the plantation. He it was who taught us the fine points. An expert and an unusually strong swimmer, he took pleasure in showing us how to improve ourselves in this necessary art.

"Cousin Ned," as we affectionately called him, used also to take us hunting. Equipped with a good gun, and an extra fine hunting dog, we always brought home large strings of birds. It was not long before we boys were allowed to own small guns, and soon we hunted on our own, bagging birds, squirrels and rabbits. In those days small game was much in evidence on the plantation, and there were no game laws to bother us. We regulated things to suit ourselves.

Once I shot a wild cat—or so it was thought to be—near Bayou Le Butte, a meandering little waterway back of our place. The stealthy, powerful looking animal was crossing the bayou on a fallen tree and I happened to be concealed nearby. It was indeed an exciting moment. I shot but the distance was too far and the bird shot scattered. With a terrific snarl the animal leaped into the air, then, fortunately for the boyish hunter, left the field to him and his little bird-shot gun.

In another hunting experience I remember coming suddenly on a big fat opossum lying, apparently dead, in our back yard. This time there was no danger. Feeling him still warm, I went off to get help in bringing in the prize. When I returned the big fellow was gone. He had had presence of mind enough to play that "possum" trick—when he found I was right on top of him. It was quite evident that he was preparing to invade our chicken roost. Well, I had to learn. Our colored retainers would have greatly enjoyed a "possum and taters" dish, had the young hunter used a club to finish off the marauder at once.

At Retreat the first thing you heard in the morning was the coffee grinder as Aunt Josephine prepared the coffee which was roasted fresh every morning. We youngsters of course did not get morning "coffee in bed", southern style, like the older folks, but we did get it at breakfast, served with hot milk. I still remember how good it was. No one serves coffee like that now. Coffee in those days was not "assembled" or blended with chickory—it was all Mocha and Java. At regular intervals our New Orleans agent, W. B. Bloomfield, shipped us two hundred-pound bags of coffee—one Java

and one Mocha. Every day Grandma with her big bunch of
keys made a trip to the storeroom. She would give out, along
with other provisions like flour, meal and sugar, the green
coffee for the next day—equal amounts of each variety which
"Aunt Josephine" mixed that afternoon, roasted and then
ground the first thing next morning. It has been years since
this writer smelled the delicious aroma of coffee roasting on
top of a stove, but the memory lingers.

I mentioned the gumbo filé with shrimp, but overlooked the
crayfish bisque which was one of Josephine's specialties—and
crayfish were plentiful in the big plantation drainage canals.
Mother would often take us crayfishing when we were very
small. All that was needed was a few little chunks of salt meat,
a piece of string and a short pole, together with a good net on a
long pole. Another specialty of Josephine's was okra gumbo,
using shrimp, chicken or crabs as a base. It was superior to
gumbo filé and one of the most delicious dishes I ever tasted.

Once I found a "cap and ball" revolver in the "Retreat"
attic. This was one of Colt's earliest efforts and was really
an antique. I saw one like it recently in a collection of old
guns, and the owner valued it at $250. Now a collector's item
they are very scarce. We boys would load it with powder and
shot, then stick on the required percussion caps. Occasionally
all six chambers would go off at once. When that happened
the only safe place in the neighborhood was immediately behind it. While most of the hunters of those days were still
using the old-fashioned "muzzle loaders" with ramrods,
powder horns and caps, we possessed one of the early-model
Parker double-barrel breech-loaders. This was a hammer
gun but a really fine piece, and man-size. There were no
ready-loaded shells in those days, and we bought empty shells,
powder and shot, loaded our own shells with a set of tools that
came with the gun. All of this outfit had belonged to our
deceased father.

My brother Alfred and I used to take this practically-new

gun and the ancient revolver and go hunting accompanied by our two colored retainers, Ike and George. We would take turns shooting. It is a wonder no one ever was injured. We frequently brought in fairly good bags of game—I do not recall a single mishap. We could not have been over nine and ten, respectively, when we started using these weapons. What would a person think today of two little boys of nine and ten going hunting with a double-barrel, twelve gauge, shotgun and a forty-five caliber Colt revolver.

Resourcefulness and determination are almost necessary attributes of the small boy on a plantation. At a young age one learns to develop initiative and not to be afraid. I well recall, while hunting alone on the riverfront, shooting my first wild duck and then seeing the much coveted duck—big game to me at that time—floating down the Mississippi river about 75 feet out from shore. To go home and tell of my prowess without the duck would get me nowhere. Having no "retriever" dog, notwithstanding winter weather and icy cold water, it was up to me to do the retrieving, or see my duck disappear in the offing. So, without hesitation I took off my shoes and clothes and swam out into the big river. Soon I was back on the shore with my prize. I dressed and went happily on the way home at a warm-up trot, none the worse for my experience.

It might be a little difficult for city-bred boys to believe that such crazy, life-risking experiences were ordinary happenings for youngsters like us out in the country. However, sometimes the country man with his careless "gun play," came to grief as parish records show.

I must chronicle here a boyish sporting event in which my little colored retainer, Ike, appeared as hero. He was somewhat malformed. His left hand was what he himself called a "nub," almost useless. In addition to good use of his extra strong right hand, he could whip larger boys by butting them with his extremely hard, bullet-shaped head. In fact, he achieved considerable local fame for butting pickets off of the fence, which tour de force he would perform for a dime. "Billy," the plantation goat, one of my much-loved four-footed pets, had also acquired quite a reputation as a "butter," having vanquished all the goats and rams in the neighborhood. One day a group of the plantation boys were discussing the powers of the two champions. A purse of 25c was subscribed and Ike agreed to swap butts with Billy for the championship and the purse. He got down on his hands and knees and awaited for the onslaught, after emitting a challenging B-a-a! Billy took time out to think things over. He took so long that Ike looked up to see what was the trouble, just then Billy reared up and came down with a crashing butt square on Ike's forehead. Billy scored a knock-out and complete victory. Ike had to be rescued from further mayhem.

I don't remember ever "learning" to ride a horse—I rode and had horses to ride as far back as memory goes. But I do remember many of the horses, including the mountainous-in-size, Pet, the smaller Prince, Lookout and a wiry little Indian mustang pony used as transportation to school. I remember a lot of the mules too and some of the names, including "Fashion," the mare mule that killed Aunt Josephine's only boy, a sad and terrible happening. Most mules are stolid, easy going, rather safe animals to deal with. However, the child somehow enraged this powerful and somewhat "ornery" animal. By a sudden rear-end kick, she broke his neck causing almost instant death. This seems to have been the only mule-engendered fatality of the kind that occurred on the plantation during my time. The tragedy may have had something to do with the fright that came later when one of a party of little girls—cousins visiting "Retreat"—on being dared by her playmates, suddenly ducked her head and ran under one of the mules standing in the backyard. Fortunately nothing happened except a resultant reprimand and stern lecture to the little one, who in this case was no less a personage than the future Mrs. Anna Gay McClung, daughter of Andrew H. Gay, of nearby St. Louis Plantation.

I remember also the great excitement created when one of the mules fell into the underground cistern at the nearby big barn, and the futile efforts to rescue it. That scene, on a cold winter's night, with a dim lantern on a rope throwing its fitful glare on the poor mule thrashing around in the water twenty feet down — uttering strange and awful cries — while the hostler and the Negroes made vain attempts to get ropes under it, is as vivid in my memory today as if it had happened last night.

I also remember that big snow in 1889, when the whole country seemed to freeze. It killed our beloved orange trees and did much other damage. It was the first snow I ever saw, and the last, until that still greater one in New Orleans, years later in 1895, the time when the Mississippi river was full of floating ice cakes.

"OPEN KETTLE" SUGAR MILL OPERATION

My earliest recollection of sugar making on the plantation was of a little mill that had run for many "grinding" seasons during the time of my father and grandfather. The Clement mill, however, was dismantled in later years, and the cane sold to larger mills nearby. But when I was a little boy the old fashioned sugar mill operated in all its glamour, and for the last two or three months of the year it was the momentous concern of all the plantation people, white and black, young and old. Big slabs of wood, from nearby stacked cords of this home-produced fuel, thrown or pushed into blazing fires under the big old-fashioned boilers, was a spectacle in itself. A cane "carrier" brought the great piles of juicy looking "ribbon" cane to the crushing rollers. The cane juice flowed in a small river to the row of "batteries" where the boiling and "skimming off" of impurities took place.

These batteries of "open" kettles or cauldrons with steam

coils underneath were arranged in order. The transfer of the hot juice from one to the other was done by a hand-operated ladling process, amid a steamy surrounding, with much sampling and testing to find when the point of proper cooking had been reached. Great long sweeps with wooden buckets were the ladles that carried the boiling cane juice from one cauldron to the other and to the final-process vat before it was transferred to coolers in the "cooling room." There the soft sugar mass was left to solidify into the brown sugar, the finished product. Later, men with ordinary spades dug the brown sugar out of the coolers and filled sugar barrels and hogsheads for shipping to New Orleans. Some of the juice ended up as our Retreat Plantation *Delectable* brand of molasses. Molasses of course was handled differently, and was poured into a tighter barrel. After each boiling when the molasses was cooled off there remained at the bottom of the kettle a thick substance called *cuite*. This ropey, taffy-like confection was a table delicacy with the flavor of sugar cane and was much enjoyed during the season. It could not be kept long without turning into sugar. Cuite is now almost a non-existent product. Once in universal use, the "open kettle" system such as ours is now extinct. At one time there were hundreds, now only one or two left — if that.

All these little old-time mills, one on practically every sugar plantation — some horse operated, some steam — making the simplest form of plain brown sugar, had their own cooper shop attached. There barrels were made and put together. The work was done by home-trained expert Negro coopers. After the barrels were filled four-mule carts hauled them out along the road in front of our house, over the levee and down to the boat landing where they were loaded on a steamboat to be taken to New Orleans.

The transport of the weighty hogsheads of sugar was effected by a special lifting apparatus, which hoisted the great casks and hung them under and between two big wheels to

Left—Planter Edward J. Gay and author W. E. Clement at the St. Louis Plantation, Iberville Parish, "grinding" time.

t—Messrs. Charles Ed-l Grace, Notary (left); oh Allain Grace (cen-Clerk of Court of Iber-Parish for nearly 30 s and brother of Albert race, author of "Heart e Sugar Bowl, the Story berville"; and Stuart O. ry (right) of New Or-. This picture was taken ront of the Grace law e at Plaquemine by W. lement when the author gathering material for book.

Above—Pre-Civil War "Court House" at Plaquemine, former "temple of justice" now houses the City Hall.

Below—MAMMY LIZZY, a slave bought by planter Gervais Schlater from the Davis family to nurse his children. On being set free this faithful and much loved "Mammy" nursed succeeding generations of babies in the Schlater and Clement family.

form a novel conveyance. Queer looking rigs these were, generally pulled by oxen, traveling at a slow pace with the big barrel-shaped container hanging only a few feet from the ground. In bad weather, when the roads were deep with mud, hauling entailed great difficulties. But there was no trouble in getting steamboats to take on this freight as it stood on the bank of the river. I remember freight agents from the boats coming to our home and pestering our people for business.

The forest in rear of our plantation did not supply quite all the wood that was needed to "take off" the sugar crop. So each spring, when the river-rise brought great logs down the river, a gang of our colored workers using four-oared skiffs would go out into the stream and bring to shore some of the largest of the constantly passing uprooted trees. These logs, some of them of great size, were drawn from the water edge to the working area high on the bank by means of hand windlasses. Round and round the men went pulling out the logs. Some times a small horse was used to pull the big lever around. The logs were then sawed in proper lengths by hand, two men with cross-cut saws. By using axes and wedges, the sawed sections were split into "slabs" for the sugar-house furnaces. They were then piled to dry for the coming "grinding" season. I remember going out to the river-front one cold freezing day to watch the colored workers do this fast-moving "assembly line" work. I asked the foreman why the men did not have a fire burning. His answer was, "when we get going we don't need no fire, we heats up on the job." The Negroes have an old saying that "when you'se young you heats from the inside out, when you gits old you heats from the outside in." In talking recently with former U. S. Senator Edward Gay about this rather primitive fuel operation of the sugar making process of many years ago, when compared to modern oil burning equipment now used in most all the big sugar mills, he said, "Yes I remember the old method." "But in those days," he said, "The sugar mills made a lot more money than they do at present."

LANTERNS ON THE LEVEE

The levee played an important role in the lives of all. I must tell of the tension and fear which weakness in these little levees provided us with in the old days in Iberville Parish. The effectiveness of these small dykes, built by hand labor with wheel barrows, against the power of the great river they were dedicated to holding back gave us much concern each year. I recall vividly the anxious days and weeks our people went through each season when the river kept rising and rising, and "revetment" by means of outside planking and sandbags became necessary. I saw the hungry waves lapping over a little at places when big boats passed, thus softening and weakening still further the narrow little barriers which kept us and our belongings from being swept away. Men with lanterns constantly patrolled the levees night and day, watching for the beginnings of breaks, the crayfish holes and "boils" which sometimes spouted up under the hydrostatic pressure. It was only when these leaks could be found that there was a possibility of foreseeing or preventing a break. After even a small section of the levee "went out" there was seldom any stopping the rush of water. Fortunately for us no break-through or "crevasse", occurred at our place during the time I was there. This was due perhaps to the fact that the crevasses that occurred above us took the pressure off our poor little levee about to collapse.

The levees at that time were kept up by assessment of the property owners in the various levee districts. Not much money was available for this purpose. Of late years this job has been taken over by the national government and the machine-made embankments of today are very different looking affairs from those of seventy years ago. But even as late as 1927 when the river rose to record breaking heights there was loss of life and widespread property damage.

SCHOOL DAYS

When the time came for school, we boys and girls of the neighborhood were fortunate in having available the services of Cousin Eliza Kent, a widowed grand-daughter of the late planter, Nicholas Wilson, and a great grand-daughter of the developer of the section, Captain Joseph Erwin. On our mother's side we boys of Retreat Plantation were also Erwin descendants, as was Edward Gay on his father's side. The six, school-age Dickinson youngsters and the five boy-and-girl Craigheads were also scions of the same stock. In fact most of us were "two way" cousins. Besides these youngsters there quite a few others of the neighborhood, making a fair sized school attendance. The little one-room school was on our Uncle Andrew Gay's property and, to reach it, we of Retreat, were forced to ride about four miles on horseback. Cousin Eliza, let me respectfully say, was something of a martinet, maintaining strict discipline and order. However, she was a most able and experienced teacher, having taught many of the previous generation, our fathers and mothers.

As I look back on the instruction given there as compared to the general teaching of today, the high ideals our teacher very determinedly and ably tried to implant in the minds of her young flock, I cannot but give thanks that my early views and training were so much influenced by the teachings and morals of our strong-minded Cousin Eliza. There was no slurring over anything.

Recently there has been a revival of interest in the McGuffey Readers that were used in the schools all over America. In studying them I was influenced by the emphasis placed on the fundamentals of truth, honesty, fair dealing, invention and self-reliance. The preposterous and destructive idea that "everybody is entitled to a living at the expense of the state" has no place in these splendid books. McGuffey's first reader had a little poem which conveyed a valuable hint on the virtue of work:

The Lark is up to meet the sun,
The bee is on the wing,
The ant its labor has begun,
The woods with music ring.

Shall birds and ants and bees be wise,
While I my moments waste?
Then let us with the morning rise
And to our duties haste.

Maybe all this sounds old-fashioned and out of harmony with the educational ideas we hear today. Moreover I would have felt sorry for anybody who delivered himself of any such modern educational theories before Cousin Eliza. That would have been heresy indeed.

Discipline as I have indicated was strictly enforced. Never was there a chance for revolt of any kind. Our parents stood solidly behind Cousin Eliza. They knew she was the epitome of all that was right and fair.

In the large pasture playground surrounding the school there was ample room for ball games, Indian fighting, and foot races. The writer of these lines one day distinguished himself when playing "catcher" by running too fast to a big fence post. At high speed he scraped against a barb-wire fence. The barbs tore a large piece of flesh out of his leg near the knee. A long, livid scar from that encounter remains until this day. The big flow of blood was stanched by using pretty much all the cobwebs the school ceilings could muster, and the wound was bandaged with two handkerchiefs. Wonderful indeed is youth. I even rode home that evening on horseback. Not much coddling in those days.

After lessons we boys would saddle our ponies and start gayly for home. Quite frequently a race would take place, sometimes with casualties that, as we look back on those falls from speeding horses, came desperately near being broken necks. Often the ride home would be interrupted by a swim in the river. Once this nearly resulted in tragedy. The river was rising rapidly and the place we selected for the swim that day was perhaps the most dangerous along the river. A headland or old "levee point" reached out obliquely into the big stream, partly enclosing a "batture," where the rising water swirled in to fill the partly empty space between an old and new levee.

Brother Alfred, elected to swim out a little way from this outside point to a partly submerged oak tree and then come back to where the group was disporting itself. To our horror we saw that on his return he was unable to breast the strong current and that he was too exhausted to go around the long way to safe ground. Immediately one of the boys, Alvin Dupuy and myself swam out to save him. Alfred was going under for the last time when we reached him. All he could say was "Leave me, save yourselves." We seized him one on each side, and endeavored to make headway to the nearby point of land against the rushing stream. Charles Dickinson helped by meeting us with a log. Though we were unusually strong swimmers, we couldn't do any more than hold our position, and it began to look like we could not do that much longer. Soon we would all go under and three or more names would be added to the river's long list of victims.

Fortunately a lad, Sam Mathews, who had remained on shore, ran out on the point with a long pole. He reached out as far as he safely could and shoved the end of the pole to us. I was able to grasp it, and thus the group, holding to each other, were pulled back to safety. Alfred was laid on the incline of the levee with his head down so the water could run out of his lungs. In a short time a bunch of scared and contrite boys was ready to resume the journey home. At the time we said nothing about this to our mother. I have often thought how awful it would have been if, on that day news had been carried to the recently bereaved widow — that she must now face the death of her two children in a double tragedy.

With racial conflict arising between white and blacks today, being promoted sometimes, as I believe, for political reasons, I like to think of the harmony and good feeling that existed between the two races on our place following the stresses
and strains of the Civil War. I remember one Christmas
when, because of bad weather and consequent impassable
roads, there appeared to be no chance of a visit from Santa
Claus. A heart-breaking disaster for the children. The only
way to get to town was to walk there on the top of the levee.
"Young Anthony," son of our yardman and ex-slave, Anthony,
did this for our mother. Putting on big boots it required all
his strength to walk in the mud against a freezing rain and
cutting wind. He made the trip and brought back the presents.
The big day was thus saved for us through help of a colored
man who could not bear to see the white children saddened
and disappointed.

Christmas was always the occasion for a fire works display
at the Big House (not very big, but that was planter's par-
lance for a plantation owner's home). Not only did we boys
enjoy shooting off fire crackers, but the entire neighborhood
joined in, including the colored children from the nearby
"quarters." Sometimes there were a few burns and casualties from the ample number of small Chinese crackers, cannon
crackers, skyrockets, roman candles and pin wheels, but nothing serious ever happened. We not only enjoyed the show
ourselves, but enjoyed seeing the other children so happy.

Recently there has come into vogue a theory that the
romantic writings of Sir Walter Scott have had a fuedalistic
and unhealthy influence over the elders and youth of the
South. Our reading as youngsters was largely of these great
books and similar romances found in our father's library. But
many southerners feel that only good came from such old-
fashioned and high minded reading as Scott's Ivanhoe and his
other books in the formative years. One result of this was that
we boys made long "jousting spears," with guards near the

handle to catch the rings as we darted around the jousting courses on our horse — a la Knight Errant style. In fact we were not alone in this predilection towards medieval pagentry. Others of the youthful South, engaged in joustings and had for years, prior to the Civil War, all modeled on Sir Walter Scott's stories.

ENTERTAINMENT, SPORTS AND SOCIAL AFFAIRS

Because travel was slow and rather difficult, those who lived on plantations had to be largely self-contained in the matter of entertainment. With no picture shows, radio, or automobiles, we had to get along with far less outside diversion than now seems necessary. There were no "utilities," no electric service, no gas, no city water, no telephones and few conveniences, but life had its gaieties.

One of our forms of amusement was horseracing. The races were mostly trotting races in which the driver sat close-up behind his horse, legs stretched out to a kind of stirrup in the shafts, in a light and very uncomfortable looking racing sulky. It so happened that the course used most often was on the main river road in front of our plantation. This road was selected because it afforded a good, straight mile-course, with no curves, and was wide enough for racing vehicles to pass each other.

On race days, usually Saturday afternoon, people would flock to our Retreat Plantation levee, which elevation formed an excellent grand-stand. It would of course be specially crowded nearest the finishline. I remember vividly two of the main contenders. One was Mr. James A. Ware, a handsome, wealthy planter from the great Belle Grove Plantation near the town of White Castle about twenty miles below us. The other was Mr. Nahun L. Bruce, a well-known and plucky merchant from Plaquemine, five miles away. The two, driving their own horses, raced at terrific speed. Their two magnificent steeds would come thundering down the home stretch amid great acclaim.

A famous race I recall was that between Mr. Bruce's mare, "Lady", and a splendid looking horse owned by my cousin, Mr. William Schlater. "Lady" won the best two out of three. It was pleasing to us to be able to have ringside seats on the levee by merely walking out to the river-road. No admission charge, plenty of excitement, betting on the race (but no betting for us), pop selling, popcorn, the inevitable organ grinder with his monkey, and the jolly crowd.

Most of our entertainment came through attending the few traveling stage-shows, political rallies and lectures held in Plaquemine at the "Opera House" or on the open square in the center of the town. Showboats or "Floating Palaces" came along occasionally, but during my time there was not much of this. My father in his day was quite a good actor, frequently appearing in amateur shows in Plaquemine.

Once in a while medicine-men, patent medicine sellers, came along with their "Kickapoo Indian Shows." I will never forget the various wild contortions of these, buckskin-clad, tomahawk handlers, their fierce, blood curdling Indian yells, and — as these subsided — the fakers' efforts to sell patent-medicine. These outdoor exhibitions usually took place on a roughly-built, raised platform, from which the Kickapoo-medicine salesman afterward proclaimed the merits of his wares.

The medicine man would make an amazing spiel, or "pitch" as it is now called — a somehow believable story of his cure-all. He would have a big brown bottle in his hand with a large stock, well displayed on the platform. Always he had an excellent voice and a friendly personality. Dozens of bottles of the "wonderful" Indian herb prescription would be sold. All the buyers got was often a raw alcohol concoction mixed with water and flavored with green herb bitters. It merely intoxicated, worked as a *narcotic* and did not cure anything.

Modern spielers are often reminiscent of the old-time patent medicine men with their exciting Kickapoo Indian yells, fiery incantations and then the ingratiating "pitch" of the master salesman.

As a little lad I once saw one of these medicine salesmen mounted on a box haranguing the colored folks in the confines of our plantation "quarters." In a nearby cabin lay a poor colored boy dying of tuberculosis — consumption as we called it in those days. This heartless faker, after making his lying appeal, took the last dollar this poor emaciated youth possessed. To do this, he had to go into the cabin and harangue the sick boy as he lay dying in his bed.

A feature of the old days was the frequent passing on the main road of little bands of romantic-looking gypsies. They too practiced a genial rascality, telling fortunes and selling nostrums. They often camped for the night on our levee front with campfires lighted, near the big trees. More stable and honest passersby were the occasional peddler with packs on their backs. Selling trinkets, cheap jewelry, and ten-cent-store gew gaws, some of these later developed into important businessmen with large stores in New Orleans or elsewhere. Most of these travelers who camped by night near the levee, particularly the peripatetic immigrant workers, carried dangerous-looking double-barrelled shotguns. For hunting game, self-defense, or maybe something more sinister, these guns looked quite formidable.

The social life of plantation people was limited, and yet there were always a few families of proud lineage who were careful in their social contacts. Among the dear friends of my family were the Randolphs, of *Forest Home, Nottaway* and *Blythewood* plantations to the south of us at Bayou Goula. M. Liddell, son of the highly placed former Virginian, John Hampden Randloph, was my father's very close friend. "Nottaway" the imposing looking Randolph-built home is still considered one of the finest and largest of the great plantation homes on the river. The ball-room in this 40-room-house is one of the finest, and most luxurious of the kind I have seen in the south. The Iberville Parish authority, Edward Gay, says that both Nottaway, and the elegant and spacious old colonial type Gay manor house at St. Louis Plantation, were built in the same year, 1856 or 1857. These were prosperous years and planters had good crops along with high prices. In the golden decade before the Civil War many of the beautiful homes along the Mississippi River were constructed.

Later, a young scion of the family, M. Liddell, son of John Hampden Randolph, established himself comfortably and happily in his lovely *Blythewood* home, on the plantation of that name in the rear of the Bayou Goula settlement. It was there that I went to weekend parties and was captivated by the gracious manner of living and the lovely people who made up the big Randolph-Conner family. There was a cutoff road from the rear of our place through *Dunboyne* Plantation, thus reducing the distance to the Randolph place by many miles. The story goes that my father in driving home from a dance at Nottaway, on this unfrequented road ran over a sleeping cow. The cow got up quickly and turned the buggy over. Badly shaken he was not hurt seriously.

Nottaway still stands, and the present owners have kept the great and imposing-looking mansion in good repair. *Blythewood*, the smaller Randolph home, burned to the ground as the family barely escaped with their lives. Many beautiful heirlooms belonging to the Randolphs perished in the flames. The house took fire in the dead hours of the night and before help could arrive everything was destroyed.

It is thought that many lovely old southern homes were destroyed by fire because of defective chimneys. After many years of use, the mortar around the bricks in the chimneys, particularly in the upper part which goes through the attic, has a tendency to disintegrate, leave an opening between the bricks. Quite frequently the joists or other supports are anchored in the outer edge of this chimney masonry. When sparks finally reach these dry-as-tinder wooden supports, a fire starts in the attic and gains such headway that, out in the country, nothing can be done to save the home. That is the way we explain the loss of the more-than-a-century-old Clement home at Retreat, so dear to us. From what the farmer who lived in the much emasculated old house, after we had moved away from the country, later told us about the fire it is reasonable to suppose this is what happened. Our house was much changed in looks before it burned. My recently deceased cousin, George Bright of New Orleans, and I used to visit the old place, and wander nostalgically through the rooms, but we found the house a little difficult of recognition. The two "ells" had long been taken down, the lovely front garden demolished. The drastic change in general appearance was partly caused by the levee having been moved in almost a half mile, due to encroachment by the great and always changing Mississippi.

One of the many pleasing recollections that come to me is my memory of the old Pleyel upright piano in our plantation living room and the joy it often gave a small boy with a love for music. At times when our visitors included Cousins Lottie and Nettie Miller from New Orleans, Anna Gay, her two sisters and her brother Andrew would spend the evening with us. Andrew would always bring his banjo to enliven the proceedings. It was then we heard our first college songs, very enchanting indeed. As I read Anna Gay's (now Mrs. McClung) reference to the Retreat Plantation musical group of long ago when Uncle Charles Clement, deceased before my time, used to play the flute, with his sister Lodoiska accompanying on the Pleyel, it reminded me of later days when we used to visit Aunt Lodo at her lovely home following Uncle Andrew Gay's death. She was then well up in the eighties. Even so our remarkable aunt would say, "William, don't you want to hear me play the piano?" I, of course, would quickly assent. Then, she would dash off a brilliant piece of music with zest *sacre feu*, and wonderful technique. Until shortly before Aunt Lodo's death, at the age of 90 whenever I called she would always play the piano for me.

In our "Retreat" living room, there was a rather striking looking bust of the famous physician, Dr. Luzenberg. It occupied a commanding position above the old-fashioned writing desk. We were told that the deceased doctor was an especially good friend of Grandfather Clement. Later when I came to New Orleans and learned that Dr. Luzenberg's son (a prominent attorney and later district attorney of the parish) was named Chandler Clement Luzenberg, I appreciated the impress of our grandfather's character on other people. I had heard also of his friendship with the then prominent and wealthy, Story family of Saxonholm plantation and New Orleans. Later I was to meet a Mr. Clement Story* who, it seems

---

*After the publication of this book in 1952 I was pleasantly surprised one morning to be called upon by Mr. Henry Clement Story of New Orleans. I learned that he was a direct descendant of Henry Clement, brother of my grandfather, Dr. Charles Clement. This Henry, however, was named after *his* grandfather, Gen. Henry Clement Story. On page 133 there appears a letter written to a relative just before the Battle of New Orleans in January 1815 by Mrs. E. Clement, wife of Henry Clement of New Orleans. I thus knew of the early Henry but did not know it was his daughter who married Benjamin Story, New Orleans' first banker and progenitor of the well known Story family.

One of Benjamin Story's sons, a West Pointer, rose to high distinction. He was General Henry Clement Story of the U.S. Army. When secession started and the "War between the States" loomed, Gen. Robert E. Lee endeavored to persuade Gen. Story to take sides with the Confederates. This he felt he could not do. On the other hand his wife and family were supporters of the Southern cause and a terrible rift was certain if he took part on the Northern side.

Gen. Story explained the circumstances and laid the matter before President Lincoln. It was then decided that he should, as a "Neutral", *retire* to his Louisiana Plantation, a few miles below New Orleans. From his grandson, Henry Clement Story, I learned that when the Federal gunboats breached the New Orleans defenses, and steamed up the river, they

was also named in honor of my progenitor, the owner of Retreat Plantation, another tribute to the worth and potent character of Dr. Clement and evidence of his wide professional and business connections throughout Louisiana.

The use of telephones in Iberville began about 1886. I remember the erection of the first poles in front of our plantation and the stringing of the wires. All this was quite a curiosity, of course, and we—in our immaturity—greeted it with the doubt and contempt any such fool enterprise should properly merit. People like us, with swift horses always ready could send messages, or visit around at will. We were getting along fine, saw no use for crazy innovations such as telephones. It was just a fad and would soon die out.

Shortly after the line was installed I was contentedly whiling away a rainy, stormy afternoon, helping to shell corn for the mules and horses in the big stable along-side the river-road, close to and almost up against the new telephone line. All of a sudden there was a terrific thunder-clap, a blinding light and a rending noise. I thought the Judgment Day had come. Realizing that I was all right, I rushed out of the barn to find that the poor, new telephone line was in ruins. Not knowing much about lightning arresters in those early days, they had built the line without necessary protection. For the first time I saw great poles still standing, but split like kindling wood, some pieces thrown clear across the levee. A small boy pondered over the foolishness of men and their gadgets.

---

were surprised to note a plantation home in front of which flew *both* the Union and Confederate flags.

A boat was immediately sent ashore to investigate. They were met at the landing by Gen. Story in his general's uniform. The officer in charge saluted, and was quickly shown the "Neutrality" paper by Pres. Lincoln. As a consequence Story's plantation suffered no depredation. In fact the Federal Commander placed guards around the property to see that no damage was done. All of the surrounding plantations lost much of their stock, equipment and stores requisitioned by the conquering Federal forces.

He was glad he got off with nothing worse than a bad scare.

The main barn and its big bins of corn and oats, racks of hay, and room for the stock to seek shelter, was evidence that we of Retreat used to raise all the food for our many draft animals, riding horses, cows, sheep and other animals. We developed our own motive power on the farm. There was no buying of gasoline or crude oil to run machines. We were a good balanced economy, a self-contained unit. The machine age with tractors, cultivators and harvesters of course, was changing all that. Whether for better or worse only time can tell. The annual harvest of oats was made by the use of hand-operated sickles.

When I was about 10 years, I once went out to show the men how to properly garner the grain. Reaching out with the left hand to gather in a great bunch of grain, I then gave a swift pull with the right hand of the sharp sickle, to cut the oat stalks. My mistake, however, was in not cutting lower than the handgrip. Three fingers of my left hand caught the full cutting impact of the sharp blade. With my fingers deeply gashed, apparently nearly off, and a hand gushing blood, I rushed home across the pasture. With the application of large amounts of the much-used spider web—a blood stancher supposed to have some mysterious quality—the bleeding stopped, and my fingers in a short while were quickly healed. That oat-field scar, however, I have carried to this day. A reminder ever before me as it is even at this writing—how *not* to do things.

OLD-TIME LIVING CONDITIONS

I learned to read—indeed some of my best reading was done by coal oil ("insurance" oil it was called) lamps—which needed daily filling and trimming and whose wicks gave strange, and devious trouble, sometimes smoking horribly and disastrously, throwing forth a sooty deposit. Our household

menage was quite innocent of plumbing—in fact we had none
at all. Drinking water came from the immense, unscreened
cistern, partly open at the top for air ventilation. It held the
rain water which ran off the roof of the house. Sometimes,
to our consternation "wiggle tails" were found in large numbers. Small snakes occasionally got into the big wooden, rain-
water reservoir. Fortunately these were the harmless kind
that disported themselves, obligingly, on the water surface,
where we could in our righteous indignation quickly get at
them.

During the old days there were no window or door screens
to keep out flies and mosquitoes. We got along with palmetto
fans, used mosquito "bars" or netting over the beds. Thank-
ful indeed were we for that haven of rest from the annoying,
irritating and blood-sucking mosquitoes. The first screened
porch, or "gallery mosquito house" erected in our section about
1888 was at the Plaquemine home of our Uncle Jacob Mc-
Williams. Only this porch was screen-protected, nowhere else
were they used in the house. In the summer it was a popular
spot—indeed quite a step forward in home comfort. The first
bathroom, too, was quite a curiosity. Somehow I at first
looked upon that new innovation as "sissy," encouraging soft-
ness. I saw one at the home of our more affluent uncle,
Andrew H. Gay, Sr., where this epochal installation first came
to my notice.

If we were hot, we thought nothing of it, we either stayed
hot or cooled off with palmetto fans. Never did we seem to
miss the electric fans of the future or air-conditioning now so
essential in some quarters. If we were cold we summoned
yardman Anthony to come with more armfuls of wood for the
big log-fire. We then moved in closer. If no objections were
raised the boys liked to stand in front of the fire—warm their
backs, very delightfully. When Saturday night came we did
not turn on the hot and cold water. Instead we luxuriated in

the embrace of a big tin bathtub, carried into the bedrom for that purpose—the portable kind, with a raised, roundish back and curved arm rests. Something a good deal nicer to use than the ordinary, round washtub of the laundry type. A refinement that, at the time it came into use was probably thought to be quite an advance in bath technique.

CHANGE IN IDEALS

In the old South, as "Lanterns On The Levee" signalled so fatefully to us, we have "lost the old ideals, the old strength." But there's time ahead, and believing that there is an underlying, God-denying, and entirely correctible reason for this disintegration, it is pleasing to read a recent Roger Babson news letter, in which he says quite cogently, that the answer will come through fundamental work now going on in the sphere of scientific human research. Through the study of Man, much neglected in the past, we can and must develop a science of living, both for the rural and city dweller. We must discover what "environmental stimuli and idealized goals are universally acceptable." While Babson does not go into that particular phase, it is reasonable to suppose that land-use, and man's more equitable and "satisfied relation" adjustment to the land and natural resources of his country, will be an important phase of this great study. A glimpse of the old plantation, self-contained way of life may be of help as we go along with this idea and influence the changes which perforce are coming.

Nobility of character, love and compassion, beauty and innocence are not lost, they will return. It is said that the great Henry Ford Foundation contemplates a thorough study of these matters. Certainly, to survive we must concern ourselves very vitally with the great problem of our time—our natural resources and human relationships. It is good to know that those engaged in research like the Babson, Ford,

ove—*Palatial* NOTTAWAY, situated in Iberville Parish near Bayou Goula, was built
John Hampden Randolph—formerly of Virginia and one of the great planters of the
e-Civil-War period. Dr. Whyte Owen, a relative of the Craigheads, purchased the
me and renovated it completely. Fronting on the Mississippi it has long been one
the show places of the River Road.

low—TALLY HO. a stately and beautiful mansion, in the Bayou Goula section of Iber-
le, was built by George M. Murrell in the late 1850's. The property is still owned
his descendants. It fronts the Mississippi River and is in a grove of lovely oaks.

A group of Ibervillians of the old days: *Left:* Charles D. Craighead, owner of "Tennessee Plantation"; *standing*, M. Liddell Randolph, son of John Hampden Randolph and owner of "Blythewood"; *right*, Alfred H. Clement of "Retreat Plantation."

and other organizations who seek to benefit mankind, feel as they do about this great problem. As I look back rather delightfully, into the old days and study the manner of living of other times, it seems to me that we must take from the past much that will help men of today.

CHAPTER II

JOSEPH ERWIN — AN IBERVILLE PIONEER

Among Louisiana's plantation barons of the first quarter of the Nineteenth Century was Joseph Erwin. Originally of North Carolina, later of Nashville, Tennessee, he came to Iberville Parish in 1807. He accumulated great wealth for those days and at one time owned five miles of river-front property below Plaquemine. He had a large family and his descendants are numerous and widely scattered. Many of them have been senators and congressmen, judges, professional men and business leaders.

Let us look into the background and family history of this remarkable man.

Joseph Erwin came from Guilford County, North Carolina where he was born in 1761. The Erwins were a Scotch-Irish family who belonged to the "North Buffaloe Creek Presbyterian Church".* The creek was named "Buffaloe" because of the large herds of wild buffalo that formerly ranged through that section. The Church of today is located two miles north of the center of Greensboro.

The forefathers of the Buffalo Church Presbyterians had seen much persecution and had endured trials both in Scotland and Ireland. To quote Mr. Rankin: "These trials had made them strong in character and tenacious for the principles of

---

*The History of the Buffalo Presbyterian Church and its people was written by the Rev. S. M. Rankin and published in 1935 by Joseph Stone Co., printers of Greensboro, N. C. It is an interesting and informative book, and we are indebted to it for much information given here.

civil and religious freedom. They were not mere adventurers, seeking worldly fortunes in new places, but they were real men, strong and true, who were seeking a place where they and their children might enjoy personal and property rights, and be permitted to worship their God they loved according to the dictates of their own conscience, without fear or molestation."

Between 1610 and 1625 King James dictated measures that were oppressive to the Presbyterians in Scotland and many emigrated to Ireland. However, he did one wise thing. Instead of bestowing the forfeited lands of North Ireland upon courtiers and soldiers in large tracts, he divided it into small portions, which he granted to settlers, especially ordaining that "no one shall obtain grants of land which he is unable to plant with men." This was the essential feature of his plan. It is in accord with truly fundamental economic theories.

For two generations the Scotch who had moved to Ireland were not molested. Then the English Parliament began passing restrictive laws. In 1704 it passed the Test Act and in 1714 the Schism Act. These laws infringed on the religious beliefs of the Presbyterians and other religions and were enacted to make them conform to the rules of the Established Church.

The Scotch-Irish now began to come to America. Most of them landed in Philadelphia. By 1740 they were coming into Pennsylvania at the rate of 10,000 a year. The heirs of William Penn, who owned the Colony, instructed their agents not to sell any more land to the Scotch-Irish because they were afraid that the new-comers would get political control of the Colony. Some of the ancestors of the Buffalo Creek people had come to Pennsylvania around 1740 and others of the more recent arrivals were not allowed to buy land in Pennsylvania. They then moved on down through Virginia to North Carolina.

The Erwins belonged to this group. The first settlers in

North Carolina got their land from Lord John Carteret, the
Earl of Granville. Each land grant or contract specified 640
acres but was more like a perpetual lease. Each rentor agreed
to pay an annual rent of three shillings per 100 acres in two
equal semi-annual installments, one on the day of the "Feast
of the Annunciation of the Blessed Virgin Mary" and the
other on the day of "the Feast of Saint Michael the Arch-
angel." The first settlers of the Buffalo Region must have
arrived around 1753 as the deeds are all dated December 1753.

The Scotch-Irish Presbyterians who settled around Buffalo
Creek were real pioneers. When they arrived the land was
heavily covered with oak, chestnut and other trees. As late as
1781 General Greene in his report of the Battle of Guilford
Courthouse, said: "The greater part of this country is wilderness, with a few cleared fields interspersed here and there."

When the early settlers arrived, they had to clear the land
and build houses. Only a few acres could be cleared a year.
The houses were the crudest log cabins, with floors of dirt.

Says Rankin in his description of the Buffalo Settlement:

> Their patches of wheat were cut with a small hand
> sickle, flailed from the straw, then separated from the
> chaff by pouring it from a platform on a windy day; and
> both wheat and corn were pounded into meal, or ground
> with a small hand mill, like our old coffee mills. With
> such crude methods of harvesting and handling wheat
> they could raise only small patches. Wheat bread was a
> rarity to be enjoyed only for breakfast on Sunday morn-
> ing. Corn was the main crop and supplied bread for the
> family and feed for the stock.

> These trying conditions lasted for only a few years. It
> was not long until their homes were enlarged and im-
> proved. Small grist mills were soon built on the bran-
> ches. Shops and small stores were soon opened. Living
> conditions were constantly being changed for the better.
> However, for more than fifty years practically all the
> clothes for men, women and children were made at their

. homes from cotton, wool and flax. The seed had to be
picked from the cotton by hand. This was a slow and
tedious job. The task for each member of the family in
the evening after supper was to pick his shoe full of seed
cotton, then the lint was carded, spun and woven into
cloth.

These pioneers were men of true character, with some
education, and all had some money, but money could not
buy the comforts and conveniences. They were not on
the market and had to be made at home.

Everybody had geese from which the down was picked
to make feather beds. It was a custom for the parents to
give their daughters a feather bed when they married. It
has been handed down by tradition that sometimes a
young man would carry a turn of pelts of wild animals to
Philadelphia on his pack horse in order to get money with .
which to buy his marriage license.

But do not think for a moment that our ancestors were
unhappy in those hard pioneer days. They had never
known anything but hardship and privation. They and
their fathers had come to America primarily that they
might have civil and religious liberty. This was the
dearest thing to them and they were happy in this freedom. They were a religious people and rejoiced in the
worship of God. No doubt there were many family altars
in this community before there was a church. Their
libraries consisted of a Bible, the Confession of Faith,
Matthew Henry's Commentary, Baxter's Works, Bun-
yan's Pilgrim's Progress and Buck's Theological Diction-
ary. There may have been a few other books in some
homes, but they were all of a religious or historical
nature.

Robert Erwin (sometimes spelt *Arvine* in the Records)
bought 640 acres of John McClintoch in 1758 located on Reedy
Fork. His wife was Martha and his children Isabella, Robert,
Richard, *Joseph*, Mary, Jane and Sarah. On August 7, 1760,
it is recorded in Orange County House (Orange County was

four miles from Rowan County and later Guilford County) that Robert Erwin was given a grant of 217 acres, the southwest side of the Enoe River, (deed #590, book 14, page 398).

Joseph Erwin was the son of Robert Erwin and his wife, Martha. The month and the day of his birth are not known, but that it was in 1761 we know because on his Iberville Parish tombstone his age is given as 68 and he died in 1829. The Buffalo Church group was organized in 1756, after proper petition to the Court. At that time Protestant dissenters, which included Presbyterians, were not permitted to organize without permission of the local court.

The governor of the state was appointed by the English Crown and he in turn appointed all local officials, sheriffs, judges, clerks and so on. The organization of the Regulators in the back country was brought about because the sheriffs, clerks of court, and registrars of deeds demanded from one to five times as much as the legal fees for their services. The legal fee for recording a deed was one dollar, but the clerks often collected five dollars. The sheriff and his deputies would go out to collect, and if a citizen did not have enough money on hand to pay, his horse was taken and placed on sale with no one present but officers of the law. One would bid in the horse at his own figure. The sheriff would sometimes sell the clothes off the backs of members of a family.

Petitions were sent to the governor but there was no relief. This condition existed from 1765 to 1771. It went on until the good Scotch-Irish lost all patience and organized "The Regulators" who began to handle the sheriffs pretty roughly. They ran one judge out of town. They captured one court clerk and whipped him. Finally Governor Tryon brought over the militia to put down the Regulators. They met his armed force in battle on May 16, 1771. The governor's forces numbered 1,100 men and the Regulators about 2,000. Dr. Carruthers in his life of Dr. Caldwell says that they were not prepared for battle. Many on both sides were killed and wounded. Among those killed were Robert Thompson who was the father of Lavinia Thompson who first married James McKemey and then Joseph Erwin. Robert Thompson was shot down by Governor Tryon in cold blood and was a martyr to liberty. (A five page article about this little affair, known as the Battle of ALAMANCE, appeared in the Saturday Evening Post May 19, 1951).

Now this McKemey family were connected with Andrew Jackson. His mother's sister married a McKemey. In fact Andrew Jackson is supposed to have been born at the McKemey house. The dispute about his birth has been described and analyzed very well by Marquis James in his "Border Captain," the biography of Andrew Jackson.

In any event, there was some connection between Andrew Jackson and Joseph Erwin. Jackson was a constable and deputy sheriff of Guilford County. Having been appointed district attorney for Western North Carolina (now Tennessee) he went there in 1788.

Undoubtedly Joseph Erwin later went to Tennessee on the invitation or advice of Jackson; just when Erwin moved his family there is not known. The records of Davidson County (Tenn.) show that in October 1790 Joseph Erwin traded a horse for a town lot in Nashville.

Nashville is one hundred and eighty three miles from Jonesboro. The road ran through a gap in the Cumberland Mountains and then entered a wilderness more dangerously infested with hostile Indians than any portion of the Western country —not even excepting the dark and bloody land of Kentucky. Joseph Erwin experienced great danger and risk of life in his travels to and from Nashville.

According to Alice Pemble White* it was the year 1800

---

*"The Plantation Experiences of Lavinia and Joseph Erwin 1807-1836," Louisiana Historical Quarterly, Oct. 1944.

that Joseph Erwin with his wife, six children and a few slaves crossed the mountains and settled in the Nashville Basin near the junction of the Cumberland and Stone Rivers in Davidson County, Tennessee, about three and one half miles from Nashville, the capital and trading center for that fast-growing section.

At first things did not go so well for the Erwins. Tradition had it that they were sometimes short of food in their simple log cabin. Once, according to an elderly cousin of the writer, whose grandmother, Eliza Wilson, was about nine years old at the time of the incident, the family was sitting around the dying embers of the large fireplace hungry and despondent when they were suddenly alarmed by the appearance of several large bundles that had fallen down the chimney scattering ashes over them all. Hastening to open the bundles they found hams, salted meats, bread and other provisions. These had evidently been thrown down the chimney by kind hearted neighbors who did not want to offend the pride of the Erwins.

On one occasion, according to Miss White, who got this story from one of the great-grandchildren of Joseph Erwin, the larder got low and there was no money to buy food. "Captain" Erwin suddenly disappeared with a friend. His wife and family were frantic, but he did not return for six months. When he did he had money. It was said that he made this money by speculating in gin seng for which a sudden demand had arisen at that time. He was lucky and made enough to start him on the way to the wealth which he later accumulated.

By the year 1806, Erwin was the owner of a flourishing cotton plantation, situated in the County of Davidson, State of Tennessee and lying on the waters of the Richland Creek, "beginning at two oak trees on the north side of a knob, the original northeast corner of Hodges pre-emption, running west with the old line, seventy-one poles to an Elm and a Walnut— John B. Craighead's corner, thence on the west side of the road leading from Nashville by Cockrill's spring, thence following the meanders of the road—including in all about one thousand acres." The other fork leading from Cockrill's Spring to Richland Creek was known as the Harding Pike. "The first man of note on this road was Capt. Joseph Erwin who settled on this place in 1805. He later was a very wealthy man having large plantations at Plaquemine, La., though he resided in Tennessee. He was the father-in-law of Charles Dickinson who was killed by Gen. Jackson in a duel and was buried on this place near the turnpike. Dickinson also lived in this neighborhood in sight on the opposite side of the road."*

At about this time the Aaron Burr excitement was at its height and Jackson was supposed to have been mixed up in the affair with Burr. He had entertained Burr at his home and corresponded with him. On January 3rd 1807 Aaron Burr was burned in effigy in the courthouse square at Nashville, and among those who harangued the crowd and inveighed against Burr as well as Jackson were Joseph Erwin and Thomas Swann.

Joseph Erwin, probably from his desire to get away from his former friend, Jackson, and to go to a country where his speculative faculties could have a wider "play", started for the lower Louisiana Country in 1807, leaving behind in Nashville his sons and daughters. He and his wife Lavinia and a few slaves made the long journey by flatboat propelled by hand-sweep down the Mississippi River to a newer frontier, the Territory of Orleans. Joseph Erwin was then forty-six years old. There is no record of how long it took him to get to Iberville Parish. But it is certain that it was a dangerous trip because of the Indians and the river pirates who lay in wait all along the route. Furthermore, travel on the river itself afforded a certain element of danger. The banks in many places would fall into the river throwing whole trees into the moving stream. Floating tree trunks and "sawyers"—hid-

---

*From Ramsey's History of Davidson County, Tenn.

den logs or trees caught in the bed or projecting from the banks under water—were a danger to navigation. Barges and boats going down the river were often sunk by these obstructions.

Louisiana was purchased from France in 1803 and already the eyes of the "Americaines" of Tennessee, Kentucky and Ohio glanced expectantly toward the Territory of Orleans and the City of New Orleans. The race to win fame and fortune began at once and Erwin was in the van. The population of Louisiana (Orleans Territory) increased rapidly from about 50,000 in 1803 to 76,576 in 1810, of which nearly one-half were slaves.

Iberville Parish had been an early settlement but the census of 1810 shows nearly 2679 people. Of these about half were slaves. Travelers, however, had pointed out that the soil of Iberville Parish was rich, some of the richest in the State. Erwin, with his knowledge of farming and his shrewd evaluation of land, found this site an opportunity for him to amass a fortune.

Around Iberville Parish both cotton and sugar could be grown and when Erwin arrived, his original idea was to grow cotton. But sugar was developing and soon Erwin's plantations produced more sugar than cotton. Joseph Erwin acquired his first real estate in Louisiana in June 1807 when he bought 1170 arpents for $10,000 cash. With this as a basis, he began to pyramid his property holdings which finally extended five miles along the river front and spread backward on Bayous Plaquemine and Grosse Tete. At one time he had property in Iberville, Pointe Coupee, Ascension and West Baton Rouge parishes. The parish records show scores of deals totaling over a million dollars. Hundreds of slaves passed through his hands, many in connection with land transactions and others by separate bills of sale. Joseph Erwin speculated in land and "traffiked" in slaves. However, he was not a designing speculator, but was honorable in his dealings, wronged no one and was trusted by all. His headquarters were at the "Home Plantation" where he lived the life of a planter, but gave his various interests his personal attention although he employed agents and overseers. The Home Plantation is situated about two miles below Plaquemine. Erwin bought it June 3, 1822 from Warner Washington of Frederick County, Virginia for $28,000. There were 3000 acres and 90 slaves. The witnesses to the act of sale were Fairfax Washington, Herbert Washington, and Hamilton Washington. He then built a fine house near the river front.

The "big house", dubbed "Castle Dangerous" by the local inhabitants on account of its unusual height, was happily typical of the houses that were built later in that section. It was a substantial, square two-story mansion, the first two-story house built in Iberville Parish. Four large rooms, with a great central hall entered from the front porch, formed the ground floor. Every room portrayed solidity and simplicity with a certain share of beauty. There were mermaids painted on the doors, and gilded cornices around some of the rooms, and marble mantelpieces and hearths throughout the house.

In accord with the general tone the furniture of the house, made of cypress, massive mahogany, dainty bird's-eye maple, beautiful cherry and walnut, fitted the rooms harmoniously. Eastwick Evans in his "Pedestrious Tour" up the Mississippi in 1817 says, "The dwelling houses of the planters are not inferior to any in the United States, either with respect to size, architecture or the manner in which they are furnished."

Captain Erwin's old home site and the river battled for decades and the river won many years ago. The Mississippi now rolls cruelly over the once beloved spot, just across the road from the beautiful mansion built in 1858 by Edward J. Gay to replace the original. It is now owned and occupied by the Gay family who are direct descendants.

Joseph Erwin prospered in Iberville Parish, yet he had

many ups and downs. By 1823 he had acquired large holdings but in that year he was forced to put a mortgage on his property. This was probably necessitated by the panic of 1819, the yellow fever epidemic of 1820, and the freeze of 1823.

In the latter year on February 16, after a spell of warm weather, a severe freeze set in. "The water near the banks of the river was frozen, and persons skated on the marshes. All the orange trees were killed, water men in their boats, Negroes in their cabins, cattle in the forests perished from cold." The cold was so intense that the planted cane froze in the ground.

In 1828 the River overflowed his plantation and Erwin believed himself a ruined man. He then sold the greater part of his property. He sold the Home Plantation to Durham Tudor Hall for $222,000, and the Irion property for $100,000 to Robert Irion and Alvin B. Clark, while Francis Neuralt and Louis Dardenne bought the Portage property.

After having sold the Home Plantation Erwin left it to reside in the home of his daughter, Eliza Wilson, on the adjoining Evergreen Plantation. There in the presence of Samuel Spragins, his old friend and agent, Erwin made his last real estate transaction. This was on March 21, 1829 when Isaac Erwin of Davidson County, Tennessee, bought his father's share of the Grosse Tete Plantation — 1490 acres at $10.00 an acre.

Upon Joseph Erwin's death the estate was almost insolvent because the principal debtors could not pay. Mrs. Lavinia Erwin, the widow, now a woman of sixty years old, undertook to administer the estate and carry on the activities of the plantations. She employed her son-in-law, John B. Craighead of Nashville, to act as her general agent and attorney. Mrs. Erwin and Craighead ran the plantations successfully, but they had many setbacks.

In 1835 Cholera broke out in the cabins back of the Home Plantation, and 28 slaves and the overseer died within four days. Mrs. Erwin cared for the Negroes during this serious sickness. Dr. Charles Clement was the regular plantation and family physician.

The Erwin estate often suffered loss from runaway slaves. In one year Mrs. Erwin paid Col. Andrew Hynes $200 for bringing back Negroes who had run away from the Irion Plantation. She paid the parish Prison in New Orleans $85.70 for arresting and keeping runaway slaves.

Mrs. Erwin and Craighead managed this business thriftily and economically and a large amount of supplies was raised on the plantations. However, every year such staples as pork, corn, oats and potatoes had to be purchased additionally. The slaves usually received fixed amounts of meat, meal and molasses with occasional additions of fish, flour, also vegetables from the big garden. The slaves had their own garden patches which they were permitted to cultivate, and they were allowed to sell the produce and keep the money themselves.

It is interesting to know what the slaves wore. Actually the clothing cost much less than the food. Each slave was given every year several shirts and pantaloons, a woolen overcoat for winter, a pair of shoes and a pair of blankets. The shoes were clumsy and home-made but Mrs. Erwin bought many pairs. One time she paid $273.58 for Negro brogans. Another time the shoe bill was $392.94. Blankets were distributed to slaves in November. In 1833 she paid $517.88 for a hundred pair, and two years later the blanket bill amounted to $964.00.

Strange as it may seem, the prices did not vary greatly from the prices of one hundred years later. A suit of clothes cost $46.00, a hat $5.00 and a pair of shoes $2.50. Coffee was 15½ cents a pound and sugar 6½ to 8 cents a pound.

Mrs. Erwin and Craighead took over the estate when pressed by onerous debts, credit at low ebb and the estate on the verge of bankruptcy. By their industry, prudence and good business management they placed the estate in a firm and solvent position. When Mrs. Erwin died on February 13, 1836, her half of the estate was valued at $262,105. Against this was a debt of $140,891, thus leaving $121,313 to be divided among her heirs. Considering the obstacles Mrs. Erwin had done well. With the assistance, advice and cooperation of Craighead, she had restored the estate to solvency and left something for the children.

When Mrs. Erwin died she left her entire estate to the six remaining heirs. By compromise, in 1837 the estate was divided as follows: The Peachblossom Plantation in Tennessee, which Erwin had always reserved for Mrs. Erwin in case he should lose his money in Louisiana, together with the Home Plantation and 219 slaves went to the Hynes, Craighead and Isaac Erwin heirs. The Irion Plantation and 74 slaves was divided between the Robertson and Wilson heirs. Each of the heirs assumed responsibility for the debts on his portion of the estate.

Joseph Erwin lies buried with his wife in what was the private cemetery on the Home Place. The quaint little graveyard in rear of the St. Louis Plantation may be seen from the main highway which it borders. In it are buried likewise his daughter, Eliza; his planter son-in-law, Nicholas Wilson; and their son-in-law, the Rev. David D. Chesnut. Joseph Erwin wrote an epitaph for Nicholas Wilson which was engraved on his marble tomb. Now almost obliterated by the rain, winds, and sunshine of a hundred and twenty-five years it is a tribute not only to Nicholas Wilson, but is in fact a fitting epitaph to the life of brave, daring, honest Joseph Erwin. It reads in part:

> In every relation of life
> He acted well his part
> He was a dutiful son,
> A tender Husband,
> An affectionate Father,
> A sincere Friend & Humane Master.

CHAPTER III

THE DUEL BETWEEN ANDREW JACKSON AND CHARLES DICKINSON

In my boyhood days I heard older members of the family speak reverently of "Grandpa Erwin" and his success as a sugar planter. I also remember brief references to the duel in which Gen. Jackson killed the son-in-law of his former friend and neighbor, probably the determining factor in the relocation of the Erwin family in Louisiana. It was not, however, for many years after leaving Plaquemine that I read in detail the story of the tragic duel and realized its impact on the affairs of Joseph Erwin and the various members of his family. The Charles Dickinson of my youthful days, the great-grandson of the duellist, was my particular chum, a close friendship lasting to this time.

The famous duel between Andrew Jackson and Charles Dickinson in 1806 had a direct bearing on the history of Iberville Parish and the development of plantation life there. Because of this duel, Joseph Erwin of Nashville came to Louisiana to become one of the early settlers of the parish. Later came his grandson and ward Charles Dickinson, son of the deceased duellist. Then other members of Erwin's family his sons, John and Isaac, his sons-in-law, Wilson, Robertson, Craighead, Hynes and Col. Hynes' son-in-law, Edward J. Gay of St. Louis, whose descendants still own much of the former Erwin properties. Joseph Erwin also persuaded the able young physician Dr. Charles Clement of Duchess County, New

York, to locate there to become later one of the parish's leading citizens.

While Andrew Jackson never visited Iberville Parish, the chain of circumstances resulting from his irascible nature terminating in the celebrated duel has extended down through the years and has affected the history and development of the great Parish of Iberville.

Much has been written about the duel between Jackson and Dickinson. Parton in his three-volume life of Jackson made quite a study of this event and in the "Life" tells about the duel in detail. Over forty pages of his book are given to it.

As everyone knows Jackson was hot-blooded and "quick on the draw". He got into many disputes. The Encyclopedia Britannica says: "His combative disposition led him into numerous personal difficulties—a succession of personal acts in which he showed himself ignorant, violent, perverse, quarrelsome and astonishingly indiscreet."

During his presidential campaign one writer made a study of General Jackson's disputes, and collected nearly one hundred incidents of fights or violent and abusive quarrels in which Jackson had taken part. Seventeen of these affairs were of a serious nature.

Jackson was a follower of the *code duello*. Duelling, that strange system of satisfying honor between gentlemen, was introduced into America by the French at the time of the American Revolution. Many French officers were located at Charleston, South Carolina for a period, and they imbued the young bloods of that city with the idea of fighting with pistols and swords to avenge one's honor.

Charleston was a city of culture and its people were more urbane than most Americans including New Englanders. It was said that the young Charlestonian officers in the American Army took pleasure in picking quarrels with the Yankee officers whom they made fun of as being awkward, crude and ill-mannered. Charleston became a duelling center, but in

JOSEPH ERWIN, 1761-1829

The pictures of Mr. and Mrs. Erwin were made from paintings now owned by Senator E. J. Gay. They still hang on the walls of the old Mansion at St. Louis Plantation.

MRS. JOSEPH ERWIN, 1762-1836
The former Lavinia Thompson

Gen. Andrew Jackson about the time of the Battle of New Orleans. Drawn by C. M. Luria.

New Orleans more duels were fought than in any other American city. While duels were fought in England, they were never popular or as prevalent in Anglo-Saxon countries. The system never was well established in the northern part of the United States, and the killing of Alexander Hamilton by Aaron Burr created a wave of feeling against duelling particularly in the North.

However, in the South duelling became even more prevalent and continued in great favor up until the time of the War Between the States. Army and Navy officers used to fight duels, but none was fought in the armed forces of the United States after 1861, although several duels were fought between Confederate officers after that time.

It will be remembered that Andrew Jackson when a youth spent some time in Charleston. There he became acquainted with many of the young men of the town. He adopted their code of living, learned how to race horses and attend cock fights and to defend his honor with pistols. He carried this idea with him to Tennessee.

Andrew Jackson fought several duels before the one in which he killed Charles Dickinson. The direct cause of this last duel was dispute over a proposed race between Jackson's horse, "Truxton," and Joseph Erwin's "Plowboy," which race was never run. Some trivial details connected with the payment of the forfeit for not running the race were blown up into matters of great importance, and brought on the duel.

Indirectly, however, as some think, the reason for the duel was the ill feeling between Jackson and Charles Dickinson because of remarks he is alleged to have made about Jackson's wife. As these criticisms were based on general gossip, it was said that Jackson became greatly incensed and wished to make an example of some highly placed individual so as to intimidate others and stop the talk.

Jackson married Mrs. Rachel Robards, formerly Miss Donelson. She had left her husband, and they both had heard that he had obtained a divorce by an act of the Legislature of Virginia. This act, however, was not an act of divorce, but it only authorized the courts to determine whether or not there were sufficient grounds for divorce and to grant or withhold it accordingly. In his plea for the divorce Robards accused his wife of adultery. This had not been proved. It was more than two years afterwards that the divorce was actually granted and only then because of the fact that Jackson and Mrs. Robards were living together. Jackson had the marriage ceremony performed the second time.

Naturally, there was a great deal of gossip about the affair. His enemies particularly criticized him and made sly remarks. Jackson let it be known that he would fight or kill anyone who cast suspicion upon his honor or that of his wife and he meant it.

Jackson had met young Charles Dickinson while he was a member of Congress on a visit to the home of a friend in Maryland. Impressed with young Dickinson, he invited him to come to Nashville. Dickinson was a lawyer, handsome, young and possessed of means. He loved horse racing and soon became the "catch" of the town. He married Joseph Erwin's beautiful daughter, Jane.

Jackson and Erwin were rival owners of blooded race horses. At the opening of the fall races of 1805, Captain Erwin offered to bet $5,000 on his *Tanner* against all comers at a race to be held at Cloverbottom. Jackson accepted, and trained 16 horses, *Truxton* and *Greyhound* among them. *Greyhound* won in three heats. Jackson and his adherents made much money on the race. In fact, Jackson was able to pay debts that were embarrassing him. After *Tanner* was defeated Erwin then offered to run *Plowboy*, his famous stallion, for the best two out of three two-mile heats for a stake of $2,000, forfeit to be $800.00, payable on the day of the race in notes which were to be "due." It must be explained that in those days there was not much cash in circulation and responsible business men gave their notes which circulated as cash.

Truxton was a beautiful bay sired by an imported horse *Diomede* with a thoroughbred mare, *Nancy Coleman*, "which said horse is in high estimation of any horse ever imported into the State of Virginia." Jackson had purchased this famous horse, said to be the finest in all that part of the West.

But Joseph Erwin was also proud of his horse, and so the great race was arranged to be run at *Cloverbottom*, near Jackson's property, and not so far away from *Peachblossom*, Joseph Erwin's plantation.

Six persons were interested in this race. Those backing *Truxton* were General Jackson; Major W. P. Anderson; Major Verrell and Captain Pryor. The backers of *Plowboy* were Joseph Erwin and his son-in-law Charles Dickinson. Before the day appointed for the day of the race, *Plowboy* developed a lame leg and Erwin and Dickinson decided to pay the forfeit and withdrew their horse, which was done amicably and the affair was supposed to be at an end.

The duel between Jackson and Dickinson was brought on indirectly by Thomas Swann. Swann was a young lawyer from Virginia, a graduate of William and Mary College, who had just arrived at Nashville with letters of introduction from prominent people. Actually he belonged to a better family than Jackson, but Jackson would not recognize him as his social equal and attempted to cane him rather than fight a duel, accusing Swann of being a horse jockey.*

Swann carried gossip emanating from Jackson's friends to Dickinson and Erwin which alleged that Erwin acted in bad faith in the matter of the notes given in payment of the forfeit. Dickinson resented this, and after several meetings and correspondence, with Swann trying to get Jackson into a duel with him, and letters to the paper, Jackson challenged Dickinson.

Gen. Jackson and Capt. Erwin were the leading turfmen of the Middle West. They both had fine stables and Jackson owned the Clover Bottom race course. In spite of the differences between Jackson and Erwin's son-in-law, Dickinson, the "races must go on."

After the Fall races of 1805 and the withdrawal of Erwin's *Plowboy* from the proposed race of November, 1805 when Erwin and Dickinson paid the forfeit with notes which brought on incidents that later caused the duel, another great race was arranged for the Spring.

---

*An officer or a gentleman would not fight a duel with a social inferior, or with some one whom he would not invite to dine in his home. He would cane or horse whip such a person who insulted him.

Here is an advertisement taken from the Cumberland Repository (Nashville) of March 15, 1806.

CLOVER BOTTOM RACE

On Thursday, the 3rd of April next, will be run the greatest and most interesting match race ever run in the western country, between General Jackson's horse.

TRUXTON,

six years old, carrying 124 pounds, and Capt. Joseph Erwin's horse,

PLOUGHBOY

eight years old, carrying 130 pounds. These horses run the two-mile heats for the sum of $3,000. No stud horses can be admitted within the gates, but such as contend on the turf, and persons are requested not to bring their dogs to the field, as they will be shot without respect to the owners.

The day of the Truxton-Ploughboy race was cloudy. *Truxton* had an injured thigh. Some of his backers wanted to call the race off, because they had plenty of money bet on him. A large crowd was present at the Clover Bottom track, in fact, Gen. Jackson said it was the largest crowd he ever saw assembled.

Truxton won the first heat, but he was limping badly. Jackson insisted that he run the second heat. He did and beat Ploughboy by 60 yards in a heavy rain, running the two-mile course in a few seconds less than four minutes. Jackson and his friends won $10,000. Capt. Erwin paid his debt promptly. This saved Andrew Jackson financially, and he withdrew his property which he had offered for sale.

On the 20th of May, Dickinson returned to Nashville after a trip down the river to Natchez and New Orleans. On May 22, General Thomas Overton rode out to General Jackson's store at Cloverbottom with the information that Dickinson had written a scurrilous attack upon Jackson which was in the hands of Mr. Eastin, the editor of the paper, and that it would appear in the next issue. Overton told Jackson that he should not overlook it. Jackson mounted his horse and rode to the office of the Impartial Review and looked at the letter which Mr. Dickinson had sent. Thereupon Andrew Jackson challenged Dickinson. We now follow Parton's interesting account.

Before the day closed, Jackson received, through Dr. Hanson Catlett, a reply to his challenge. "Your note of this morning", wrote Dickinson, "is received, and your request shall be gratified. My friend who hands you this will make the necessary arrangements."

The seconds immediately conferred, agreed upon the time and place of meeting, and drew up their agreement in writing:—"On Friday, the 30th instant, we agree to meet at Harrison's Mills, on Red river, in Logan county, State of Kentucky, for the purpose of settling an affair of honor between General Andrew Jackson and Charles Dickinson, Esq. Further arrangements to be made. It it understood that the meeting will be at the hour of seven in the morning."

On the same day the seconds met again, and agreed upon the following: "It is agreed that the distance shall be twenty-four feet; the parties to stand facing each other, with their pistols down perpendicularly. When they are ready, the single word, FIRE, to be given; at which they are to fire as soon as they please. Should either fire before the word is given, we pledge ourselves to shoot him down instantly. The person to give the word to be determined by lot, as also the choice of position. We mutually agree that the above regulations shall be observed in the affair of honor depending between General Andrew Jackson and Charles Dickinson, Esq."

This was Saturday, May 24th, 1806. The duel was not to take place till the Friday following. The quarrel thus far had excited intense interest in Nashville, and the successive numbers of the *Impartial Review* had been read with avidity. The coming duel was no secret, though the time and place were not known to any but the friends of the parties. Bets, I am informed, were laid upon the result of the meeting, the odds being against Jackson. Dickinson himself is said to have bet five hundred dollars that he would bring his antagonist down at the first fire. Another informant says three thousand. But I have small belief in *any* of the ill things said of this man.

THE DUEL

The place appointed for the meeting was a long day's ride from Nashville. Thursday morning, before the dawn of day, Dickinson stole from the side of his young and beautiful wife, and began silently to prepare for the journey. She awoke and asked him why he was up so early. He replied that he had business in Kentucky across the Red river, but it would not detain him long. Before leaving the room, he went up to his wife, kissed her with peculiar tenderness, and said:

"Good bye, darling; I shall be *sure* to be at home tomorrow night."

He mounted his horse and repaired to the rendezvous where his second and half a dozen of the gay blades of Nashville were waiting to escort him on his journey.

General Jackson and the party that accompanied him were worried. General Thomas Overton, an old revolutionary soldier, versed in the science, and familiar with the practice of dueling, had reflected deeply upon the conditions of the coming combat, with the view to conclude upon the tactics most likely to save his friend from Dickinson's unerring bullet. For this duel was not to be the the amusing mockery that some modern duels have been. This duel was to be *real*. It was to be an affair in which each man was to strive with his utmost skill to effect the purpose of the occasion—disable his antagonist and save

his own life. As the principal and the second rode apart
from the rest, they discussed all the chances and proba-
bilities with the single aim to decide upon a course which
should result in the disabling of Dickinson and the saving of Jackson. The mode of fighting which had been
agreed upon was somewhat peculiar. The pistols were
to be held downward until the word was given to fire;
then each man was to fire *as soon as he pleased*. With
such an arrangement, it was scarcely possible that both
the pistols should be discharged at the same moment.
There was a chance, even, that by extreme quickness of
movement one man could bring down his antagonist without himself receiving a shot. The question anxiously
discussed between Jackson and Overton was this: Shall
we try to get the first shot, or shall we permit Dickinson
to have it? They agreed, at length, that it would be de-
cidedly better to let Dickinson fire first. In the first place,
Dickinson, like all miraculous shots, required no time
to take aim, and would have a far better chance than
Jackson in a quick shot, even if both fired at once. And
in spite of anything Jackson could do, Dickinson would
be almost sure to get the first fire. Moreover, Jackson
was *certain* he would be hit; and he was unwilling to subject his own aim to the chance of its being totally destroyed by the shock of the blow. For Jackson was resolved
on hitting Dickinson. His feelings toward his adversary
were embittered. "I should have hit him, if he had shot
me through the brain," said Jackson later.

A tavern kept by one David Miller, somewhat noted in
the neighborhood, stood on the banks of the Red river,
near the ground appointed for the duel. Late in the afternoon of Thursday, the 29th of May, the inmates of this
tavern were surprised by the arrival of a party of seven
or eight horsemen. Jacob Smith, then employed by Miller
as an overseer, but not himself a planter in the vicinity,
was standing before the house when this unexpected
company rode up. One of these horsemen asked him if
they could be accommodated with lodgings for the night.

They could. The party dismounted, gave their horses to the attendant Negroes, and entered the tavern. No sooner had they done so, than honest Jacob was perplexed by the arrival of a second cavalcade—Dickinson and his friends, who also asked for lodgings. The manager told them the house was full; but that he never turned travelers away, and if they chose to remain, he would do the best he could for them. Dickinson then asked where was the next house of entertainment. He was directed to a house two miles lower down the river, kept by William Harrison. The house is still standing. The room in which Dickinson slept that night, and *slept* the following night, is the one now used by the occupants as a dining-room.

Jackson ate heartily at supper that night, conversing in a lively, pleasant manner, and smoked his evening pipe as usual. Jacob Smith remembers being exceedingly pleased with his guest, and, on learning the cause of his visit, heartily wishing him a safe deliverance.

Before breakfast on the next morning the whole party mounted and rode down the road that wound close along the picturesque banks of the stream.

About the same hour, the overseer and his gang of Negroes went to the fields to begin their daily toil; he, longing to venture within sight of what he knew was about to take place.

The horsemen rode about a mile along the river; then turned down toward the river to a point on the bank where they had expected to find a ferryman. No ferryman appearing, Jackson spurred his horse into the stream and dashed across, followed by all his party. They rode into the poplar forest, two hundred yards or less, to a spot near the center of a level platform or river bottom, then covered with forest, now smiling with cultivated fields. The horsemen halted and dismounted just before reaching the appointed place. Jackson, Overton, and a surgeon who had come with them from home, walked on together, and the rest led their horses a short distance in an opposite direction.

"How do you feel about it now, General?" asked one
of the party, as Jackson turned to go.

"Oh, all right," replied Jackson, gayly; "I shall wing
him, never fear."

Dickinson's second won the choice of position, and
Jackson's the office of giving the word. The astute Overton considered this giving of the word a matter of great
importance, and he had already determined *how* he would
give it, if the lot fell to him. The eight paces were measured off, and the men placed. Both were perfectly collected. All the politeness of such occasions were very
strictly and elegantly performed. Jackson was dressed
in a loose frock-coat, buttoned carelessly over his chest,
and concealing in some degree the extreme slenderness of
his figure. Dickinson was the younger and handsomer
man of the two. But Jackson's tall, erect figure, and the
still intensity of his demeanor, it is said, gave him a most
superior and commanding air, as he stood under the tall
poplars of this bright May morning, silently awaiting the
moment of doom.

"Are you ready?" said Overton.

"I am ready," replied Dickinson.

"I am ready," said Jackson.

The words were no sooner pronounced than Overton,
with a sudden shout cried, using his old-country pronun-
ciation, "FERE!"

Dickinson raised his pistol quickly and fired. Overton,
who was looking with anxiety and dread at Jackson, saw
a puff of dust fly from the breast of his coat, and saw
him raise his left arm and place it tightly across his chest.
He is surely hit, thought Overton, and in a bad place, too;
but no, he does not fall. Erect and grim as Fate he stood,
his teeth clenched, raising his pistol. Overton glanced at
Dickinson. Amazed at the unwonted failure of his aim,
and apparently appalled at the awful figure and face
before him, Dickinson had unconsciously recoiled a pace
or two.

"Great God!" he faltered, "Have I missed him?"

"Back to the MARK, Sir!" shrieked Overton, with his hand upon his pistol.

Dickinson recovered his composure, stepped forward to the peg, and stood with his eyes averted from his antagonist. All this was the work of a moment, though it requires many words to tell it.

General Jackson took deliberate aim, and pulled the trigger. The pistol neither snapped nor went off. He looked at the trigger, and discovered that it had stopped at half cock. He drew it back to its place, and took aim a second time. He fired. Dickinson's face blanched; he reeled; his friends rushed toward him, caught him in their arms, and gently seated him on the ground, leaning against a bush. His trowsers reddened. They stripped off his clothes. The blood was gushing from his side in a torrent. And, alas! here is the ball, not near the wound, but above the *opposite* hip, just under the skin. The ball had passed through the body below the ribs. Such a wound could not but be fatal.

Overton went forward and learned the condition of the wounded man. Rejoining his principal, he said, "He won't want anything more of you, General," and conducted him from the ground. They had gone a hundred yards, Overton walking on one side of Jackson, the surgeon on the other, and neither speaking a word, when the surgeon observed that one of Jackson's shoes was full of blood.

"My God! General Jackson, are you hit?" he exclaimed, pointing to the blood.

"Oh! I believe," replied Jackson, "that he has pinked me a little. Let's look at it, But say nothing about it *there*," pointing to the house.

He opened his coat. Dickinson's aim had been perfect. He had sent the ball precisely where he supposed Jackson's heart was beating. But the thinness of his body and the looseness of his coat combining to deceive Dickinson, the ball had only broken a rib or two, and raked the breast-bone. It was a somewhat painful, bad-looking wound, but neither severe or dangerous, and he was able to ride to the tavern without much inconvenience. Upon approaching the house, he went up to one of the negro women who was churning, and asked her if the butter had come. She said it was just coming. He asked for some buttermilk. While she was getting it for him, she observed him furtively open his coat and look within it. She saw that his shirt was soaked with blood, and she stood gazing in blank horror at the sight, dipper in hand. He caught her eye, and hastily buttoned his coat again. She dipped out a quart measure full of buttermilk, and gave it to him. He drank it off at a draught; then went in, took off his coat, and had his wound carefully examined and dressed. That done, he dispatched one of his retinue to Dr. Catlett, to inquire respecting the condition of Dickinson, and to say that the surgeon attending himself would be glad to contribute his aid toward Mr. Dickinson's relief. Polite reply was returned that Mr. Dickinson's case was past surgery. In the course of the day, General Jackson sent a bottle of wine to Dr. Catlett for the use of his patient.

But there was one gratification which Jackson could not, even in such circumstances, grant him. A very old friend of General Jackson writes to me thus: "Although the General had been wounded, he did not desire it should be known until he had left the neighborhood, and had therefore concealed it at first from his own friends. His reason for this, as he once stated to me, was, that as Dickinson considered himself the best shot in the world, and was certain of killing him at the first fire, he did not want him to have gratification even of knowing that he had touched him."

Poor Dickinson bled to death. The flowing of blood was stanched, but could not be stopped. He was conveyed to the house in which he had passed the night, and placed upon a mattress, which was soon drenched with blood. He suffered extreme agony, and uttered horrible cries all the long day. At nine o'clock in the evening he suddenly asked why they had put out the light. The doctor knew then that the end was at hand; the wife, who had been sent for in the morning, would not arrive in time to close her husband's eyes. He died five minutes after, cursing, it is said, with his last breath, the ball that had entered his body. The poor wife hurried away on hearing that her husband was "dangerously wounded." and met, as she rode toward the scene of the duel, a procession of silent horsemen escorting a rough emigrant wagon that contained her husband's remains.

The news created in Nashville the most profound sensation. "On Tuesday evening (afternoon) last," said the *Impartial Review* of the following week, "the remains of Mr. Charles Dickinson were committed to the grave, at the residence of Mr. Joseph Erwin, attended by a large number of citizens of Nashville and its neighborhood. There have been few occasions on which stronger impressions of sorrow or testimonies of greater respect were evinced than on the one we have the unwelcome task to record. In the prime of life, and blessed in domestic circumstances with almost every valuable enjoyment, he fell a victim to the barbarous and pernicious practice of dueling. By his untimely fate the community is deprived of an amiable man and a virtuous citizen. His friends will long lament with particular sensibility the deplorable event. Mr. Dickinson was a native of Maryland, where he was highly valued by the discriminating and good; and those who knew him best respected him most. With a consort that has to bear with this, the severest of afflictions, and an infant child, his friends and acquaintances will cordially sympathize. Their loss is above calculation. May Heaven assuage their anguish by administering such consolations as are beyond the power of human accident or change."

But the matter did not rest here. Charles Dickinson had many friends in Nashville and Andrew Jackson many enemies. The events preceeding, and the circumstances attending the duel were such as to excite horror and disgust in many minds. An informal meeting of citizens was held, who could hit upon no better way of expressing their feelings than sending the following memorial to the proprietors of the *Impartial Review*:—"The subscribers, citizens of Nashville and its vicinity, respectfully request Mr. Bradford and Mr. Eastin to put the next number of their paper in mourning as a tribute of respect for the memory and regret for the untimely death of Mr. Charles Dickinson."

Seventy-three names, many of which were of the highest respectability, were appended to this document. Mr. Eastin had no hesitation in promising to comply with the request.

Upon his couch at the Hermitage General Jackson heard of this movement. With his usual promptitude, he dispatched to the editor the following letter:—"*Mr. Eastin*: —I am informed that at the request of sundry citizens of Nashville and vicinity, you are about to dress your paper in mourning 'as a tribute of respect for the memory and regret for the untimely death of Charles Dickinson.' Your paper is the public vehicle, and is always taken as the public will, unless the contrary appears. *Presuming that the public is not in mourning for this event*, in justice to that public, it is only fair and right to set forth the names of those citizens who have made the request. The thing is so novel that names ought to appear that the public might judge whether the true motives of the signers were 'a tribute of respect for the deceased,' or something else that at first sight does not appear."

The editor, with equal complaisance and ingenuity, contrived to oblige all parties. He placed his paper in mourning, he published the memorial, he published General Jackson's letter, and he added to the whole the following remarks:—"In answer to the request of General Jackson I can only observe that, previously, the request of some of the citizens of Nashville, and its vicinity had been put to type, and as soon as it has transpired that the above

request had been made, a number of the subscribers, to
the amount of twenty-six, called and erased their names.
Always willing to support, by my acts, the title of my
paper—always willing to attend to the request of any portion of our citizens when they will take the responsibility
on themselves, induced me to comply with the petition of
those requesting citizens, and place my paper in mourning. Impartiality induces me also to attend to the request
of General Jackson."*

A week or two later, Captain Erwin, the father-in-law
of the unfortunate Dickinson, published a brief recapitu-
lation of the quarrel from the beginning, incorporating
with his article a final statement by Mr. Thomas Swann.
Swann exculpated Dickinson wholly. "I do avow," said he,
"that neither Mr. Dickinson nor any other person urged
me forward to quarrel with Jackson." He asserted in
the most solemn manner that every thing had occurred
just as in the published correspondence and affidavits it
had appeared to occur. He admitted, however, that there
was enmity between Jackson and Dickinson before his
own quarrel with Jackson began.

Here follows Captain Erwin's statement as copied in its
entirety from the *Correspondence of Andrew Jackson,* edited
by John Spencer Bassett. Vol. I, pg. 147.

June 1806

Mr. Eastin, An impartial and dispassionate enquiry
into the origin, progress and result of the dispute between
Mr. Charles Dickinson deceased and General Andrew
Jackson, is the design of this address (through the
medium of your paper) to the public.

---

*This account of the duel was compiled from many sources, verbal
and printed; but most of the incidents which occurred *on the field*
I received from an old friend of General Jackson, who heard them
related, and saw them *acted,* by General Overton. In narrating some
of the minor events, I have had to choose between conflicting state-
ments; yet I feel confident that this account contains no error of importance; no error affecting the moral quality of the principal acts.

Misrepresentations and false insinuation may, where the character of Mr. Dickinson was not known, have a tendency to make improper impressions; to repel the one and remove the other by a fair and candid statement of facts, is the object of my present purpose.

General Jackson in his letter of the 23rd of May, had exhibited a number of charges against Mr. Dickinson, which are entirely without foundation; he has attempted to show Mr. Dickinson the aggressor, when, in fact, he had made a wanton and unprovoked attack upon the character and feelings of Mr. Dickinson, he accuses Mr. Dickinson, first, of having industriously excited Thomas Swann to quarrel with him etc., secondly, of having wrote an insulting letter on the 10th of January, left the country, and caused the letter to be delivered some days after he had gone, and thirdly of having in the press a piece more replete with bl(a)ck-guard abuse than any of his former productions; to the whole of those charges I conceive the certificate of Mr. Swann is a sufficient answer, which is in the words following:

Nashville, June 16th, 1806

Capt. Joseph Erwin

Sir, In compliance with your request I commit to paper an accurate detail of all the circumstances relative to the quarrel between Charles Dickinson Esq. and Gen. Andrew Jackson, so far as at present consistent with my recollection. I do certify that having met Mr. Dickinson in Nashville some few days after he and yourself had a conversation with Jackson on the subject of the payment of the forfeit in the race between Ploughboy and Truxton, Mr. Dickinson informed me (I think at my request, for I had before heard from Samuel Jackson, that Andrew Jackson denied the statement made by me to be correct:) that Andrew Jackson did deny what I had stated to be true and further asserted that whoever was the author of a report that he had stated the notes offered by you in pay-

CHARLES DICKINSON

on-in-law of Joseph Erwin killed in
 duel with Gen. Andrew Jackson, on
ay 30, 1806. From a miniature
ainting loaned by Charles H. Dickin-
n, a direct descendant now living in
alifornia.

Right

CKINSON CREST AND COAT OF ARMS

Left—MRS. CHARLES H. DICKINSON former Anna Maria Turner of Nash wife of the duellist's son and moth the Dickinson of Civil War fame. Pi taken in 1862, Glasgow, Scotland.

Right—CHARLES H. DICKINSON, of "Live Oaks" Plantation, later of Plaquemine, Civil War veteran, distinguished civil engineer, geologist and in his younger days a Texas Ranger. At the time of his death in 1898, Federal "Surveyor General" for this section of the South.

J.B. Gillett
when Sergt of Co A

Grooms Lee

Old Bell and Bill

—Drawing by Dickinson of the
Rangers. Dickinson, b e t w e e n
s with redskins and desperadoes,
sketches. It is significant that Old
omes before Bill, because a ranger
s considered his horse first. Made
np on the Staked Plains in 1874
the men were hundreds of miles
a town. The pipe, the six-shooter,
dle, the rope, all the indispensable
nent of the ranger, are plainly vis-
the original painting which was
n water color on a piece of plain
g paper.

—LIVE OAKS. The plantation home
rles H. Dickinson on Bayou Grosse
Built about 1830, it was enlarged
widow, Mrs. Anna Maria Dickin-
1860. "Live Oaks" near the vil-
f Rosedale is one of the show
of the section.

Above—SCRATCHLEY MANSION, Plaquemine, built by the late Dr. Edward Scratchley prior to the Civil War and used since then by St. Basil's Academy. During the war years the nuns were forced to leave and the building was used as Federal headquarters.

Below—THE SCHWING MANSION in Plaquemine is one of its show places. Built by Ezra Tuttle, it was purchased from him by Joseph Schlater, one of the Schwing ancestors, in 1845. Mrs. Middleton, the former Maria Schwing, writes that, "During the Civil War a gun boat came up the Mississippi. Plaquemine was shelled and our old house got one of the cannon balls, shattering both back and west side walls." The architecture of the house is Spanish Colonial.

ment of the forfeit to be different from those which he
had agreed to receive, was a damned lyar; Previous to
Jackson's having made this declaration my name had
not been mentioned: but he then asked Mr. Dickinson who
was his informant, he told him I was, bring him forward
said Jackson, but Mr. Dickinson declined doing it. I asked
Mr. Dickinson why he had not called on me immediately,
his reply was because there was a dispute between Jackson and himself, and it would have appeared as if he
wished to shift the quarrel from him to me, to have called
on me at that time. I then observed that if General Jackson had applied those epithets to me, or had denied the
statement made by me, he was himself a damned lyar;
and I would call him to an account for his conduct; Mr.
Dickinson and myself then parted without any further
conversation on the subject; and on the next day (January 3d) I wrote a letter to general Jackson (demanding
an explanation) which he received on the 6th. And on
the day following returned an answer, not an explicit
avowal or disavowal of the declaration ascribed to him
by Mr. Dickinson; or, a confession, or denial of the statement I had made, but fraught with invective and scur-
rility against the conduct and character of Mr. Dickinson, and at the conclusion mentions that he shall set out
that morning for S. W. Point; On the 10th the third day
after having received general Jackson's letter, Mr. Dickinson replyed to it, and on the 11th having given his answer to Mr. Lee for conveyance when Jackson returned
from the Point (to which place he was supposed to have
gone) Mr. Dickinson's business called him down the river
to Orleans; during his absence general Jackson's publication made its appearance, and on its (his) return he
replied to it, they are both before the public and by the
public it will decided which is most "replete with black-
guard abuse." I do aver that neither Mr. Dickinson nor
any other person did urge me forward to quarrel with
Jackson, and should any have attempted it I would have
convinced them that I was not to be influenced (where my

reputation had been aspersed) by any man, or made the tool of any party.

I am, sir, yours respectfully

THOMAS SWANN,

Thus having summed up evidence in the dispute between Mr. Dickinson and general Jackson, I now leave the public to decide who was the aggressor. Whether Mr. Dickinson was not entirely innocent of offering an unprovoked insult or of wounding the feelings of general Jackson, until driven to it by the egregious and insufferable insults offered to himself; and whether, if he injured the general at all, the injury was of such nature that the implacable resentment of his antagonist should pursue him beyond the grave, and insult the memory of the deceased, by endeavoring to prevent that tribute of respect due to his merit, which his friends and acquaintances were about to confer.*

---

*The following were the names actually published: Hansen Catlett, Thomas E. Wagaman, Thomas K. Watkins, Boyd McNairy, John McNairy, William Tait, Duncan Robertson, John H. Smith, Thomas Williamson, William T. Lewis, John Nichols, Thomas C. Clark, Daney McCraw, John Maclin, Jeremiah Scales, Timothy Demonbrum, Elisha Johnson, James P. Downes, William B. Robertson, William Lytle, D. Moore, Robert Soteart, J. Gordan, J. B. Craighead, P. Boum, Alexander Craighead, John Read, Robert P. Currin, Roger B. Sappington, Roger B. Currey, Thomas Swann, Ernest Benoir, William Y. Probert, C. Wheston, J. Baird, Hervey Lane, Samuel Finney, William Black, R. Hewett, Thomas Ramsey, Nathaniel McCairys, Thomas Napier, Robert Hughes, James King, Robert Bell, Felix Robertson. One sheet of the issue of the Impartial Review is missing dater June 7, 1806. On the margin has been written in pencil, "The portion of this paper torn off contained a request by many citizens that the editor place the paper in mourning, and Gen. Jackson's call on the editor for the names of the persons."

In a letter to the *Impartial Review*, July 5, 1806, Corbin Lee, who seems to have had in charge Captain Erwin's horse Ploughboy, and was, therefore, not biassed toward Jackson, declared "Jackson had fought agreeable to the stipulations, and that having done so, instead of being aspersed he deserved to be honored." Corbin Lee was present at the duel.

It may not be improper before this subject is dismissed
to enquire, whether the proceedings on the field were
strictly proper? and whether general Jackson had a right,
according to the law of duelling, to recock his pistol after
having snapped it? It is said it was agreed that a snap
should not be considered a fire; granted, but was it not
also agreed that nothing which was not committed to
writing should be considered as binding or having effect?
a snap not to be considered as a fire was not committed
to writing, consequently, it was not one of the stipulations in the agreement, 3 neither was it warranted by the
usual practice; yet such was the cruel fate of the unfortunate Dickinson, he gallantly maintained his ground,
and fell a victim to this unguarded, illiberal and unjust
advantage. Peace be to his name, respect to his memory,
which will be ever dear to his friend.

                                        JOSEPH ERWIN

Other accounts of the duel between Jackson and Dickinson
vary considerably from that given by Parton. For instance,
Alice Pemble White in her article on Joseph and Lavinia Erwin in the Louisiana Historical Quarterly states that "Jackson previously placed a thick memorandum book in his pocket,
right over his heart . . . . . . The bullet which would have been
fatal only for the book, glanced and caused only a flesh wound.
Jackson had never raised his arm. According to the rules of
duelling, a wound that brought blood ended the fight; however, Jackson concealed his wound, deliberately took aim and
pulled the trigger, but the hammer stopped at half cock. Dickinson all the time was standing at the peg waiting to be shot.
Jackson once again took accurate aim and killed his oppon-
ent."

The public soon forgets. At first Jackson felt that public
opinion was against him, although he implies in his letter to
Editor Eastin demanding the publication of the names to the
mourning announcement for Dickinson that it was otherwise.

But he seriously thought of leaving Tennessee and tried very hard to be appointed Governor of the Mississippi Territory. This appointment he did not get, and Fate then began pushing him up towards fame and the presidency. The war against the Creek Indians made him popular again and the Battle of New Orleans made him president. The matter of the Dickinson affair was soon relegated to the background. Most people thought of it as a personal quarrel, and in those early days when violence, fighting and killing were common they overlooked Jackson's peccadilloes such as the killing of Charles Dickinson.

Among the relics preserved at the Hermitage are the duelling pistols used in the famous duel. Gen. Jackson kept those pistols to the day of his death, on the mantelpiece or on top of a table in the living room. A visitor chanced one day to pick up one of the pistols. The General said in an ordinary conversational tone, "That is the pistol with which I killed Mr. Dickinson."

It would seem that Andrew Jackson gloried over the death of Dickinson all his life, just as a primitive tribesman was proud of the scalp of his enemy. Thus embittered Jackson could not have been a happy man. In the end it was an old wound, the bullet of Dickinson, that eventually brought about his death.

CHAPTER IV

THE DICKINSONS OF IBERVILLE

Among the able and outstanding men of Iberville Parish
was Charles H. Dickinson, grandson of the Charles of Davidson County, Tennessee, who was killed in the duel with Andrew Jackson. He was the father of my boyhood chum, and
aside from his interesting background and heritage, won renown and prestige in the community.

The Dickinson of the duel came from Maryland. It was in
the year 1780 that "the marvelously beautiful boy," Charles
Dickinson, was born in Caroline County of that state. If his
mother had been able to read the horoscope of her infant son,
she would have brooded over his future. His sad fate has been
a matter much talked of even to this day.

It is probable that he went to Nashville on the invitation of
Andrew Jackson. In *Maryland's Colonial Eastern Shore*,
edited by Swepson Earle (1916), it is stated:

Andrew Jackson, of Tennessee, attending the sessions
at Philadelphia of the Fourth Congress as a Representative, and of the Fifth as a Senator, is said to have visited
Caroline County, Maryland and to have been a guest at
the Daffin home, as well as at others on the Eastern bank
of the Chesapeake. Here he made the acquaintance of
young Charles Dickinson, whom he successfully urged to
move to Tennessee. The sequel to their one-time friendship and business relations, which did not survive the
exigencies of Tennessee politics and social life, was the
duel on the Red River in Kentucky in which Dickinson
fell.

In Buell's "Life of Andrew Jackson," it is stated that Charles Dickinson settled in Nashville in 1801 when he was twenty-three years old. Buell says that Dickinson was a scion of an old Maryland family in whose veins flowed the blood of the Carrolls and the Claytons and that he was college bred and studied law under Chief Justice Marshall.

A lawyer and a man of some means, Dickinson was well received in Nashville. He was handsome and popular. He was fond of horse racing and owned blooded stock. He married Miss Jane Erwin, the "belle of the town"—the beautiful daughter of Capt. Joseph Erwin.

At first he and Jackson were great friends but soon their friendship cooled. The death of Charles Dickinson whom the General killed in a duel was told about in the previous chapter. He left a young son named Charles.

In 1828 this young son, now grown to manhood, came with his bride from his native Nashville to become a pioneer on Bayou Grosse Tete at Rosedale, in Iberville Parish, seventeen miles west of Baton Rouge. He came to Louisiana probably at the urging of his grandfather, Joseph Erwin. Young Dickinson was able to make the entire trip from Port Allen, across the river from Baton Rouge, to Rosedale by boat—the entire region had just been inundated by the great crevasses of 1828. The wide acres that were to be his demesne were all under water, and he got out of a skiff to climb a tall tree to survey his property. Today that tree, some twenty-nine feet in circumference and well over 300 years old, is the vice-president of the Southern Live Oak Society. Appropriately the plantation that Dickinson moved to is known today as "Live Oaks Plantation." At the time of Dickinson's arrival Bayou Grosse Tete was populated almost solely by Indians of the Bayou Goula and Houma tribes.

At his father's death, Charles Dickinson became the ward of his grandfather, Captain Erwin, whose "Home," later the St. Louis Plantation, with other holdings, made him the most extensive real estate owner in Iberville Parish. Dickinson was twenty-two when he was persuaded to leave Nashville for the Bayou Grosse Tete Country. Erwin had before this deeded his ward a large tract of land on the bayou with its fertile acres in a region long known as the "garden spot of Louisiana."

The first house young Dickinson built at Live Oaks Plantation consisted of four rooms. This was later incorporated into the present structure, which remains in a nearly perfect state of preservation after more than a century. The lumber was hauled from the nearby swamps, virgin cypress hewn and dressed by slave craftsmen; the bricks were dug in a neighboring pit and burned in a kiln that was still extant on the premises up till about thirty-two years ago.*

Austerely simple in its architectural lines, the house contains two and a half stories, its double galleries, supported by slender square pillars of wood. Typical of the sturdy construction of ante-bellum days, its brick wall, resting on massive sills 24 x 24 inches, were plastered within and faced with beaded weatherboard without. Typically, too, the heart cypress framework is pegged throughout, not nailed. The great windows, in design suggestive of French provincial casements, are ten feet, four inches tall, and, including the lovely sidelights, well over eight feet wide, with massive cypress blinds thick enough to repel the fiercest onslaught of the sun. The mouldings of windows and doors, in keeping with the general style of the house, are diffident and chaste, the only decorative note being the expert chamfering and the effective placement of an occasional simple panel to break the monotony of the rectilinear scheme.

There are four spacious rooms on the ground floor and the same number on the second story, though the two floors are not identical in groundplan. A vast hall, 20 feet or more

---

*This information was taken from "The Progress" of January 6, 1939.

wide, traverses the center of the house from front to rear. Every chamber is furnished with a beautiful handwrought cypress-wood mantel of the pedestal type, with ornament cut in low relief.

The dining room and one of the bedrooms upstairs are furnished with antique cupboard presses, built into the walls to conserve space. Another quaint touch is an arrangement in the ponderous sliding doors between the parlor and dining room whereby the knobs are concealed in niches, with flaps that come down to give the frames the appearance of an unbroken surface. The knobs, incidentally, are heavily silver plated, and each door is fitted with a slave-made key of hammered brass.

But the most striking feature of the historic house is, without question, the exquisite spiral staircase which rises in an alcove in the rear hall. Not a few of the old plantation homes of Louisiana boast similar stairways, for they were much in vogue in ante-bellum days, but none that bears the stamp of a master builder, as does this one. Decorated with a simple scroll design, with a graceful mahogany rail imported from France, it sweeps upward in a magnificent curve without bolster or buttress, seemingly balanced more by architectural wizardry than by its casual jointure with the wall.

In general aspect, at least, the grounds of the old homestead suggest the original layout. To the west is an orchard and truck garden, to the east a broad pasture. The plantation proper stretches away to the south and west, and formerly a lane of great pecan trees led back from stables (now demolished) behind the house to the back line. Though the storms of yesteryear have taken many of the venerable live oaks that set the house off like a park, there is still a wealth of priceless shade trees about the place. And before the doorstep the waters of the bayou flow as placidly as of yore.

Of the ancient outbuildings, two remain standing, their

warm red brick crumbling beneath the thick layers of white-wash. One is a two-storied structure, a combination kitchen and house-servants' quarters, which used to be connected with the main house by a latticed walkway. There was a companion structure to it some yards away, but that too is gone. The other relic of the old times is a brick chapel, located in the pasture. Dickinson built it for his slaves, and it used to accommodate 200 or more for Sunday worship, led by itinerant preachers the planter was accustomed to engage as occasion offered.

Although never given to such princely entertainment as was his more spectacular grandparent at the "Home" place (now the St. Louis Plantation), Dickinson, who made a gratifying success at sugarcane growing, did in one instance give a banquet that has become legendary along Bayou Grosse Tete. The immense attic at Live Oaks was transformed into a colorful dining hall. One hundred and fifty guests were invited, and behind the chair of every one Dickinson placed a small slave boy in livery, to act as a personal servant throughout the sumptuous meal.

Charles Dickinson, former Tennessean and builder of Live Oaks, died in 1846, an untimely demise. This successful planter and community builder was then at the height of his career, only 40 years old. He left a wife and three children. According to family records he died from dysentery (called "stomach trouble" in those days). Dickinson's widow, the former Anna Maria Turner of Nashville, married at the early age of 14, survived him by about forty years, becoming a leader in community affairs and principal stockholder in the Louisiana Central Railroad. One of her children, a daughter, Mary, married the widely known Iberville Parish planter, Andrew H. Gay.

Live Oaks Plantation, which was bequeathed to Charles and Mary at Mrs. Dickinson's death in 1886, passed some years later into the hands of Mrs. Lavinia Davis, and through her to Mr. and Mrs. J. R. Mays. The Mays, gentlefolk of the old Southern School, since their occupancy in 1915, made every effort to maintain the historic residence in the manner it deserved. To them belongs much of the credit for its continued excellent condition and the attractiveness of the grounds. They furnished the stately rooms with fine and gracious antiques, heirlooms of their own family. They restored the gardens, which in season flame with narcissus, Easter lilies, ligustrums, wisteria, crapemyrtle and other semi-tropical shrubs and flowers.

Live Oaks today, lovingly cared for by its new owner, Mr. Lee Merrill who purchased the mansion about five years ago, remains a beauty spot and a Mecca for people interested in historic ante-bellum homes. It is the kind of plantation home that Charles Dickinson, more than a century ago, peering from his high perch in the now famous tree, visualized, despite the flood-waters that rolled temporarily around him, as the fitting abode for his Tennessee bride.

Charles H. Dickinson of the Civil War and Reconstruction Era

Charles Dickinson of "Live Oaks" plantation left a son Charles H. Dickinson who had an interesting and romantic life. His career of danger and daring began even in childhood.

When a little fellow, twelve years old, he went through the great and dangerous "Isle Derniere," Last Island Storm, one of the worst disasters of its kind recorded in Louisiana history. Young Dickinson, his sister and mother were among the few survivors. (See Chapter IX about this storm).

The widow, Mrs. Dickinson, was occupying a cottage at Last Island when the storm struck. She had quite a retinue of relatives and servants with her, and as she was a Scotch Presbyterian, she would not tolerate the dancing and flirting that went on at the "Tradewind Hotel," the huge building which was destroyed with loss of all occupants. When it became evident that a hurricane was raging, Mrs. Dickinson invited some friends from the hotel to stay at her cottage, which was located on the highest and safest spot on the island. It was one of the staunchest buildings there.

The event left an indelible impression on Charles, her son. In fact, to the day of his death he was always nervous in a storm—probably the only thing that he was ever afraid of. In telling of the terrible storm Dickinson—in later years—said that he was not particularly frightened by the howling wind and the rising tide, but while watching the storm through the doorway on the leeward side of the home the door on the windward side suddenly burst open, creating a terrific draft through the house which carried him bodily outdoors. As he was being swept along by the wind and waves, he grabbed hold of a gate post and clung to it. His mother saw him and rushed to his assistance. Of course she could not do anything but hold on to the post too, while keeping his head out of the water.

Tom Shallowhorne, one of the family slaves, saw their plight and went out to them with a long rope tied to his waist. By some miracle he mastered the wind and tide and reached the mother and child. He and Mrs. Dickinson and young Charles were then pulled back into the house by the people there.

After the storm and waves had subsided the survivors were in a pitiful condition and thoroughly demoralized. They could see the battered mail steamer aground nearby. Not only was she in distress, but there was no drinking water on board. Wandering around, the boy Dickinson noticed that the faucet of the cistern belonging to the cottage was running and rapidly wasting the only drinking water remaining on the island. He succeeded in shutting it off, thus saving the remaining water. When he told about this the little fellow was proclaimed a hero by the survivors for having almost equalled Tom Shallowhorne's performance. Tom's son later became Dickinson's "body servant" and served him faithfully all during the Civil War.

The grandson of the Tennessee duellist, a youngster of the age of 16, enlisted as a scout in Captain Allen Jumel's Company formed at Iberville during the Civil War. The youthful but always game fighter was wounded alongside his cousin, Nicholas Edwards, of Plaquemine (uncle of this writer) at Morgan City, in a hopeless charge against the Yankee fort there. Edwards, shot through the stomach from "side-to-side" and given up as a "goner," recovered miraculously. The surgeon said he was saved by an empty stomach, he having had nothing to eat for several days. According to these young soldiers, so bad were "foraging" conditions and so scarce the food, that special guards were posted to prevent the men from stealing the corn from their horses on the picket line at night.

Dickinson was captured and taken to New Orleans. He escaped from a prison on Camp Street, and after reaching the lake front, paddled a canoe twenty-two miles across the dangerous waters of Lake Pontchartrain to Mandeville. This remarkable exploit was accomplished after wading around in what was then a lake front swamp for several days. When one considers the mosquitoes, snakes, and alligators, that Dickinson was exposed to, the lack of food and the remarkable feat of crossing the lake in a canoe—a trip never equalled in peacetime, so far as we know, it seems a wonder that he lived to tell the tale.

Another incident of Dickinson's Confederate Army war service was that in which he, Gervais Kleinpeter and Edward (later Judge) Talbot held a bridge near Indian Village against a Yankee Cavalry force which later captured two videttes and raided the fort in Fortville (Plaquemine). Dickinson shot the arm off Yankee Colonel Hawkins, and Gervais

Kleinpeter was injured so badly he bore scars forming a perfect cross, on top of his head, the rest of his life. A dramatic sequel to this war-time meeting was that the man who many years after handled the matter of paying Dickinson's life insurance claim, on the occasion of his untimely and tragic death in 1898, was no less a personage than the same Col. Hawkins who had lost his arm in the scrimmage.

It must be said also that Dickinson by holding the bridge at Indian Village caused the Federal gunboats in the river to shell Plaquemine, and nearly wreck the fine old Schwing Mansion. The marks of cannon ball breeches in the brickwork remain to this day. Because of the consequences of their intrepidity the over-enthusiastic young soldiers of the C.S.A. were later put in the guardhouse by their Iberville Parish Commander, Captain Jumel.

After the war was over Dickinson was sent to Europe to complete his civil engineering education. He attended the University of Edinburgh, where he was graduated as a civil engineer and geologist. He later toured Europe.

While en route to Edinburgh, in a sailing vessel, Dickinson became bored, and made friends with the crew, who taught him a lot of useful things such as splicing and coiling ropes, taking in sails, and other nautical skills. He became quite self-confident and bet the captain he could climb the ropes to the topmast quicker than a sailor. He did all right, but the sailor then proceeded to truss him up to the mast as a warn-to keep out of the rigging. While the sailor was busily tying his legs Dickinson reached over his shoulder, took the knife out of the sailor's belt sheath, cut the rope and slid down the rat-lines to the deck, a la Jim Hawkins in Treasure Island, thus spoiling the joke for the chagrined sailor.

In the 1870's Dickinson went to Texas for his health, joined a surveying party that built the Texas & Pacific R. R. to Marshall. When the Indians got too bad and broke up the party he joined the Texas Rangers there. He was engaged in many fights with Apaches and Comanches as well as desperadoes. Dickinson's "Ranger" service record is officially as follows: "Private, Company E., Frontier Battalion, Capt. W. J. Maltby, Commanding. Enlisted May 30, 1874 honorably discharged November 13, 1874." A word about the Texas Rangers is now relevant.

Few people today know about the celebrated Texas Rangers of eighty years ago. At that time Texas was a land of unoccupied plains where herds of buffalo and droves of wild horses, cattle and deer roamed over the vast expanse of unfenced land. There were Indian tribes, however, who moved in and over the plains pitching their tents or tepees by streams, moving their camps when they wanted more game. These Indians would ride bareback on their little ponies. Naturally they soon came into conflict with the white men who were moving out into Texas.

The Texas Rangers were organized in 1823 by Stephen F. Austin to protect the frontiers against the Indians. A more or less loosely organized troop of Rangers existed from that time until Texas joined the Union, then the Federal Government was supposed to protect the frontier and the Ranger organization was disbanded. The U. S. Government did send troops out into Texas, but the infantry was so unaccustomed to Indian warfare that the Rangers were reorganized to give them help.

During the Mexican War the Texas Rangers took part in the fighting. They were used as scouts and "intelligence" units. In Mexico they were called *Los Diablos Tejanos*—The Texas devils.

The Texas Rangers were disbanded again during the Civil War. Many of the troops fought in the Confederate Army. In 1874 the Rangers came back into service again. In the seventies the Texas frontier not only suffered from Indian depredations, but "bad men," cattle thieves and train robbers made the frontier country hazardous for peaceful citizens.

The Rangers not only protected the settlers from Indian raids, but they preserved law and order and took care of the "bad men." The fighting of Indians took up some time but hunting desperadoes and criminals was even more important and more difficult. Gangs of thieves and murderers would terrorize the country.

The "bad men" were of the man-killing type and the local peace-enforcement officers had great difficulty in handling them. In 1874 it was necessary to put 450 Rangers on the frontier to preserve order. One of these "bad men" was only twenty-two years old and he had killed 23 white men as well as Indians.

Charles H. Dickinson came from Louisiana to join the Rangers. He was a member during a most exciting time, and he enjoyed this career of danger and daring. Dickinson was something of a geologist and predicted that coal and oil would be found in West Texas. He was also a painter and often when the boys were in camp, he would paint them and their mounts and make drawings of camp scenes. He was very popular, and, years later, an old member of the Rangers in an interview in the Dallas Times mentioned Charles Dickinson as one of the famous members of the organization.

The stories of the Texas Rangers are plentiful in the history of Texas. The Rangers are still in existence as a division of the State Dept. of Safety, and they are charged with putting down riots and insurrections and in detecting and arresting major criminals.

Charles Dickinson, his son, now living in California writes: "I have my father's Winchester rifle and six-shooter that he used as a Ranger, bows and arrows, Bowie knives, sketch books, etc., which he kept as souvenirs of his experiences in Texas, and remember distinctly his account of the fight in which Webb was killed by the Taylor Gang; the Lost Valley Battle, etc."

Charles Dickinson returned to Louisiana in time for the

battle of Canal Street on September 14, 1874 with the Metropolitan Police, and helped the White League to win.

Later when 500 Metropolitan Police were sent by steamboat from New Orleans to cut the dyke at Plaquemine to relieve the pressure of high water on New Orleans and the lower levees, Col. Sam Matthews organized an armed company of Plaquemine citizens composed of such men as Judge Talbot, Andrew Gay, Judge Wailes, Dr. Schwing and Charles Dickinson to protect the Iberville levees. They dared the Metropolitans to come ashore, but the soldiers returned to New Orleans, post haste, without accomplishing their purpose.

Dickinson was parish surveyor for a number of years and at one time, mayor of Plaquemine. His map of the parish is still a splendid example of map making. He was finally appointed Surveyor General by President Cleveland.

Dickinson used to bring his children apples, bananas, and candy when returning from a trip to New Orleans. He would secretly scatter the "goodies" under the fruit trees and then persuade the youngsters, under one pretense or another, to hunt for eggs. Imagine their delight at finding "sugar plums" on the branches of orange trees. Somehow it seemed perfectly natural a la "Alice in Wonderland." He was the one who promoted—among the children—the "sham battles" between his Indians and the "settlers,"—in which the fort was generally carried by storm and ammunition captured, despite a herioc defense by the beleagured garrison.

Ironically Charles Dickinson, the much beloved pioneer civil engineer and soldier of the Civil War, having survived so many dangers was accidentally killed while on a hunting trip in 1898 at the early age of fifty-two.

His son of the same name true to family tradition, and in

PEACH BLOSSOM, Nashville. Built by Joseph Erwin in 1905. His son-in-law, Charles Dickinson, after the duel, was buried on the grounds. *(Courtesy Ashley Wilson)*

the same year, enlisted in a cavalry division during the Spanish American War. However, his unit was still in training, not yet called into active service when the war terminated. This Charles Dickinson of the fourth generation—scion of the duellist who lost his life many years ago—left Iberville, moving first to New Orleans and then in later years to the Pacific Coast. An amateur sketch artist of no mean ability which skill seems to run in the family, he now lives near Los Angeles and has retired from active business.

In a recent letter Dickinson reminds this writer of an incident of more than 50 years ago when, following a long-to-be-remembered deer hunt in the Bayou Grosse Tete section, William and Alfred Clement, Edward J. Gay and he, Charles Dickinson, all youthful hunters and scions of the Iberville pioneers, slept in an upstairs bedroom in the otherwise empty and temporarily unused Dickinson "Live Oaks" mansion. The single furnished room in the house, the one the hunters occupied for the night, had a large fireplace and a mantel piece over which was hung numerous "Texas Ranger" trophies, such as Indian war-bonnets, bows and arrows, sabres, bowie knives, horse pistols (big pistols carried ordinarily in large scabbards hung from saddle attachments on the horse's back), spurs, antlers, powder horns, etc. After amusing ourselves by firing the big, and somewhat unfamiliar to us, horse pistols through the open window and engaging in other pranks, the tired hunters slept all together in the immense "four-poster" bed. Dickinson is said to have later caught "whatnot" for not straightening the room up before the visitors' departure.

At that time the Dickinson family had left Grosse Tete and "Live Oaks," moving about 1880 to the old Leftwich place in the town of Plaquemine, a fine old home with large grounds facing Bayou Plaquemine. This change was made because

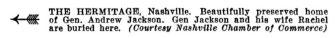

THE HERMITAGE, Nashville. Beautifully preserved home of Gen. Andrew Jackson. Gen Jackson and his wife Rachel are buried here. *(Courtesy Nashville Chamber of Commerce)*

the Morganza levee on the Mississippi broke repeatedly, the water flooding the entire "back country," destroying crops, drowning cattle and causing much sickness. Live Oaks was later sold, and fortunately for posterity, it has been maintained in perfect condition.

LETTERS FROM CHARLES DICKINSON

Shortly after his marriage Charles Dickinson, a close business associate of his planter father-in-law, Erwin, went to Louisiana on one of the big "flat boats" of those days, on a long and dangerous trading expedition. This was his last trip, before leaving on which, he had written Andrew Jackson a letter that brought a challenge for the duel. While on the voyage he wrote the following letters to his wife in Nashville:

Natchez—17th Feb. 1806

My dearest Wife:

We arrived at this place on Thursday last, after the most long & disagreeable voyage that was ever experienced, but after difficulties the most hazardous, having run over every sawyer, and falling-over board in the middle of the Mississippi River. I, and a number of the negroes, all landed safe at this place, never was a woman nearer being a widow, than yourself, and would have been, had not the delight I anticipated in seeing you, my dearest Jane, with our little Charles in her arms, who I hope before this time has happily landed in Tennessee. I shall leave this place in a few days, we have sold seven or eight of our slaves, at very good prices. Stephen, Joe & Clement at six hundred dollars each. Susan at five hundred & Peter McNairy and Harry at five hudred-fifty, and Morgan and Perry at four hundred and Andrew & Bill who I bought the night before I started at four hundred & fifty each; we hope to sell more before we start from here. Let me hear from you and my buntling; direct your letter to Natchez, Mississippi Territory, and inform me if your father has gone to Maryland. Please have my horse in readiness against my arrival, as I leave in a great hurry for Maryland.   Give my dear little Charles a kiss for his Papa, and tell him I long to see him, but when I cannot guess, but rest assured as soon as possible you shall see your loving husband.

Charles Dickinson

New Orleans, 17th April, 1806

My dearest Wife;

Your disappointment in not hearing from me for so long a period, I make no doubt has given you many weary moments, but you will be informed thro this medium why I have not written to you more frequent.   I have been in Louisiana territory ever since the date of my letter to you from Natchez by Mr. Nathaniel Scales, through which there is no post.   I arrived here four days ago and have sold all the slaves but Charles and Alice; Charles I have hired out at one hundred and twenty dollars per year; Alice is at Natchez and I hope I shall be able to dispose of her on my arrival at Natchez for which place I start tomorrow on my way for Nashville, I hope to see you by the 12th or 15th of next month.   I have been extremely uneasy for fear you have had some accident with our darling child who will add greatly to my happiness, my anxiety to see my little Charles and Mama is greater than I can express, tell our little boy where his Papa is, that he has told you to give a sweet kiss for him.   My hurry is so great you must excuse my scrawl.   I should have started on home a day or two ago but bad weather had prevented me.   Have my horse taken care of, I shall be at home in a little while after you receive this.   Give my best respect to Corbin Lee and hope he beat with Ploughboy very easy.   I remain my dearest Jane,

Your loving and affectionate husband,
Charles Dickinson

N.B. I have been tolerably healthy since I had the pleasure of seeing you tho' it is very sickly here.

CHAPTER V

COL. ANDREW HYNES, SOLDIER SON-IN-LAW
OF JOSEPH ERWIN

The Nashville Tennessean, through Silliman Evans, publisher, a recent visitor at the famous Tennessee-Maryland football game in the Sugar Bowl, ran a full page advertisement in the New Orleans States December 31, 1951. In this he called attention to the rescue of the imperilled South by Andrew Jackson and his "Tennesseans". Hand-propelled flatboats, almost a century and a half ago, brought a thousand or so Tennessee riflemen to New Orleans. The advertisements said they "donned their leather-fringed breeches and their coon-skin caps, they shouldered their long rifles and set off toward the beautiful Crescent City, their heroic victory is history." Old papers telling of Col. Hynes' part in this victory have recently come to light. Hynes' father-in-law, Joseph Erwin, naturally, was much concerned over the apparent imminence of a British victory and the losses which this was certain to bring him.

When word was received of the expected landing of British troops at New Orleans Capt. Samuel Clement immediately placed himself and steamboat "Vesuvius" at the disposal of Gen. Andrew Jackson. While proceeding down river to the threatened city he passed Gen. Carroll's brigade of some 1500 men embarked on the slow moving, sweep-propelled flatboats. Later Clement stopped to take on board Col. Andrew Hynes who wanted to get to New Orleans ahead of his troops, probably to arrange headquarters for his commander, Gen. Carroll.

On November 14, 1814 Col. Hynes, Adjutant General of Tennessee and Aide-de-camp to Maj. Gen. William Carroll, had received orders to start on this expedition to save New Orleans and the Mississippi Valley. He thus addressed his hastily summoned militia at Nashville:

> The embarkation of the troops will take place this day on board the transports now in the Cumberland River. The general invokes the benediction of heaven, for the Army and for its safety—its glory and honorable return —humbly knowing that the strong arm of power is alone derived from the Almighty.

The rough and ready Tennessee riflemen enthusiastically completed preparation for the trip to New Orleans. The entire valley was alarmed because the British, it was said, threatened to sack and burn the Crescent City and take over the whole Mississippi Territory.

In gathering material for this book I asked Sen. Edward J. Gay of St. Louis Plantation, Iberville Parish for information about his great-grandfather, Col. Hynes. The result was the unearthing of some new side-lights on the Battle of New Orleans. This came about while Mr. Gay was "rooting" in the attic of one of his plantation out-buildings in search of a harness. There he found a box containing a large bundle of letters, papers, maps, hand bills, and military orders evidently gathered together by his highly respected ancestor, Col. Hynes.

It consisted of personal correspondence, mementos, and old newspapers, all of course with a strong Tennessee viewpoint. The collection turned out to be, according to a recent article in the Times-Picayune, "one of the most important discoveries of original Battle of New Orleans material found in many a day."

These Hynes papers give an excellent insight into the terrifying situation as it then obtained. The delays incident to slow, flatboat, transportation, and the fear of not getting to Chalmette in time to help stop the British are emphasized.

The decisions of Gen. Jackson are mentioned, the feeling of local people about the Tennesseans, and the suffering and agonies endured by the Tennessee troops in the swamps outside the city in the cold winter are told about. Comments on the herioc conduct of these men at the Chalmette breastworks during the furious British attack and tributes to their bravery are a part of the collection.

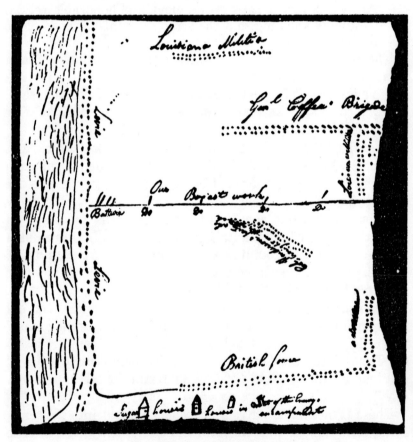

Col. Hynes' plan of the Battle of New Orleans.

Col. Hynes wrote this for General Carroll to be read to the troops:

The City of New Orleans is the grand depot of the products of our country, and every one of us ought to feel a strong interest in defending this great mart of trade and source of wealth to the upper country.

In Captain Samuel Clement's story of the Battle of New Orleans are several references to the fine soldierly conduct of Col. Hynes. After the battle was over the Colonel wrote a letter to Gen. Blount which shows his sense of humor.

The unfortunate Lt. Gen. Sir Edward Pakenham, bro-ther-in-law of Lord Wellington, and Maj. Gen. Gibbs are each put into hogsheads of rum and sent home to England in good spirits.

The Times-Picayune story goes on to say that the collection contains newspapers of the day, both New Orleans and Nash-ville sheets, which describe the general rejoicing, as well as eloquent, long-winded speeches of praise. Several copies of the rare New Orleans newspaper. "Friend of the Laws," con-tain published texts of Gen. Jackson's important orders.

On Jan. 21, 1815 Jackson said that he was "at length en-abled to perform the pleasing task of restoring to Tennessee ... the brave boys who have enacted such a distinguished part in the war. . . ." and he ordered Gen. Carrol to march his command back to its home state.

Col. Hynes, later a prominent merchant and manufacturer of Nashville, married on March 2, 1817, Nancy, a daughter of Joseph Erwin, who as we know, had already moved to Louisi-ana and accumulated the "Home" and other extensive planta-tion properties in Iberville Parish.

After the tragic death of Joseph Erwin, Col. Hynes was a frequent visitor to Iberville Parish, and aided Mrs. Erwin in her excellent and effective work in restoring to solvency this much involved Erwin estate. He later acquired much of the Erwin properties by purchase.

The record shows that Hynes, an excellent business man and an interested party, of course, was of much assistance in holding the great Iberville Parish properties together. Colonel Hynes had a fine home and large business interests in Nashville. There still stands today the handsome old brick mansion built by him in the long ago.

In May 1825 Gen. Lafayette was entertained at Nashville. There was a public dinner at the Nashville Inn at which Gen. Jackson presided. Col. Andrew Hynes toasted Timothy Demonbreun as the patriarch of Tennessee and the first white man to settle in Tennessee.

When Andrew Hynes died in 1849 in St. Louis, he owned in Iberville Parish 223 slaves appraised at $86,000. He was the largest slave holder in Iberville and one of the largest in the United States. (In 1860 out of 384,000 slave owners in the U.S. only 312 owned more than 200 slaves). The estate of Hynes on St. Louis Plantation in 1851-52 produced 495 hogsheads of sugar, one of the largest producers in Iberville according to Champomier.

The Hynes family came from Ireland to Maryland then to Kentucky. Andrew Hynes was one of the founders of Louisville in 1780. He was delegate to the Constitutional Convention of Kentucky in 1792. He later went to Nashville and the Col. Andrew Hynes who fought at New Orleans in 1815 was his son.

EDWARD J. GAY 1814-1889

Later Hynes's son-in-law, Edward J. Gay, grandfather of the present Sen. Gay, came to Iberville Parish from St. Louis, Missouri, and it was under his able management that the former "Home" property was greatly augmented by purchase of adjoining properties and the name changed to St. Louis

Plantation. Generally speaking these were plantations held previously by other Erwin heirs, but which owners either wanted to sell in order to move elsewhere, or because they were financially in distress. The properties were then in danger of being taken over by other nearby interests.

It was the young Missourian, Edward J. Gay, Hynes's son-in-law, who in 1857 built the present Gay mansion and laid out the lovely gardens which surround the house. This fine old residence sits well back from the river and is one of the showplaces of that section. I remember quite well the quiet, reserved and dignified Congressman Edward J. Gay, who, in my time in the eighties, spent many months each year in Washington, D.C. Mr. Gay's reluctance to take part in the politics of Reconstruction days was overcome when Louisiana leaders assured him that only thus could the Kellogg carpet-bag rule be abolished. On the death of Mr. Gay the people elected his son-in-law, Andrew Price, to represent the District in the Congress.

My youthful admiration for the Congressman was of course increased by the fact that one of the big river steamboats of that day, the "Edward J. Gay," had been named after him. Mr. Gay's son, Andrew Hynes Gay, 1841-1914, in addition to owning and operating the great St. Louis and Union plantations, was proprietor of the former Isaac Erwin "Shady Grove" and other places on Bayou Grosse Tete.

Sen. Edward Gay's son, Andrew, (named after his uncle, Andrew Price, who was elected to U.S. House of Representatives, succeeding his father-in-law, Edward J. Gay) is a Gay of the fourth generation to own this big estate. His father entrusted to him the direct management of the sugar farming and stock-raising activities of this famous property.

The following memorandum contributed by Mrs. Anna McClung concerning the Nashville homes of Joseph Erwin and Col. Hynes is of interest.

Nashville, Tennessee
August 12, 1934

Aunt Nannie Price took Margaret Weaver and me on a
tour of three old ancestral homes in Nashville. The first
was the home of Capt. and Mrs. Joseph Erwin on Craighead Avenue, called "Peach Blossom" farm. It is of
brick, painted white and is more than 125 years old.
Charles Dickinson went from this house to fight the
famous duel with Andrew Jackson on May 30, 1806. He
was buried in a tomb on the grounds, but this has since
been moved. He married Jane Erwin, Joseph Erwin's
eldest daughter and left one son, Charles Henry Dickinson, born March 9, 1806.

Margaret and I went inside the house and saw the
lovely big hall 19' x 42' with a beautiful winding stair at
the rear and a little balcony upstairs on which the bedrooms open. We went into the large parlor on the left,
which has a handsome wood mantle and large paneled
doors. We next visited the old Hynes home on Church
Street. The house is of brick painted gray with a queer
round tower. St. Mary's Catholic church now owns it.

Grandma Gay (Lavinia Hynes) daughter of Col. and
Mrs. Andrew Hynes was married in that old house October 22, 1840 to Edward James Gay of St. Louis, Missouri.
Her wedding dress and slippers are still in a perfect state
of preservation and are in my possession. Her dress is
of white (ivory) satin and was made at Thompson's in
Nashville. His wedding vest of blueish white satin and
made by hand is also in perfect condition.

We drove in the grounds and looked at the house. She
was born in 1821 in a house situated on the public square,
long since disappeared. She died in New Orleans in
1891. The last one we visited was the funny little two
story red brick house where Great Grandma Turner lived
and where Grandma Dickinson was born, 1814. It is at
514 Cedar Street, corner of Summer Street, just opposite
the side corner of the State Capitol building. It has stone

steps and is in a very dilapidated condition. Grandma Dickinson (Anna Maria Turner) was married in that house April 17, 1828, at the age of 14 years and 6 months. Born October 4, 1814 and died January, 1886. She married Charles Henry Dickinson, son of the Dickinson killed in a duel with Andrew Jackson.

He was born March 9, 1806—died July 5, 1846. Her wedding dress was Empire style, of cream moiré and with an over-dress of fine net, trimmed with narrow bands of satin. The wedding veil is of lace. She gave me her wedding dress when I was quite a young girl, and it is still in my possession. I also own a miniature on ivory of her mother, Mrs. Ann Williamson Turner, who owned the little house and lived there. She was born in Virginia 1788—died in Plaquemine, Louisiana, 1847.

CHAPTER VI

ISAAC ERWIN OF "SHADY GROVE"

Only a few miles away from Live Oaks on the beautiful Bayou Grosse Tete road there was, until it was torn down recently, the Shady Grove Mansion, almost a hundred years old, built by Isaac Erwin, a Dickinson cousin and neighbor. This great Erwin ante-bellum manor was for many years used by the parish as a school. A new and modern school building has taken its place.

Isaac Erwin* when a young man came by flatboat from Nashville to take possession of the Bayou Grosse Tete Plantation. His slaves were forced to clear the canebreak so he could land and his command to the Negroes was, "Clear the way for here's where we die." Isaac, a son of Joseph Erwin, prospered and became quite a "big man" in his own right. He later built Shady Grove Mansion, a house of magnificent proportions. The big rooms, thirty feet square with high ceilings, were exceptionally large due to Erwin's having a big family and, it is said, his desire to get around "without stepping on any of the children." This was the "house the Jack built," so wrote a granddaughter "Cousin Mary" Erwin whom this author well remembers. She said:

Grandfather Isaac swapped his place on the Franklin Turnpike in Nashville, Tennessee for an uncleared wild-

---

*Isaac Erwin's diary from 1848 to 1868 is now at the La. State Library, Baton Rouge. The diary refers mostly to his farming operations, but some entries are interesting. Among them is a beautiful prayer written at the end of a disastrous year.

erness in Louisiana on the banks of Bayou Grosse Tete as early as 1825. He came with slaves and chattels in a flatboat, had to cut his way thru canes that overlapped the Bayou and at night built large fires and tied out dogs to keep off the wild beasts.

He built the old log house and it was added to as needed, they baked their own bricks and cut timber from the Erwin-owned forest of trees. Those were the days when people did not consider clothes and houses, but set a value on people. Those, the days of dipped candles and not of gas and electric lights. All but two of Grandfather's children were born in this log cabin. A frequent visitor was Cousin Amelia Chesnut, who afterwards married S. Omer Landry. Dr. Garrett [father of the late Mrs. Cammie Garrett Henry of Melrose] and Aunt Jane were married in this house. The big new house "Shady Grove" was not built until 1859.

Grandfather was very fond of having family reunions at his home. Once he made up his mind to give a Mayday party. The supper was served in a tent in the front yard. The hall was built for dancing. The tree was so fine he hated to cut it down. So he built it in, not in the room proper, but at one end and just inside. All the relatives from Plaquemine and some from Nashville came in a little steamboat owned by Cousin James Robertson (son of Aunt Leodocia Erwin Robertson).

One day we came home from school we found all the front gallery canvassed in, and a long, wide table made the length of the gallery. This was the wedding feast. Your grandfather insisted that a whole barrel of flour be made up into pound cake and they brought Cousin Tenn. Sharp's fine servant and she and Ma worked at the pound cakes. This was Dr. Garrett and Sister Jane's wedding. All the whole county was bidden and came. A grand affair it was.

It might be well to visualize Bayou Grosse Tete as it was in the days of Dickinson, Erwin, and other residents of that sec-

tion. The sugar, cotton, and other produce which had to be
shipped to market and railroads had not yet come in to the picture. The Bayou waters therefore, plus little, light draught
steamboats, rendered a service which made it possible to carry
on trade and social contacts.

"MISS CAMMIE" OF MELROSE—FRIEND OF AUTHORS

Among the distinguished descendants of Isaac Erwin was
Mrs. John Henry (Cammie Garrett) of Melrose, known to
thousands as "Miss Cammie". She was Erwin's granddaughter, and her mother was married at Shady Grove Plantation.
I can best tell the story of Miss Cammie by reprinting an
article written by Vera Morel for the "New York Sun" back
in April of 1938. Miss Morel, when she went to interview her,
said that Miss Cammie came forward, peering over gold-
rimmed spectacles and waving a garden trowel in greeting.
Miss Morel wrote:

A short, sturdy figure of a woman in black serge skirt
and stiff white waist; her thick white hair rebellious under a black straw. Behind her was a heart shaped garden, and beyond, "the big house" built over a century ago,
with outdoor stairways and wide galleries that overlooked
several thousand acres of cotton plantation over which
this remarkable woman ruled.

Mrs. John Henry of Melrose, La., more familiarly
"Miss Cammie," is a cotton planter, scholar, historian,
weaver, gardner and helpful friend to writers. Many creative workers have been able to produce better work because of her very practical aid. She had permitted them
the peace and seclusion of her home as a workshop, and
provided them with a valuable reference library of her
own making. How this library and its scrapbooks grew
is a story that began a long time ago.

Before the advent of modern paved highways, many
plantations were inaccessible except by boat. Traveling

was an infrequent event. Children usually had to make their own amusement, some diligently creating patchwork quilts, others doing crochet and knitting. Little Cammie found her great delight in making scrapbooks, for this pastime engaged her brain as well as little fingers.

Painstakingly she clipped newspapers and magazines, carefully dating her cuttings. She collected pictures and letters, anything and everything that was news of events, of people, and of places was grist for her scrapbooks. Thus was her own interest in Southern history born and stimulated.

Nor did this eagerness and quest for historical data lag after her marriage and widowhood. In addition to raising a large family and managing a large plantation, she found time to develop her library and to keep the scrapbooks up to date. These now number over two hundred, all carefully indexed.

Soon writers and artists made a beaten path along placid Cane River to Melrose. Here Lyle Saxon wrote his "Fabulous New Orleans," "Father Mississippi" and "Old Louisiana", which was dedicated to Miss Cammie, who supplied much of the material for this valuable book. Here worked Roark Bradford, whose "Old Man Adam" furnished the story for "Green Pastures." To Melrose came Rachel Field, author of "Hitty—Her First Hundred Years," and Ruth Cross, Ada Jack Carver, Marie Stanley, E. H. Suydam, Caroline Dorman, Ellsworth Woodward, Will Stevens, Henry E. Chambers, John P. Coleman and others. [Later Harnett Kane and Ross Phares.]

Miss Cammie shared with them the search for factual and fictional material that abounds in this section of the South. Melrose is but a few miles away from Natchitoches, oldest settlement of the Louisiana purchase, and said to be the third oldest town in this country. She stimulated the efforts of these serious workers and protected them from interruptions while at work.

Indefatigable in her determination to preserve what is good of the old, Miss Cammie's tireless pursuits have salvaged much of historic value. Assembled at Melrose are valuable manuscripts, collections of old letters and rare volumes. In the library will be found the first map of the Southwest, made for one of the Law brothers in 1721, and possibly figuring in the "Mississippi Bubble."

In the clubhouse, formerly the old slave hospital of the plantation is the slave-branding iron said to have been used by none other than Simon Legree. The site of the original cabin of Uncle Tom is not far distant from Melrose, and Miss Cammie had collected valuable data about Harriet Beecher Stowe's visit to Louisiana prior to her writing of the sensational "Uncle Tom's Cabin." Miss Cammie also collected cabins and has a number of interesting constructions that have been moved to Melrose from miles away.

Much information had been gathered from the passing generation by word of mouth and from the few remaining ex-slaves who were among her charges, for digging after facts was "second nature" to this energetic woman. Miss Cammie found time to weave and to teach the women of the plantation the old craft of making homespun. One cabin served as a loom room where are primitive hand-made frames and spinning wheels. Cotton and wool were spun into threads for weaving rugs, blankets, draperies and material for garments.

And there's the garden, her creation and sole handiwork. It dips down to Cane River whose banks are lined with native iris and willows. In spring, there are redbuds, periwinkles, wild haw and jonquils for color, and summer brings gay hollyhocks, poppies and annuals to mingle with rare specimens of exotic plants. Old iron lanterns and Andulusian oil jars suggest travel, but Miss Cammie declared she had never found time to leave the parish, not found the need to, as so many interesting people came to Melrose.

COLONEL ANDREW HYNES,
1786-1849
Son-in-law of Joseph Erwin

Right—EDWARD J. GAY, 1814-1889, Iberville Parish planter and financier, originally of St. Louis, Missouri. Mr. Gay, son-in-law of Col. Andrew Hynes, for many years represented his Congressional District in the National Congress.

Below—Steamboat EDWARD J. GAY was named in honor of Congressman Gay. She w 251 ft. long, 41 ft. wide with a draft of 7.6 ft. and built in 1878 for the New Orlea and Bayou Sara trade. The big, roof-bell, of the "Gay" came from the old "Brilliar built in 1850. The Gay burned while laid up at First Street, New Orelans, July 30, 18:

(Courtesy of Leonard T. Hub

Aunt Cammie, while not a blood relation, was one of Lyle Saxon's most devoted friends. She restored one of the old cabins, once a slave hospital on the plantation, and Saxon used it many years as a refuge and a place to write. In THE FRIENDS OF JOE GILMORE by Lyle Saxon, Hastings House, Publishers, Inc., we read:

Although the cabin was a simple building, the interior, under the Saxon influence, acquired a certain elegance, with white panelling, antique furniture, books, and pictures. At the back was a semicircular garden fenced off from the cotton fields by a screen of banana trees. Saxon planned it as a white garden, which would be at its best at night and on which he could lookout, beyond the large expanse of lawn, to white lilies, moon flowers, and altheas bright under the Melrose moon. On another side of the cabin was a large mint bed planted with a variety of mints for juleps. The bed, appropriately enough, was outlined with alternate whiskey and milk-of-magnesia bottles.

An endlessly busy woman, she [Mrs. Henry] sometimes wrote letters with one hand while watering flowers with the other. The letters were telegraphic, usually containing certain stock phases and clichés which she had picked up over the years. One of these was: "This too will pass," which she always used after relating one of the more violent upheavals on the plantation.

Her letters were always warm invitations, urging him [Saxon] to come to Melrose. Hurry Home, she would say, doors always open. You need rest. Frequently such messages were written on the outside of the envelopes of letters addressed to him at Melrose which she forwarded to New Orleans.

Saxon delighted to tease her and would sometimes reply, imitating her style, or write letters to a few friends who knew them both, signing her name. This for instance, he scribbled on the back of a letter addressed to a friend in his care which he forwarded:

"Come home. Roof always open. Can't hardly
wait. Chickens and children dying. I don't care.
This too will pass. Love.

AUNT CAMMIE."

Mrs. John Henry died November 17, 1948. The Joseph
Erwin descendants have always been proud of their connection with "Cousin Cammie" Garret Henry of Melrose.

CHAPTER VII

DR. CHARLES CLEMENT,
A FRIEND OF JOSEPH ERWIN

A little over 125 years ago a young man arrived at New Orleans on a sailing vessel from New York. He was on his way to visit his brother, Samuel Clement, one of the early steamboat captains on the Mississippi River and—as we tell later—a participant in the then recent Battle of New Orleans, rendering special help to Gen. Andrew Jackson. Captain Samuel Clement was living the life of a plantation owner in Concordia Parish, across the river from Natchez. Dr. Charles Clement of Duchess Co., New York who had just been graduated from the Poughkeepsie Medical School, was looking for a place to locate and practice his profession, and he thought that Natchez offered an opportunity for professional advancement.

Natchez was even then quite a settlement and while the town itself was small, there were many rich and prosperous planters living in the city or in the vicinity. The beautiful homes still existing today are proof that Natchez was the center of culture and wealth, at a time when most of the United States was backwoods or pioneer country.

The steamboats at that time, only a few years after the steamer NEW ORLEANS had made its first trip down the Mississippi, were rather primitive and were not the floating palaces that plied the river many years later. Passengers on these little steamers soon became acquainted and, just as on a trans-Atlantic liner, they begin to make friends with the other voyagers as soon as the ship leaves port. It happened that on this particular trip that Captain Joseph Erwin, prominent planter and one of the wealthiest men not only in Louisiana but in all the United States, was going to his home near Plaquemine in Iberville Parish. Captain Erwin and the young doctor soon became good friends and Dr. Clement told the older man something of his plans and his dreams for the future.

Joseph Erwin explained to the young doctor that there was great opportunity in Iberville Parish and gave reasons why he should get off the boat at his plantation. This he did and young Doctor Clement even lived for a while in the home of his patron, Captain Erwin.

The Quaker-bred Dr. Clement, on coming to Iberville Parish and the town of Plaquemine, was quite scandalized and disturbed by the lack of Sunday observance, the drinking habits of the men, horse racing, cock-fighting, and the continental idea of having a good time, that prevailed. In letters written home to his family in the North the young doctor several times called attention to this sort of thing. Perhaps the situation he found can best be summed up by reference to an old letter, written more than a hundred years ago (when New Orleans and the South Louisiana section had already passed its first century mark) by an Englishman traveller, one, Colonel Creecy, "a man of parts and great gusto."*

Have you ever been in New Orleans? If not you'd better go.

It's a nation of a queer place; day and night a show!

Frenchmen, Spaniards, West Indians, Creoles, Mustees, Yankees, Kentuckians, Tennesseans, lawyers and trustees;

Negroes in purple and fine linen, and slaves in rags and chains.

Ships, arks, steamboats, robbers, pirates, alligators, assassins,

---

*A copy of this letter was given to me by Dr. W. H. Butterworth, former British subject, but for many years a leading physician of New Orleans.

Gamblers, drunkards, and cotton speculators: sailors, sol-
   diers,
Pretty girls, and ugly fortune-tellers, pimps, imps,
   shrimps, and
All sorts of dirty fellows;
A progeny of all colors—an infernal motley crew; yellow
   fever
In February—muddy streets all the year; many things to
   hope for,
And a devilish sight to fear! gold and silver bullion—
United States banknotes, horse-racers, cock-fighters, and
   beggars without
Coats, snapping - turtles, sugar, sugar - houses, water -
   snakes,
Molasses, flour, whiskey, tobacco, corn and johnny-cakes,
   beef,
Cattle, hogs, pork, turkeys, Kentucky rifles, lumber,
   boards, apples,
Cotton, and many other trifles. Butter, cheese, onions,
   wild beasts.
In wooden cages, barbers, waiters, draymen, with the
   highest
Sort of wages.

It was not long, however, before Doctor Clement became
quite successful. About this time Louis Derouzelle Desobry,
the family who had moved from San Domingo to Cuba then to
New Orleans, came to Plaquemine to superintend the building
of Joseph Erwin's "big house," the first two-story residence
in the Parish of Iberville. He brought with him materials and
workmen to build the house. Family records, however, indicate that—in addition to Desobry—Mr. Michael Schlatre, an
expert builder, and a planter of that section, also helped to
superintend the erection of the Erwin Home.

Not long after the charming young Desobry sister, Henrietta, who had been born in Baracoa, Cuba in 1804 came to visit
her brother Louis. Henrietta's Parisian born parents had been

sugar planters in turbulent San Domingo and after a thrilling escape from slave uprisings, and the loss of much of their property, left their home and numerous possessions and moved to Cuba and then to Iberville Parish. Of course, she soon met young Dr. Clement and it was love at first sight. Although he was a Quaker and could speak no French and she a Catholic and could speak no English, that did not prevent the two young people from falling in love and in 1826 they were married.

It is said that he taught his young wife English by reading Scott's novels to her or with her. On May 2, 1828, a daughter, Mary Fort, their first child was born. A crevasse occurred that same day on the St. Louis Plantation and Dr. Clement was unable to return to his wife for hours.

Charles and Henrietta had eight children. There were six daughters and two sons. Mary married Gervais Schlater of Plaquemine. Minerva married Jacob McWilliams of New Jersey. Maria married George L. Bright of New Orleans. Laura married Henry Carlton Miller of New Orleans. Henrietta unmarried, and Lodoiska married Andrew H. Gay whose son Sen. Edward J. Gay still lives on the ancestral estate, the St. Louis Plantation. Charles never married, and died in the north while travelling for his health. Alfred married Ida Edwards of Plaquemine.

When Dr. Clement married he built a small residence near the plantation home of Joseph Erwin. But prospering and circumstances warranting it, he soon moved to Plaquemine where he built a handsome two-story brick house on a large piece of ground near the riverfront. A commodious doctor's office adjoined the lovely plantation type home and both buildings remained there for seventy years when the river encroached on the property and they were finally demolished, to make way for the new levee.

It was from this home that three of Dr. Clement's daughters were married before the Civil War. One of these, Minerva,

married Jacob McWilliams who at that time built on the land
in the rear of Dr. Clement's home a large and comfortable
house with ample grounds, carriage houses and outhouses.

"Aunt Minerva" and "Uncle Mac"—as everybody in town
called them—lived in the same house in Plaquemine for sixty
years and when their sixty-first wedding anniversary occurred, instead of giving a grand entertainment, they donated
most generously of their wealth to many orphanages, homes,
for old ministers, and other worthy causes. They were "blue
stocking" Presbyterians and the main support of the little
church across the street in which they had been married. Jacob
McWilliams was born in New Jersey in 1827; he came to
Plaquemine in 1849 and died there in 1917 on his 90th birthday. "Aunt Minerva" lived to be eighty-five.

Mr. McWilliams was a prominent citizen, a merchant, banker and plantation owner. He owned Myrtle Grove Plantation,
2800 acres, which he sold in 1899 to Wilbert and Sons. He was
the founder of the Bank of Plaquemine and President also
Vice-President of the Peoples Bank. He served six years as
president of the Police Jury. In 1851 Mr. McWilliams established the firm of Roth and McWilliams (C. N. Roth was born
in Plaquemine in 1836). This firm always paid "dollar for
dollar", even during the Civil War, and never asked for an
extension. Jacob McWilliams was high in Masonic Orders, a
good church member, and loved by all the citizens of Iberville
Parish.

Plaquemine is French for persimmon and I always thought
when a young boy that the town might have been named after
a large grove of persimmon trees in Uncle Mac's backyard, the
favorite hunting ground for us when the fruit was ripe.

Plaquemine is situated on the west bank of the Mississippi
in the bend of the river. Many years ago a cave-in occurred in
front of the town, affecting the main street which ran parallel
to the river. The property and buildings along this street were

ruined, bringing great financial loss to many since it was advisable to build a new levee. This was necessarily located two or three blocks in the rear of the town's older business section. Among the fine buildings outside the new levee and which eventually fell into the river were Jacob McWilliam's large brick store, the biggest building in town at that time, a bank building and Dr. Clement's old home as well as many other stores and homes.

The town of Plaquemine was made the "seat of government" of Iberville Parish in 1835. Dr. Charles Clement it should be noted was a member of the governing body, or "Police Jury," which brought this about. Family papers, and items in the Iberville Gazette show that the town of Plaquemine was then forging ahead in rapid progression—as compared to Point Pleasant, a smaller center where the seat of government had for many years been located. People were asking for quicker contact with governing authorities and that Plaquemine be given the recognition it seemed to deserve. In response to this the Police Jury met to consider the matter and —courageously—ordered removal of the county seat to the town of Plaquemine. The fact that young Dr. Clement was a member of the important governing body which brought about the removal is another indication of the doctor's prominence in the community, and the high measure of general confidence he enjoyed during his long residence in the Parish.

Plaquemine is said to have become a banking center way back in 1837, when the Exchange & Banking Co., of New Orleans established a branch there with Augustin T. Leftwich as president. Dr. Charles Clement was pressed—or shall we say drafted—into being cashier and held the post during a seven-year formative period. This may be now considered a little out of line for a busy practicing physician, with much horse-and-buggy traveling to visit patients. However, Dr. Clement was "commandeered", so to speak, for the job by the prominent people of the Parish. Many there were whose confidence he enjoyed and who looked upon his freedom-from-business connections as an absolute guarantee of fairness to all, and a safer banking situation under conditions then existing. The Quaker-bred Dr. Clement fortunately, and notwithstanding the expense of raising a large family, was able to save and, being a good business man, to invest wisely. This is evidenced not only by his purchase of a plantation five miles below the town of Plaquemine complete with operating sugar mill, slaves, equipment and appurtenances, but also his ownership at one time of a valuable piece of commercial property in New Orleans.

In common with everyone else, however, the Civil War brought devastating loss. Even so, the doctor managed to hold on to Retreat Plantation upon which he and his remaining family lived until the time of his death in 1874, at the age of seventy-seven.

There remains today a parcel of land on a prominent corner in Plaquemine with what some call a "freak title." In 1840, or thereabouts, this prominently located town-lot then becoming valuable was sold by Dr. Clement to James Johns to be used for a church or school. The deed reads: "Besides the cash consideration of $100, the lot is here sold for the purpose of its becoming the site of a Protestant church and is never to be destined to be used for any other purpose than as a site for a church or house of education for the use of the public."

Strange was it not that the doctor's grandson, and many others of his descendants, were later benefactors from this donation! This writer, it might be said, in the early nineties, attended the very excellent Plaquemine public school built on this lot. That was of course long prior to its removal to the present location, one of considerably greater size.

Dr. Clement, the much beloved physician and plantation owner of the old days, having passed on to his reward four years prior to this writer's appearance on earth, my earliest impression of grandfather's former presence in the house were the many book shelves and the large library of medical books, which remained to tell in some degree of our progenitor's labors and problems. The big musty-looking volumes of the medical lore were, of course, quite uninteresting to me.

A few months ago I talked to my cousin, George Clement Bright (89) * of New Orleans, well known New Orleans insurance executive, about Dr. Clement whom he had personally known. Mr. Bright said, "Oh, certainly I remember Grandpa Clement. At times when I spent my vacation periods on *Retreat Plantation* he used to make bows and arrows for me." This indicates the doctor's human and kindly attitude towards boys, something that was present notwithstanding the disabilities of old age, and troublesome plantation problems that would seem to have barred out any such extensive whittling job. Another cousin who, as a visitor during Dr. Clement's time, recalls pleasant experiences on *Retreat Plantation*. She is Mrs. Horatio W. Turner (87) of Princeton, N. J., daughter by a previous marriage, of Henry Carlton Miller, prominent New Orleans lawyer and later Associate Justice of the Louisiana Supreme Court. After the demise of his first wife, Mrs. Turner's father married Dr. Clement's daughter, Laura. Mrs. Turner recalls that, as a young girl, the always cautious doctor allowed her to fulfill her desire of going in swimming, in the big, swift and dangerous Mississippi River, but *only under condition that a rope be tied around her waist*, and the end held securely by a strong female guardian on shore.

At that time in some states doctors were permitted to practice after "reading" medicine. Dr. Clement belonged to the school which thought that students who took the essentials of a medical reading course, and who were to go into practice, should finish the course by clinical observation at the bedside and in the operating room. It must be remembered that in those days a good country doctor nearby was an essential for

---

*Died February 27, 1952.

safe living conditions. Even at that, with the recurrent menace of yellow fever, cholera and malaria, our pioneering ancestors, needed lots of "back-bone" to take up residence in the then rather miasmatic country under primitive conditions. The good doctor knew well the value of tranquility and when his active days in the medical field were over he retired to his sugar plantation and the quiet life of farming. He acquired extensive knowledge about the production of sugar and this, together with his love of books, interest in the education and well-being of his large family of children, brought him happiness, and he lived to the then somewhat exceptional age of 77.

Dr. Clement was a man of character and man of parts. I am sorry that I cannot pay a better tribute to his memory than the sketchy outline of his life that I have given here.

The Desobry Family Came To New Orleans In 1809, They Later Helped Build Iberville Parish

According to a story told by Mrs. Lodoiska Clement Gay to her stepdaughter, Anna Gay McClung in 1918, Felix Desobry and Henrietta Abelard both were born in France and were married there. They left France and went to San Domingo Island, presumably with the idea of acquiring sugar estates and becoming wealthy. Their first son, Joseph, was born there.

About 1791 or '92 a threatened insurrection occurred among the Negroes of the Island of San Domingo and Mr. and Mrs. Felix Desobry and their eldest son, Joseph, left the island and went to Baltimore where their second son, Louis De'rouzelle, was born in 1795.

The insurrection not amounting to much, the family returned to San Domingo where they remained until the awful insurrection took place in 1799. Mrs. Desobry actually saw two of her brothers (Abelards) struck against a tree and killed. During the horrors their lives were threatened, but a faithful Negro slave named Zoe warned them in time to escape. In a small boat they crossed the narrow channel carrying only a few clothes and some silver, and reached Cuba. Their only daughter, Henrietta, was born there in Baracoa, Dec. 23, 1804.

During the time of the insurrection Napoleon sent his brother-in-law General LeClerc to quell the disturbances.

While at Baracoa, Mr. Desobry died, and when Henrietta was about four the widow left Cuba with her three children and three slaves and came to New Orleans. The slaves were the faithful Zoe, and her sons Isaff and Francois. The reason they left Cuba was because the Spanish oppressed the French and demanded they take the oath of allegience to Spain. This they refused to do, and numbers of French emigrated from Cuba to the United States, going to New Orleans, Charleston, Baltimore and Savannah.

In New Orleans there was quite a colony of refugees—pure French—and not identified with the Spanish in any way. Paul Tulane, 1792, who settled later at Princeton, N. J., the Audubon and Poydras families were among them.

CHAPTER VIII

SAMUEL CLEMENT, EARLY STEAMBOATMAN AND CRITIC OF ANDREW JACKSON

In 1911, the hundredth anniversary of the voyage of the "New Orleans", a replica of the first steamboat that came down the Mississippi River, made the trip from Pittsburgh to New Orleans. There was a great deal of interest in the anniversary and appropriate ceremonies were held as the boat landed at various cities on the Ohio and Mississippi Rivers.

The late Mrs. Andrew Hynes Gay of Plaquemine, Louisiana, who was then 70 years old, gave an interview at that time to a New Orleans paper in which she stated that her father, Dr. Charles Clement, had told her that the captain of one of the earliest steamboats to come to New Orleans was Samuel Clement, her uncle. Careful research corroborates this tradition as related by Mrs. Gay. The records show that this Clement was captain of the "Vesuvius", the third steamboat brought down the river.

Mrs. Nicholas Roosevelt, who made the first trip on the Mississippi on the steamboat "New Orleans", in company with her husband, wrote an interesting diary of the voyage. The trip is also well described by J. H. B. Latrobe, Mrs. Roosevelt's half brother. Latrobe, by the way, was the son of Benjamin Latrobe who built the capitol in Washington and the first waterworks system in New Orleans. Benjamin Latrobe's diary about his residence in New Orleans has just been reprinted.

Samuel Clement was not the captain of the "New Orleans"

on her first voyage down the river, but he may have been and probably was her captain in the later operations of the steamboat between New Orleans and Natchez. Captain Clement, together with other Clements mentioned in his book, came from Duchess County, New York. This was the home of the Roosevelts, and undoubtedly Samuel was sent to New Orleans to represent Nicholas Roosevelt in the operation of his boat.

Tradition has it that the Captain had begun life as a purser on one of John Jacob Astor's sailing vessels and had made a voyage to China. Clement made money too and had established a business in New York. When Livingston and Roosevelt in developing their monopoly of the use of steampower on the rivers of the United States wanted someone to represent them and to handle their boat, they naturally turned to Samuel Clement. Although Samuel was not on the boat, on the epoch making first trip South, it might be interesting to look at some incidents connected with the "New Orleans" on her voyage of long ago.

Built in Pittsburgh, she left there in October 1811. Mr. Roosevelt took his wife on the trip against the advice of their friends. He and his wife were the only passengers. The voyage that was to change the whole destiny of the West progressed favorably until Louisville was reached. There was not sufficient water in the Ohio to allow the boat to pass the falls nearby and they had to wait until the rise of the river.

The year 1811 was a remarkable one in the history of the West, Latrobe called it *annus mirabilis*. First, there was a remarkable comet which alarmed the superstitious. Then an earthquake occurred which extended all up and down the Mississippi Valley. As one writer says: "At that time a terrific spirit of unrest, change and fright seems to have prevailed. Animals were affected as well as man." A remarkable phenomenon was the movement of great multitudes of squirrels across the states of Indiana and Ohio in almost a solid phalanx.

Nothing seemed to be able to check their onrush until they got to the Ohio River, when hundreds of thousands or even millions of these creatures were drowned while attempting to cross. That year the rivers were unusually high and overflowed, causing much damage. Above all it was the year in which the first steamboat navigated Western waters. The Indians called the "New Orleans" PINELORE, Choctaw for "fire canoe."

The "New Orleans" in her trip down encountered many difficulties, such as the river running backward at times, changes in the channel of the river, with new channels being opened that the pilot did not know about, and the floating debris in the river caused by the earthquake. Once the little crew of the "New Orleans" was forced to frighten away Indians by allowing the steam to escape through the exhaust with a great noise. She did not have a steam whistle.

The "New Orleans" arrived at the City of New Orleans on

Advertisement on Louisiana Gazette, Jan. 15, 1812.

January 10, 1812. This was four months before Louisiana became a state. The city turned out enmasse to see the new boat. A week later the captain gave an excursion, a round trip to English Turn, charging $3.00 for the trip.

For eighteen months the "New Orleans" did service as a

packet between New Orleans and Natchez, but she was finally wrecked on a snag in the vicinity of Baton Rouge. We learn from the "Navigator", a paper published in Pittsburgh, that her accommodations were good. The fare was $18.00 from Natchez to New Orleans and $25.00 from New Orleans to Natchez. The usual number of passengers was raound 20 but she sometimes carried as many as 80. The usual freight rates were reduced 25%. It is probable that Samuel Clement had charge of this boat while she was in the New Orleans and Natchez trade.

In any event, we do know that Clement was captain and manager of the "Vesuvius", third steamboat that plied the waters of the Mississippi. The second was a small boat by the name of "Comet", built by French, not connected with the Livingston, Roosevelt and Fulton group. She did not last long and never came to New Orleans.

The "Vesuvius" was built in Pittsburgh in 1814 by Robert Fulton for a company of Philadelphia-New York-New Orleans subscribers, and was intended for the Louisville-New Orleans trade. She arrived in New Orleans on April 22, 1814, having made the trip of 1682 miles in 227 hours, or at a speed of 7.41 miles per hour. In July 1814 with cargo, the "Vesuvius" made half the distance from New Orleans to Louisville in ten days. The "Vesuvius" was 48.77 meters long, 8.53 meters in width and a draft of 1.8 meters and displaced 340 tons. She was slightly larger than the "New Orleans". In July 1816 the "Vesuvius" took fire at New Orleans and burned to the light watermark, having then on board a cargo and bound upstream. She was hauled up on land and rebuilt in a most substantial manner. When launched in January 1817 she was considered in all respects as good as a new steamboat. The history of the "Vesuvius" is found in the records of a suit of Lynch vs. Postlethwaite in 1818. (See Martin OC69287) Samuel Postlethwaite agreed to purchase the "Vesuvius" for the Natchez Steamboat Company at Natchez for $65,000. The

ove—The late Mrs. John Henry of Melrose Plantation, in whose
rary many writers have found facts and inspiration for books and
ries about the old South.

Below—MELROSE, near Natchitoches, plantation home of Mrs. John
Henry (Miss Cammie Garrett), patron of writers and descendant of
Isaac Erwin. The "cabin" where Lyle Saxon wrote "Fabulous New
Orleans" is in the immediate rear.

Above—SHADY GROVE, on Bayou Grosse Tete was built by Isaac Erwin, son of Joseph, in 1856. Visitors prior to its very recent demolishment, used to stroll through the big thirty-foot square rooms and marvel at its massive brick construction.

Below—The so-called African house on Melrose Plantation. It was once a prison and then storehouse. A Federal Archivist said this is one of the South's thirteen most distinctive buildings. *(Courtesy of N. O. Times-Picayune. Copyright 1949 by Times-Picayune Pub. Co.)*

company with 72 limited stockholders refused to accept the "Vesuvius" when she was delivered on her return trip from Louisville, saying that Lynch had misrepresented the qualities and condition of the boat. This case went to the Supreme Court and Lynch won his suit. No mention was made of Clement in connection with this suit, so he must have retired from the steamboat business by that time.

Samuel Clement, operating the only steamboat on the Mississippi River, used the "Vesuvius" as a transport in General Jackson's service helping to carry troops at the Battle of New Orleans. A story was told, and widely published, regarding a dispute which was said to have arisen between Capt. Clement and Gen. Jackson owing to a delay of the captain's boat, which at one time had to tie up because of running aground during a fog. The high-spirited sailor and steamboatman, himself accustomed to command, is said to have found the caustic remarks for which General Jackson was famous, very little to his liking, and that he answered the general in a fashion that Jackson was seldom obliged to listen to. In Samuel Clement's "Truth Is No Slander" the captain said, however, that in his dealing with Gen. Jackson there was no rupture of relations that he was always received "affably."

Samuel Clement wrote and published in 1827 a 72-page pamphlet entitled "Truth Is No Slander" in which he presented arguments against the election of Andrew Jackson as president of the United States. The book was printed in Natchez in "The Ariel Office." This remarkably well-written piece of campaign literature was not a flamboyant, bitter and scurrilous attack as were many of the broadsides and brochures issued at that time. (Some of these, such as the celebrated "Coffin Posters", are described by Irving Stone in his recent book, "The President's Lady.") But Samuel Clement's pamphlet is sane, judicial, logical and well reasoned. It is quite a literary achievement, and shows him to have been an educated man. Captain Clement's booklet makes a study of Jackson's character and analyzes his achievements. For all students of Andrew Jackson and his time, I recommend this pamphlet as necessary reading.

Here follow some excerpts from Samuel Clement's book "Truth Is No Slander."

The Battle Of New Orleans

On the 9th of December [1814], being in command of the steamboat Vesuvius, while lying to, at the bank of the Mississippi a little below St. Francis river [near Natchez], repairing some damages, and taking in wood, I was passed by general Carroll's brigade embarked on board of flatboats, amounting, as I afterward understood, to 2,-900 to 3,000 men. The next day I proceeded down the river, overtook and passed general Carroll, and, either at this place, or somewhere below, received his aid, col. Andrew Hynes, on board as passenger for New Orleans. On the evening of the 12th I arrived at Natchez, and on the following day took on board, 120 recruits, belonging either to the 7th or 44th regiment, which of them I do not remember; I then proceeded to New Orleans.

On the 15th I made a stop at Baton Rouge, where in a group of persons, who evinced a great deal of anxiety, I was told that our gunboats near New Orleans had been taken by the British; that the number of British troops upon the coast was computed at 17,000, and that they were fully of opinion that New Orleans would be captured before I could get there. I went on, and arrived at New Orleans the next day, where I found great anxiety, and much despondency prevailed; and indeed the apprehensions of the citizens are not to be wondered at, for the British forces, the amount of which was variously estimated, but by all exaggerated, were hourly expected to land; and at the time, the only defense of the place consisted of the town militia, amounting to about a thousand men, with parts of the 7th and 44th regiments, mostly raw recruits, and a small number, probably 150, sailors and marines under the command of commodore Patterson.

Here let it be particularly remarked that there was at this time, and had been for a month previous, within three hundred miles of New Orleans, a force under general Jackson's command, at different points, of more than four thousand men; one body of which, according to col. Russel's statement, consisted of the '2n, 3d, and 8th regiments; none of them," he says, "but little more than half full, and some not that; detachments of the 24th, with a few companies of artillery, and the militia." In another part of his letter, he says, "the militia were from Georgia, Tennessee, and Mississippi, with about six or seven hunred Chickesaw, Choctaw, and Creek Indians." This force was stationed at Mobile, and from the above statement we may safely conclude, that it amounted to, from three to four thousand men; indeed I understood at the time that the number was much greater than I have now estimated it. The other body was general Coffee's brigade of mounted riflemen, containing 1,550 men, stationed at Sandy-creek, a place more than 140 miles in the interior.

Again let it be remembered, that it was not until the morning of the 15th, four days after it was known in New Orleans that the British were on the coast, and two days after an attack upon, and destruction of one of the gun boats, that general Jackson sent an express to general Coffee ordering him to march with haste to New Orleans.

Now, I will ask any impartial man, whether it is not strange and unaccountable, that a place containing the wealth, and being in every way as important as New Orleans was, should have been thus jeopardized? Can general Jackson—can any man, give a plausible reason why more than three thousand men, some of them the best troops in the United States' service, and equal to any in the world, should be stationed at a place so insignificant as Mobile then was, when New Orleans (some of the ware-houses of which contained more moveable wealth than the whole town of Mobile, and all its dependencies) was left destitute. I know that general Jackson's biographer, who by most impartial persons is considered as the General's mouth-piece, or amanuensis, has said that the General was greatly concerned for the safety of Mobile, and the settlements on the Alabama and Tombigbee rivers. But who will allow this to be a sufficient reason why three or four thousand troops should be allotted for its preservation, and a place of a hundred times its value left defenceless.

What would now have been said of general Jackson's talents, had New Orleans have fallen in consequence of this injudicious distribution of the forces under his command—and it was mere accident that it did not; for had the British landed any day previous to the evening of the 19th, there would have been none to defend it, except the town militia, in whose patriotism, it has been argued, the General had no confidence, and six or seven hundred undisciplined soldiers.

Moreover, the General's biographer in defending him against the charge of having tyrannically continued martial law, after not a shadow of necessity for such a measure existed, defended him by alleging that the British were still upon the coast, and that a few hours might bring them to the shore. If he meant that in a few hours, they might land, and again attack New Orleans, in their then discomfited and greatly reduced condition, it was untrue. But when they first arrived upon the coast, they might have landed in a few days, almost without opposition; for Jackson had neglected, strangely and culpably neglected, to concentrate his force to oppose them.

On the evening of the 18th, I received orders from general Jackson to proceed up the river, with the steamboat, to meet general Carroll, for the purpose of taking as many of his men on board, as the boat would contain, and bringing then direct to New Orleans. On the morning of

the 19th I met him, about twenty miles above New Orleans; he by great and praiseworthy exertions, retarded
as he was by windy weather, descended the river much
further than could have been expected. The weather,
when I met him, having become fine, he declined letting
any of his men leave the flatboats, and that afternoon he
landed with his company at New Orleans. The following
day general Coffee, by exertions and fatigue sufficient to
prostrate both man and beast, arrived at New Orleans
with twelve hundred of his brigade, having marched over
excessively muddy roads, more than one hundred and
forty miles, in less than three days.

The General, in many instances, shows his fondness for
telling a good story; not a mere dull matter of fact tale;
but one that has pith and nerve in it. This disposition is
evinced in another part of his statement respecting the
events of the 23d [Dec. 23, 1814]. Of the New Orleans
rifle company he says, "they having penetrated into the
midst of the enemy's camp, were surrounded, and fought
their way out with the greatest heroism; bringing with
them a number of prisoners." Now one of this company
was my brother [Henry Clement*], and I am well satisfied that neither he, nor indeed any of the rest, intention-
ally, penetrated into the midst of the enemy's camp, armed
as they were with rifles and knives, although there were
as brave men in the company as any in the field. The
facts of this incident are nearly these. In the darkness
and general confusion which prevailed, this company got
divided, and separated into two nearly equal parts; one

*According to Dallas Irvine, Chief Archivist, War Records Branch,
Washington, D. C., January 11, 1952, Henry Clement served under Captain Beal, in the Rifle Company commanded by the latter, December 10,
1814, to March 14, 1815. This company belonged to General Jackson's
Army. Clement served in the campaign in Louisiana.
Warrant 62,746 for 40 acres of bounty land was issued under the act
of September 28, 1850 to Elizabeth Clement, widow of Henry Clement, on
account of his war of 1812 service.

part, twenty-five I think in number, seeing a body of men standing, took them to be Americans, and marched up to them; when very close, some of them cried out "huzza for Tennessee;" the British soldiers, for such they proved to be, ordered them to lay down their arms, this they immediately obeyed, and surrendered, for resistance would have been vain. The other part of the company took a different direction and got to the main body of the Americans, and on their way picked up several stragglers of the enemy.

From all the information which I have been able to gather, of the manner in which it proceeded [the action around New Orleans], I believe it commenced with very little concert, and ended in total confusion. "I arrived," says the General, "near the enemy's encampment, about seven, and immediately made my disposition for attack. His forces, amounting at that time on land to about 3,-000, extended about half a mile on that river, and in the rear nearly to the wood. General Coffee was ordered to turn their right, while with the residue of the force I attacked his strongest position, on the left, near the river."

This I believe is correct, as respects Coffee's brigade; but Plauche's battalion, owing to its detention, waiting for cartridges, had not yet got up. In his advance, he was met by an officer of one of the regular regiments, and ordered to repair to a certain point; but the officer was evidently so much intoxicated, that his orders were not obeyed, and, as I have been informed, and believe, Plauche took a different direction, and was fortunate in arriving at a place just in time to meet, and to baffle the right wing of the British; and probably, by his unexpected appearance, impressed them with an idea that the American force was much greater than it really was, and thus prevented a total route of our forces. The General admits there was some confusion, and the British Officer who has written upon the subject, says it was total confusion. I presume he meant on both sides.

Early on the morning succeeding the evening on which the British landed, I took the crew of the steam-boat, went down to Fort St. Charles, and offered my services to captain Humphrey, who had been in command of the fort. He told me he had received orders, and was then preparing to go down with his light artillery, to join general Jackson; he referred me to major Nix, of the infantry, who, from an accidental wound, was unable to join his regiment, and was in consequence placed in command of the fort. The Major immediately accepted of my proffered service, and captain Humphrey then went with me around the fort, to show me the condition of the guns.

He made some remarks explanatory of the reasons why some of the guns were in their ruinous state, and wished me to do what I could to render them fit for service. Two of the eighteen pounders, which ranged down the road to the point whence the enemy must come, if he advanced upon the town, were in a shameful condition; they were both loaded, and fresh primed, with match-sticks and lighted matches standing by them; they were mounted on ship carriages, with iron trucks, or wheels; the trucks of one of the guns had settled up to the axle-trees, through the platform, it being rotten, on which the gun stood, the lower part of the gun, near the muzzle, rested on the embrasure in such a manner as to give it an elevation of ten or twelve degrees; or, in other words, to point it so much into the air, that at the distance of fourteen feet from it, the ball would have passed over a man's head.

The other of the two guns above mentioned, was in a somewhat similar condition, though not so bad. These guns I afterward raised, and placed temporary platforms, of new three inch plank, under them. Before this was done, they could not be brought to bear upon any object that stood upon the ground, at a greater distance than five yards from them, and were of course entirely useless; and had the enemy advanced upon the town, firing them would have had no other effect than that of making a noise. Had general Jackson been as well skilled in the use and management of cannon, as from all accounts he is in the art of gaffing, trimming, and preparing cocks for battle, he never could have passed those guns, without seeing they were in a condition that made it impracticable to use them to any effect.

On the evening of the 27th, between 9 and 10 o'clock, Mr. Charles Harrod, deputy quarter master, came to me, and told me, that he had just received orders from headquarters, to send down immediately a quantity of thick plank and scantlings, which were in a saw mill yard, above town; that he could hire nobody, and there was no way of getting it down, unless I would, with a crew of the steam boat, take it down; of course I could not refuse, or even hesitate. I received from Mr. Harrod, written authority, to take any boat that I could find at the levee, of suitable size; I soon found one, manned her, and went up, and got the timber on board, and proceeded down river; when from the distance I had descended, I had as I supposed, approached near the American camp, I sheared in towards the land, and kept along about fifty yards from the shore, expecting to be hailed by the first sentinel that I came to, not doubting but at that time of night, it being between one and two o'clock in the morning, a vigilant watch would be kept; when hailed, I intended, after satisfying the sentinel who I was, to enquire where the timber was to be landed; the night was not dark but there was a little bank of fog resting upon the margin of the river; I soon heard men talking upon the shore, and had no doubt, but when I got abreast of them, I should be hailed, and ordered to give an account of myself; but, although making a noise with the oars that might be heard a mile, I passed them without being noticed; I began to think of hailing the shore myself; but, thought I, what, hail a military camp? I shall be considered a real bumpkin, I certainly shall be hailed when I get low enough. I kept on, under this impression, passing several groupes of men without being noticed, until not a voice was to be heard in either direction. I then concluded it would be imprudent to proceed further without knowing more of my situation, I might, I thought, get down to the British camp, in which case I had not a doubt but I should be invited to give an account of myself.

I accordingly turned the boat to the shore, and finding nobody upon the bank, was at first in doubt, whether the men whom I had passed were not loiterers, and whether I had yet descended low enough to reach camp, but I resolved to go back and enquire, I therefore, rowed up by the shore, and soon with a good deal of anger, discovered men about the breastwork; and did not fail to taunt, and reproach them for their seeming ignorance of duty; I forthwith went to headquarters, to report myself, and related to the General's volunteer aidsdecamp, this most unsoldierlike negligence of the sentinels; or unmilitary police of the camp.

Had General Jackson and his army met the enemy upon equal ground, hand to hand, and foot to foot, as general Brown did at Chippewa, and at Bridgewater, and had the British in such a contest, been defeated and destroyed, as they were at New Orleans; then might the General have been lauded with propriety. But let us for a moment consider what the real situation of the two armies, at New Orleans was; and from it draw conclusions what degree of generalship was displayed. Their positions were nearly as follows; the Americans as I have before stated, were on the upper side of a high wall, made of adhesive and slippery earth; beyond this wall at its base, was a ditch twelve or fourteen feet wide, from three to four feet deep, nearly filled with mud and water.

The British encampment was about a mile and a half lower down the river; they had at this time no breastwork, but relied solely upon their arms for safety, their business was to attack, not to keep under cover and defend themselves. In making the attack upon the Americans; they had to march up over a plain so level, that from the first step in advance, they were exposed to the American's cannon, and to the uninterrupted fire of the musketry, and riflemen, when they had arrived near enough for such arms to take effect; when arrived at the ditch, they had it to wade before they could charge the Americans; its opposite bank to climb, and then to mount the breastwork, both muddy, in doing which, their hands would unavoidably become so besmeared with mud, that they could not use a musket or any other weapon to any effect, and all this time the Americans had nothing to do, but raise their heads above the breastwork, to point their guns down upon them, and shoot them—it is proper to remark that at the river bank, and for a short distance from it, perhaps an hundred yards along the breastwork, the ditch, owing to the falling of the river since the 23rd of December, had become nearly dry, so that here the obstacles above mentioned, to the success of the enemy, or their close encounter with the Americans, was not so great as in other parts.

The numbers of the British have by some of the busy newspaper "slang whangers" been greatly exaggerated, and the numbers of the Americans as much extenuated. I have seen a chronological table printed at Boston, in which the number of the British troops on the eighth of January, was set down at thirteen thousand; and the number of the Americans at considerably less than four thousand; but why rate the force of the British at only thirteen thousand—if the object is to make a marvelous tale, why not give the round number of twenty thousand, or forty thousand, but if truth should prevail, the superiority of numbers will be found much to preponderate on the American side, for them the best sources of information respecting the numbers of the British, and indeed the only sources that are entitled to any credit, which is general Jackson's own account, and that of the British officer before alluded to, there were eight regiments of the British, and from six hundred to nine hundred marines and sailors.

Admitting all the regiments to have been full, when they landed, a circumstance totally improbable, they amounted to eight thousand, and the marines and sailors, eight hundred, the whole force was eight thousand eight hundred; it might be taken into account however, that previous to the eighth of January, there had been several conflicts, and according to all accounts their efficient force, had been reduced about eight hundred, leaving seven thousand two hundred regulars; this number, however, did not all advance upon the American lines, colonel Mullen, refused to lead his regiment to the attack; the force, therefore, that did advance to the attack on the left bank of the river on the eight of January, did not exceed six thousand three hundred men. General Jackson rates his own force at the breastwork, at three thousand six hundred men; and says nothing of the thousands which he had in the rear. There are public documents and other proofs to show, that Jackson had at his command on that day at New Orleans, more than nine thousand men; the following list will be found very near correct, or rather a low estimate.

New Orleans militia and volunteers,	1000
7th and 44th regiments of regulars,	700
Louisiana and Mississippi militia and volunteers at least,	1400
Com. Patterson's sailors and marines,	150
Coffee's Brigade Tennessee riflemen,	1250
Carrolls' Brigade Tennessee militia,	2500
Thomas' Brigade Kentucky militia	2200
	9200

[Error of 100 in addition]

Clement goes on to say that if Jackson had no more than 3600 men at the breastwork it was because he could not squeeze any more in. The works were about 1200 yards long, and men in battle need at least 3 feet, so only 1200 men were in the front line with two lines of the same number behind them. He says, "The General had more than twice 3600 men on that side of the river, but where posted, or what their condition for battle was, I do not know, at least I did not see. I was that morning employed in Fort St. Charles."

He remarks further:

> If general Jackson could not employ more than 3,600 men to advantage at the breastwork, how can it be imagined the British general could attack to advantage with a greater number, when he had no greater space to act upon than general Jackson had. The British troops could not fire while they were advancing, except the front file, and that but once without stopping to reload their pieces; and if they could have fired, it would have been mere accident if they had hit any of the Americans, for there was nothing of them to be seen by the British but their heads and shoulders, and these only when they rose up to fire.

> As I have before remarked, one thousand men, situated as the Americans were, would be equal to four, if not five thousand, situated as the British soldiers were. And where, I would ask, was there any generalship displayed by our commander? where was there an opportunity to display military skill? There was no marching; no pressing or charging upon the enemy; no bringing up of corps of reserve to strengthen any weak part, or to counteract any evolution of the enemy; there was not even any changing of position. Any of the first settlers of Kentucky, or Tennessee, would in their little forts have arranged themselves in this manner, to repel an attack of the Indians, or any other assailants.

General Jackson had on the 26th, ordered the steamboat which I commanded, to be prepared for receiving guns, to be used against the enemy; at the time the order was given, the British had not used any artillery, and it was not known that they had landed any; the boat was ready to receive the guns on or about the 2nd of January; late on that day, I got an order from Thomas L. Butler, the General's aid-de-camp, who was stationed in town, to go up the river a few miles, to take wood on board, preparatory to taking the guns on board, and to proceeding down to the lines.

I accordingly went up the river to the point of destination; when I first arrived at the pile, I concluded to lie at the place all night, and take a large quantity of wood on board, but on examing it, and finding it would not answer my purpose, I concluded to return immediately to town, and inform the aid-de-camp, and make arrangements that evening, to go early in the morning, to some other place, where better wood might be procured; on the way down it became exceeding dark and foggy, so that nothing could be seen but the faint glimmer of light on shore: I thought, however, that I could get to my usual landing place, by the aid of two lamps that stood before the custom house.

I was so unfortunate, however, as to mistake lights which stood a few hundred yards above the custom house, for the custom house lights; I had a sailor constantly heaving the lead, but the banks of the flat, which is called the batture, was so bold, that, although the engine was stopped the moment soundings were obtained, the boat forged ahead so much as to stick upon the bar; after trying to force her back by the engine, without effect, I sent out a kedge upon the starboard quarter of the boat, which moved her considerably; but at the distance of fifty fathoms from the boat, the water was from fifteen to twenty fathoms deep, and the current very rapid; I immediately tried a large anchor, but the bottom was so soft, the water so deep, and the current so rapid, that it was impossible to get a sufficient scope of cable out, to enable the anchor to hold; the flat or bar too was so soft, that it was impracticable to shore her off. Another circumstances transpired against me, the wind had for several days, been blowing from the south, which had considerably raised the water; that evening, it became calm and foggy, and the wind soon came from north-west, which caused the water to fall very rapidly.

Having worked all night, and all the next day, with my utmost strength and action, suffering the keenest mortification; and having tried every expedient which I thought likely to succeed, without effecting my object; I was compelled to yield to what I considered at that time, a great misfortune.

The above statement respecting the grounding of the steamboat, may appear to some quite superfluous; but in these ill omened days of strife and prevarication; to have omitted it would have appeared to many, that I was desirous of hiding facts; and some, who, like the modern judge of Israel, think that all is fair in politics, would eagerly seize the opportunity of manufacturing a tissue of falsehood.

Clement belittles the accomplishment of Jackson in winning the Battle of New Orleans and proves that his strategy was poor, particularly in not arranging a better defense of the right. He says further:

I saw [General Jackson] frequently in New Orleans, have been affably and kindly received by him: I know him to be an intrepid man. I thought he was in the niche which nature had best prepared him for. I suppose that the General understands the infantry exercise, knows how to form a hollow square, and how to march ecchallon, with the other evolutions appertaining to the exercise; but ask him how much elevation the axis of an eighteen pounder, would require, to carry its ball a mile before it declined so much as to intersect a line, extended horizontally the cannon, and he would not be able to give an answer; he would not know whether it required one degree and fifteen minutes, or fifteen degrees and one minute; he knows nothing of the matter; unless he has learned it since he left New Orleans.

I have said that I once respected Andrew Jackson; it

was for his bravery and his honesty; for his genius, never
—nor was it for any signal service he had done. In sub-
duing the Indians, he, and the men who were with him,
I frankly admit, did the state some service; but even that
service has been vastly overrated. In conquering and destroying the effeminate Indians of the south, who acting
without concert, incapable from the lack of provisions, of
embodying in any considerable numbers, for any length of
time, and no doubt miserably armed, there could not be
much difficulty or hazard.

Some privations for want of provisions, he doubtless
suffered. From his biographer's account, he must have
had the worst commissaries in the whole world or as I
rather think was the case, he set out on his campaign, as
some masters of vessels have set out upon a voyage; without having calculated how much water, how much bread,
how much meat, and other provisions each man would require per day, and consequently, how much would be required for the voyage. Not having made these calcula-
tions, and provided accordingly, their stock of provisions
has been soon exhausted, and they been obliged to return
to port, and refit. A similar lack of preparation, brought
general Jackson and his army into straits, and much
retarded his progress; but after he and his commissaries
had found out how much beef 3000 men would eat per
day, at two pounds each man, they took care to keep a
supply.

———

General Jackson jeopardized New Orleans, by neglect-
ing to concentrate at that place, the forces which government had placed at his command, and that it was not by
his precautionary measures that New Orleans was saved,
but that it was the unprecedented tardiness of the British
army; but admitting general Jackson's conduct was not
justly chargeable with this censure; admitting too, that
he had not permitted general Coffee's brigade, to remain
in the interior for a fortnight, after common prudence

would have required it to be at New Orleans; it would still, it appears to me, be ridiculous to call him the saviour of New Orleans.

We will suppose, that, on the morning of the eighth of January, general Jackson, instead of being only weak and emaciated by the disease of Diarrhoea, had been confined to his bed, it is to be supposed, will any one pretend that he thinks, that the men would have left the breastwork in consequence—where was Carroll—where was Coffee—where was Adair, and a hundred others equally brave with Jackson himself. It is to be supposed that these men would not have done their duty; they required no orders; every officer, and every private, knew his station beforehand; all they had to do when the British troops advanced, was to exert themselves in firing, with their greatest skill and quickness. And were it susceptible of proof I would venture almost any wager, that not one man in ten who were at the breastwork, knew, until after the British had abandoned the assault, whether general Jackson was in his bed, or standing where he did.

Jackson had acted with promptness and energy; hundreds of others have done the same thing, and thousands of others are ready to do so, when circumstances require it. Energy of action, is an animal function, but energy of mind is never found in bears or tigers; it is a quality af a much higher order. Jackson is no philosopher; philosophy never gave him even a sight of her mantel. He has always been a vindictive man. Sometimes he is meek and affable, but more frequently arrogant and despotic. He would have hung Louaillier as a spy—he would have hung the members of the Hartford Convention, under the second action of the articles of war; and I am well aware that if he had the power, he would, for thus expressing my knowledge and opinion of him, hang me, under the third section of the same articles; or under the fourth section of his own will and pleasure.

Clement tells of two cannons that Jackson sent to Natchez:

ght—Dr. Charles Clement, (1797-
'4), pioneering physician and a
ding citizen, banker, and planter of
rville Parish. A graduate of the
dical School of Poughkeepsie, New
rk, he came to Iberville at the sug-
tion of his friend and patron, Jo-
h Erwin.

ow—Plaquemine Residence of Dr.
rles Clement. The old-time doc-
s office is shown on the left.

Right—SUNNY SIDE, on the east bank of Bayou Grosse Tete, nearly opposite Isaac Erwin's "Shady Grove." A two-story mansion with lovely grounds, it was built by the late David Barrow about 1858. Now the home of Mr. and Mrs. Harry M. Row. Mrs. Row was Leonora Barrow, great granddaughter of the builder.

Below—EVERGREEN Plantation Home, Iberville Parish. Plans of this old mansion, built on the river road at St. Gabriel, now rest in the federal archives at Washington. One of the finest examples of a Louisiana planters' house of more than a century ago. The eight graceful fluted columns in the front, the beautiful fanlights, the still good plaster and the large central chambers are distinguishing features. It was erected by Jeremiah Pritchard, later bought by Julien Grassin and later by the Becnel family. A cupola that was part of the house has been torn down.   *(Courtesy Baton Rouge States-Times)*

After peace had taken place, the General took from the public arsenal, at New Orleans, two of the brass six pounders, trophies of the memorable capitulation of Burgoyne, at Saratoga with their carriages, caissons, and other appendages. These guns he sent by the steamboat which I commanded, to some friend or friends of his at Natchez; one of these trophies, which bears the heartwarming inscription of "surrendered by convention of Saratoga," is, I am credibly informed, generally to be seen standing before a blacksmith's shop door at Woodville, a little town in the state of Mississippi; and is only used to celebrate some glorious event, or memorable occurrence.

Jackson maintained martial law in New Orleans for over two months after the Battle of New Orleans, under which he arrested Louiallier, drove Judge Hall out of town, and acted in a high-handed manner, says Clement, "Finally, it has been substantially shown that martial law was never necessary for the defense of New Orleans, and that, at all events, General Jackson continued it beyond any possible necessity and exercised it with wanton tyranny."

Following the defeat of the British, Clement immediately returned to Natchez and resumed operation of his steamboat and plantation properties. Later when Jackson loomed as candidate for the presidency Clement thought it his duty to expose Jackson for what he considered the despotic continuance of martial law in the New Orleans area long after the necessity for such action existed, and as being overrated as a general. In the bitter fight between Gen. Jackson and John Quincy Adams for the presidency of the United States, Captain Clement in 1827 issued the pamphlet assailing Jackson. Political feeling ran high, the captain, however, supported only in a moderate way the candidacy of the incumbent president, the highly respected John Quincy Adams. In this connection it might be well to remember that the meticulous Adams in contending with Jackson's demagogic attack on the Bank of the United States and his appeal to the "hoi polloi," refused to make any special effort to be elected for a second term. Adams and the other members of his family, consistently took the high ethical ground that "no man should seek public office, and no man should refuse such office if offered him." It was Jackson, who coming to the presidency, changed the system to one which encouraged men to seek office and to reward their supporters with jobs and political favors.

In this powerfully written brochure Clement arraigned the General with what seems to be difficult-to-encounter logic. This long forgotten tome now reposing in the Library of Congress is only briefly quoted, but it carries much information and comment which is of interest today as we face the fruition of more than a century of the political policy of "To the victor belongs the spoils" inaugurated by Jackson, a distinct change and "counterrevolution" against the ideas of Washington, John Adams and Thomas Jefferson.

It was said at the time that Henry Clay and other statesmen saw with much uneasiness and some fear for the future the rise of demagoguery, the lowered standard of ethics in government and the danger of the trend toward a strong and dictatorial centralization of the power of the Federal government. They feared, with good reason, the later ascendency of men whose ideas were to be different from those of the revered Founding Fathers. The illuminating pages from the Clement "Truth" pamphlet are introduced as evidence of the beginning of this trend continuing to this day and leading to the weakening of the Constitution, the centralization of government and the possible coming of a dictatorship.

Captain Clement later retired from the river and settled on his plantaiton, Ravenswood, on Lake St. John in Concordia Parish, Louisiana, across the river from Natchez. In addition to Ravenswood he owned and operated both the Upper Coosa Plantation and Lower Coosa. The fine old Ravenswood home burned many years ago. Lower Coosa on Lake St. John is now a favorite fishing resort for Natchez folk. It is known as "Cool Coosa."

In a letter to a cousin, one of his admirers, Jack Willets, of Duchess County, New York (Samuel Clement's former home) the captain, cried down the idea that he was in anyway "a great man," admitted he had been in the State Legislature "two sessions," but said, "That is a weak evidence of greatness, many noodles get into the Legislature."

Captain Clement married late in life, his bride was a Miss Little, member of a well known New England family. His only child was Ellen Clement, who married Don Antonio Yznaga, wealthy sugar planter of Cuba and Louisiana. They had three beautiful daughters, Consuelo, Emily and Natica. Following the marriage of Consuelo to the Duke of Manchester the mother took her daughters to London to make their debut. "Cousin Ellen", as the Iberville Parish Clement members of the family called her, rented a house and entertained lavishly. The beauty and charm of these Southern girls attracted every one, Natica too married a title, Sir John Lister-Kaye, an English nobleman who had achieved considerable renown as a traveler in Canada and an empire builder.

"Cousin Ellen" was a great friend of the Prince of Wales, afterwards King Edward VII. He loved to attend the breakfasts she gave, where "Aunt Deborah's" buckwheat cakes and syrup were in great demand. Aunt Deborah was Mrs. Yznaga's old black cook, whom she took with her to London from her plantation in Louisiana. Deborah was once invited to a luncheon by a fashionable hostess, but declined, saying, "I ain't never eat with white folks at home, and I ain't going to begin now."

It is probable that Consuelo Yznaga was married the same year, (1876) as were Lodoiska Clement and Andrew Gay, because she sent her Louisiana cousin a beautiful gold and silver berryspoon, one of her own wedding presents. The family thought it the most beautiful spoon they had ever seen. Mrs. Gay later gave this to her daughter, Mamie Sue, the recently deceased Mrs. Herbert Doolittle of Los Angeles, California.

Before and during the Civil War many influential and conservative leaders in the east and in New York City sympathized with the South. Mrs. Yznaga spent much time in the northern metropolis. On such visits she, a strong supporter of the Southern cause, was able—so it appears—to win friends for her beloved South, even during the hectic time of fratricidal strife. In an article, appearing in the Saturday Evening Post of February 16, 1952, entitled, "A New Ray of Light on Lincoln" by Allen Nevins, is this paragraph: "A masked ball was held by August Belmont [in New York City] early in 1863, to which a young English swell, Lord Hartington, later the Duke of Devonshire, escorted a Southern sympathizer of fashion named Mrs. Yznaga. As this couple shook hands with General McLellan, [Commander in Chief of the U.S. Army] the spectators saw with amazement that Hartington had a showy little Confederate flag in his button hole."

Mrs. Yznaga, even in the Northern stronghold, was apparently trying to supplement the work of her friends, the Confederate States Commissioners in London, who were endeavoring to bring England to their side. Here we have an interesting sidelight on New York social life of the sixties and the conflict which, precipitated unnecessarily and inadvisedly by Southern hot-heads, was later to result in the sweeping away of much of the large Yznaga fortune.

How this alliance with the English aristocracy began is told by Mrs. Carter H. Harrison, in her girlhood days Edith Ogden of New Orleans, charming wife of the well-known former mayor of Chicago in STRANGE TO SAY published by A. Kroch and Sons of Chicago in 1949, with sub-title "Recollections of Persons and Events in New Orleans and Chicago." Mrs. Harrison said that her granduncle, Judge Abner Nash

Ogden, had a plantation adjoining the Iberville Parish (Yznaga) plantation of the wealthy Cuban gentleman who married Ellen Clement, daughter of Samuel. Through occasional visits to her Iberville neighbor Mrs. Harrison became the close friend of Emily Yznaga, youngest of the three sisters. These sisters were frequent visitors to New Orleans where their father was Spanish consul, and active in the business and social life of the Crescent City.

One day says Mrs. Harrison, "Emily and I met an old gypsy and crossed her palm to tell our fortunes. Well do I remember her words. She said to Emily, 'You will never marry but you will see much of the world and you will be the associate of kings.' To me she continued, 'You will marry young and to one who will help make history for his country and who will benefit the world by his influence'." Mrs. Harrison continues:

How we laughed, but not long after, see what happened! Over in England a young man, the Duke of Manchester, Baron Montagu of Kimbolton had fallen in love with a young English girl and wanted to marry her. The family considered it a mesalliance, opposed it violently, and packed him off on a trip to America. Mr. Yznaga being Spanish Consul, the young duke had brought a letter of introduction. He was later invited to spend a week on the Yznaga plantation and to meet the family's charming daughters.

By the end of the week, the young man had contracted typhoid fever. He was a long time recovering and meanwhile the family treated him the best they knew how. He very soon forgot his charmer in England and succumbed to the great beauty of Consuelo, the middle sister.

Beautiful and fascinating Consuelo loved to shock society, too. I remember she caused great embarrassment to a young cousin of mine who had asked to be her escort to a neighborhood dance. He came for her and as she was heavily cloaked, he could not see her dress. When they reached the party all the girls, discarding the wraps, were in the usual costume of the day—tight-fitting waists and bodices. My cousin's chagrin was terrible when he saw the exquisite Consuelo. She looked like an angel, as she always did, but her dress he could only describe as a voluminous thing like a balloon, a sort of Mother Hubbard gown or a big white nightgown.

He was horrified, for it made her very conspicuous. He rushed to a friend and begged her to take Miss Consuelo to the dressing room and tie a sash or a ribbon or a string around her waist—anything to confine those flowing lines. Consuelo was difficult to persuade, but finally did consent to the ribbon around the waist. Had she not consented, I believe her escort would have swooned with embarrassment.

Well, the Duke of Manchester married the lovely Consuelo and despite remonstrances from England—he refused to give her up. He sat beneath the flowering magnolias, breathing in the delicious perfume of the cape jasmine hedges and listening to the mockingbirds, and declared himself radiantly happy with his bride. This went on for a long time, but the young duke was firm in devotion to his American bride. Finally he won recognition from his aristocratic family. They went to England where she instantly proved a great success because of her beauty and charm. If she ever indulged in any further eccentricities, we never heard of them.

Later on, when Emily was grown, she joined her sisters in England. The prophecy of the old gypsy was verified in her case, for soon after her arrival there she was at a house party to which Edward VII came, and she taught him the banjo—she was expert player. The banjo craze struck England then and it lasted for a long time. She really had precipitated it. Emily never married but she owns a home in Paris as well as in England and she does mix with the high and mighty of the earth.

Captain Clement died in Natchez of cholera in 1833. It is somewhat surprising that the important part played by him at the Battle of New Orleans, the inauguration of steam-transport on the Mississippi and the interesting contribution to literature about Gen. Jackson, has received so little recognition.

A letter from Samuel Clement's brother's wife Mrs. Henry Clement, written at New Orleans three days after the battle to her brother, Jacob Wood, is appended as it appears to merit special consideration. This letter illustrates very strikingly the awful confusion and suspense which prevailed at the time of the battle. It is hard to realize what the people living in the lower section of New Orleans went through, with the ceaseless noise of cannon and musketry in their ears and the realization that the enemy might defeat our troops and sack the city. The letter from Captain Clement, too, gives an insight to his character, and an idea of the life on a plantation a hundred and twenty-five years ago.

New Orleans, La., Jan. 11, 1815

[To Jacob Wood from his sister Mrs. E. Clement]

I sit down, my dear Brother, to give you a little account of the horrible situation we have been placed in at New Orleans —On the 14th of Dec., there came an express to our worthy General Jackson to state that the enemys fleet had arrived on our water—the Genl. had not been here many days—& consequently nothing in readiness to receive them—the confusion, of course, was very great—as their fleet consisted of between 50 & 60 vessels and our force had not yet arrived, but was hourly expected of course all the citizens were called to arms, and everyone that was capable of carrying a gun was called on duty and none but invalids and old white headed men appointed to watch and guard the City. All stores were immediately shut in town, and everyone was exercising their arms the greatest part of the each day, we expected the attack on the river, & there was strict watch kept, and the fortifications made stronger, and every precaution taken to repel them —when, lo and behold!! On Dec. 23, about two o'clock in the afternoon, an express arrived in town to say the enemy had landed and only two leagues from town.

It seems there was a small canal that lead out of the swamp into lake Pontchartrain, through which the fishermen passed, it being so small and obscure, it was not thought of, but by the treachery of some one it was shown to the enemy, and they were privately conducted to our doors, consequently avoided all our strong forts, the alarm was extreme, every soul was called to arms in an instant—but fortunately for us, 3 days previous to their landing Genl. Coffee had arrived with three thousand riflemen from Tenn., who were encamped 4 miles above the City. The alarm and confusion is better imagined than described, and what added much distress to my feeling was parting with my husband, who attached himself to a rifle corps, to avoid the disagreeable company of Militia, it was a company composed of the merchants of the City, there were 62 of them. They marched in advance of the Tennesseans, or rather ran, at 4 o'clock in the afternoon they started and arrived at the encampment of the enemy a little after twilight, when they found them around their camp fires, with their arms grounded and reveling in mirth—I suppose at the idea of having taken us such an easy prey. They had no idea of being attacked that night and before the next morning would have been in town.

But their plans were interrupted, our people commenced a galling fire upon them and the action continued violently. Two vessels of war had been sent down the river to rake them with our cannon which played on them an hour—and then they retreated, they suffered considerably and so did we, but none so much as the company to which my husband attached himself, as they opened the action and were in the heat of it, nothing to obstruct the bullets. Out of the 62, 25 returned but we have heard of the death of only three, the others were wounded or taken prisoners. My husband was wounded in the leg, a ball passed through it and injured a small bone, but now he is almost well. After he was wounded he took a prisoner, made him throw down his gun and carry him off the field, if it had not been for that circumstance he would have been taken prisoner. Also our people took near one hundred British that night, the next day everything was operating on the defensive there went a requisition from Gen. Jackson to the country, for 600 negroes to work on our fortifications.

They are now as strong as it is possible to make them, the lowest is 4 miles below the City, they have made another at a convenient distance above, and still another above that. The enemy are also fortifying and seem [to be] making preparations, I am afraid for a long seige. After their repulse on the 23rd., they attempted again on the 28th and were again repulsed. Our force is pretty strong and is daily increasing. Every creature, within 300 miles, that can be spared from guarding the country, has arrived in town. We were daily expecting a strong reinforcement from Kentucky, which has just arrived 2 weeks after the enemy, they had not got here on the first of Jan. when the enemy made another attempt more bold, to force our lines and were repulsed again, as usual, but all day our people kept up a tremendous cannonading, after that they made no more advances, until the 8th when they made the most desperate attempt to storm our works with a reinforcement of 25,000 men, it, I believe, was ascertained that they have now 10,000 men and we the same.

Our house in the Faubourg, owing to a bend in the river, brings us in a straight line but 2 miles from the battle ground, so that we can hear all the battle as it rages. The battle of Jan. 8th commenced at the dawn of day and continued without cessation until 10. The cannon began firing first and it seemed like one continued peal of tremendous thunder, and the small arms roared like distant thunder. The horror of that morning is beyond my abilities to describe, if I should attempt it, I shall only say we were prepared to run as far as we could, knowing if that merciless foe got the upper hand that not only all our property, but even our lives would be destroyed. In the heat of the action, some of the enemy crossed the River, drove our men who were placed there with some large cannons from the field, but they spiked the cannon and threw the powder in the river. The enemy pursued them up to within 3 miles of our powder magazine, before they were arrested and driven back, we saw our troops flying on the other side river and thought our destruction inevitable until we heard of their retreat.

But the slaughter and carnage of that day surpasses any battle fought since the commencement of the war. The enemy are from 1500 to 2000 killed and wounded, we are only 15 killed and wounded in all. The British officers say, such fighting they never saw before, that had been in Wellington's army and have been fighting in Europe, but never saw such well directed fire and such bravery as in the Americans. They say it appeared literally to rain lead. The entrenchment before our breast works was filled with dead and dying. Lord Wellingtons brother-in-law, who is their commander in chief, is slain and three others in high command. How they will get on now I know not, 20 days have they been on our soil, our cannons are still firing on them and have been constantly—I have given you a short sketch of what my eyes have seen and ears heard—for further particulars and in better style, I refer you to the newspapers.

I am, with great gratitude to God for our preservation,

Your affectionate Sister
E. Clement

This letter was written by Captain Samuel Clement to his cousin, Jack Willets of Washington, Duchess County, New York. It was found among the papers of his niece, Mrs. Andrew H. Gay of Iberville Parish.

November 4, 1825
Natchez, Miss.

Respected Cousin:

I must beg pardon for being rather tardy in answering your letter which contained so much interesting information respecting friends and old acquaintances. This part of it I cannot reciprocate, there probably being no one here but myself of whom you have any knowledge.

I am glad to know that Jonathan [Samuel's married brother] has recovered a part of the property which he jeopardized by endorsement. I have suffered some that way myself. I am not married, and most probably never shall be, though I regret that I have not been, long since; but if I had been, or should hereafter be married, there is no guarantee that my judgment even were it really good, would guide me or enable me to gain a wife that my friends would greet with gladness, for according to what is generally said of marriages, it is the result of love, and Cupid, they say is blind—but his arrows have been so flaunted against me that I am not now likely to fall his victim. Yet there is a young widow in the neighborhood who has one son, that were she a little larger, had she a fair complexion, had she dark brown hair instead of light brown, I would acknowledge Cupid's power and gladly yield to Hyman's bands! Enough of that I will say.

Charles [Dr. Charles Clement, Samuel's brother] is practicing in his profession at Plaquemine, which lies on the Mississippi about two hundred miles below this city. I am told he has as much as he can attend to, especially when the autumnal diseases prevail, but there is only a skirt of inhabitants on the margin of the River which makes a great deal of traveling for a very little business.

In speaking of the manners and habits of the people here, I would say that they were generally industrious, something more in the habit of taking public dinners, and at such times drinking deeper than people do in the northern parts where I have been, and perhaps not altogether so familiar and sociable in their manners except at those collections, as they are in your part of the country, or in the towns adjacent.

We have no Quakers or "friends" here, or none that distinguish themselves by their plain (or singularly), and I think unearthly constructed garments of "the friends". We however, have no lack of religious sects—or rather, of places of worship. We have in this little town a Presbyterian Church, well built; an Episcopalian Church tastily and well built, also a Methodist, a Baptist and a Catholic Church.

It appears that you have heard flattering accounts of me, from which you conclude that I am a great man. I have served two sessions in the state legislature of this state, but that is a weak evidence of greatness. Many noodles gets into the legislature. At present I am not eligible for a seat in the Mississippi legislature having sold my land in this state and moved my hands [slaves] into Louisiana on the west side of the Mississippi River about fifteen miles from this place.

You apologize for inaccuracies in your letter. I however, did not to any extent discuss them, but if I had, I might say I had in this given you a Roland for your Oliver.

Sincerely your cousin,
(Signed Samuel Clement)

P.S. Remember me to my relatives.

CHAPTER IX

MICHAEL SCHLATRE'S "LAST ISLAND" STORY

Last Island on the Gulf Coast, not far from the mouth of Bayou Lafourche, a hundred years ago was a favorite summer resort of the prominent plantation families of Iberville and Lafourche Parishes and the Attakapas region. Many families, including that of Charles Dickinson whose terrible experience I have related in another chapter, had built summer homes on the island. There was also an immense, three-story wooden summer hotel, six hundred feet in frontage, which accommodated transients. As with summer resorts, the month of August was the most popular for vacationers and the population of the island was the greatest at that time.

On Sunday, August 10, 1856, a tropical hurricane struck Last Island and wiped away nearly every building—every house was unroofed and all were blown down except two or three. The wind and tidal wave made a shambles of the island, and hundreds of Louisiana's sugar planter aristocracy and their slaves died that day.

Because Last Island was frequented by prominent people from the great houses along the Mississippi and because the storms that often occur on the Louisiana coast are of perennial interest, it is appropriate to tell here again the story of this terrific hurricane that killed so many people. More particularly, a graphic story of the holocaust was written by an Iberville man, Michael Schlatre.

It was two days before the news that Last Island had been destroyed reached New Orleans. On the 16th, nearly a week afterwards, the *New Orleans Crescent* published a fairly ac-

curate account of the disaster, giving a list of those who lost
their lives. The list totaled 170, but the loss of life must have
been at least 200 or more.

The *Crescent* printed a letter written by Dr. R. B. Brashear
of Brashear, now Morgan City, which said in part:

The steamer Southern Star, which was anchored near
was blown ashore and bilged, she was thus the means of
saving [many of] those that were saved; all those who
succeeded in getting to her were saved, while [practically
all] those who preferred taking their chances on the island in preference to running the risk of being blown
out to sea on her, perished.

The scene that followed the first tremendous gust of
wind, I have been informed, beggars all description. One
tremendous cry of agony went up, and in five minutes
naught was to be heard but the howling of the winds and
the lashing of the waters—two hundred souls had perished in that short time!

From what I can learn, the force of the wind must
have exceeded anything on record. A gentleman informed
me that boards and logs would be torn from the houses
and whirled through the air like feathers, men and wom-
en were blown down and thrown about until they were
killed or stunned.

This terrible tornado only lasted about four hours, and
then subsided very rapidly; the water fell as rapidly as it
had risen, leaving dead bodies of men, women and children, mixed promiscuously with furniture and debris
from the fallen houses; in the meantime night came on
with all its horrors.

There are some incidents connected with this awful affair which I cannot refrain from giving you; among them
was the heroic conduct of Dr. Batey's Negro coachman.
This truly faithful servant, on the commencement of the
panic, seized one of his master's children, and accompanied his mother and family to the highest point of the

land; as soon as he perceived the wreck of the Star he tried to persuade his master to go aboard, but without success, and then he asked to be allowed to take the child that he had in his arms on board, but his master sternly commanded him to put the child down—he reluctantly obeyed, but in a few minutes, seeing that if he remained where he was, that he would inevitably perish, he caught up one of Mr. Pugh's children, and made for the wreck with it, and succeeded in getting there, and was saved. He says that if his poor master had permitted him, he would have saved his whole family.

One of Mr. Pugh's sons behaved like a hero, and throughout the trying time assisted his father in saving his brothers and sisters, with as much foresight, coolness and intelligence, as a man bred to battle with the elements.

Mr. and Mrs. Foley* were seen to be carried away on the crest of a breaker, locked in each others arms, and thus they died as they had lived, together.

I forgot to mention above that several of the bodies that were picked up on Last Island, were found to have been robbed, their pockets cut out, and in some cases, fingers which had had rings on them, were cut off. These outrages have been committed, it is said, by a set of piratical vagabonds who infest the bayous and swamps of the mainland. A party of gentlemen are forming here to go in search of them; if they are caught, woe unto them, no tree in the parish will be too high for a gallows to hang their despicable carcasses on.

Among those on the island from Plaquemine who survived as listed by the Crescent were: F. Marrioneau, Mr. Desobry and Family, Two Misses Clements, Mrs. Dardenne, Mr. and Mrs. Hart, two children and servant, Mrs. M. A. Leftwich, Mrs. S. M. Dickinson, two children and servant.

Another writer says: "They danced in the great ballroom

---

*From the newspaper account later it was learned that Mr. and Mrs. Foley were miraculously saved.

of the huge wooden hotel until water surged in knee-deep. Dancers and musicians climbed table-tops and danced and played on until swept screaming out to sea. Women, given a choice of which of their children they would try to save, knelt praying, paralyzed with terror, until all were swept away. Huge timbers, flying like feathers before a hurricane wind of unbelievable force, crushed many to death."

But the best account of the Last Island storm is that of Michael Schlatre,* Jr. of Plaquemine, who within a few months after the event, wrote an eyewitness description of the disaster. His narrative of the tragedy in which his wife and seven children perished is a graphic and powerful piece of writing. It is crude and lacking in style, but, written from the heart and under the spell of a terrifying experience, it grips you as you read. This narrative is good enough to be included in any collection of the writings of Louisianians, or of Louisiana literature. School children could study it with benefit. Above all it is inspirational, and shows that an indomitable will to live and a faith in God will save a man when death seems certain.

That Michael Schlatre's narrative has literary quality was appreciated by Lafcadio Hearn, who borrowed this manuscript when he wrote "Chita," a romantic description of the disaster. Hearn's classic is better written, but it is not as simple and powerful as Schlatre's account. Schlatre's manuscript is now in the Library of Louisiana State University. It was printed for the first time in the Louisiana Historical Quarterly, (July 1937 issue) after having been prepared for publication by Dr. Edmond R. Ott, Prof. of History at L.S.U. Dr. Walter Prichard wrote the introduction.

Schlatre's narrative is too long to be used in full so I have

---

*Most of the Schlatre descendants have changed the spelling of the name to Schlater and it is pronounced *Slaughter*.

Above—SAMUEL CLEMENT, originally of Duchess Co., New York. Captain of the Mississippi River Steamboat, "VESUVIUS," and under Jackson's orders a participant in the Battle of New Orleans. Later owner of "Ravenswood" plantation, Concordia Parish, La. Author of the book, "Truth Is No Slander."

Below—Replica of the steamboat "New Orleans" built for 1911 Centennial voyage. Replica was as accurate as possible. *(Courtesy Leonard T. Huber)*

DON ANTONIO YZNAGA

Owner of sugar plantations in Cuba and Louisiana, with his wife, the former Miss Ellen Clement, daughter of Samuel Clement of Ravenswood Plantation, Concordia Parish, La., and their daughter Consuelo, later Duchess of Manchester.

shortened it by leaving out certain paragraphs and, paraphrasing, or condensing others.

THE STORM OF SUNDAY AUG. 10, 1856

Well now it must be known that I commanded the Steamer *Blue Hammock*, running from Plaquemine to Last Island, but knowing that Mr. J. A. Dardenne and family were coming out the trip of the 5, of August I remained on the Island with my family, consisting of wife and seven children also 4 grown servants and three small ones, with a servant of Mrs. Robertson with us, old Hannah making it number 17 Souls of us: of these only 3 now survive,Viz. self, Ceily, and William. I had a few months previous, purchased the Summer house of Mr. Faustin Dupuy, situated between the house of Mr. Mille and Hebert, about ½ a mile from the landing.

Having been at the Island for so many seasons, and in all kinds of weather I felt no apprehension, and therefore made myself quiet. Walking backwards and forwards to and from the Hotel. Thus passed Saturday and during Saturday night, the wind blew with much the same force, strong and regular, so that we all said that the Steamer Star, due at 10 o'clock this night, would not dare venture out of oyster bayou in such a gale, the bay being white with foam and the sea running high. 10 o'clock Sunday morning I rose at daylight and went on the beach, and when I could distinguish objects across the bay, in looking casually in that direction, what was my astonishment to see the Star running parellel to the Island close on that she headed for the landing, wind heavy on the Larboard quarter yet she worked well and I soon saw that she would weather the gale and come in safely, yet I expected to see her beached as she would attempt to head to the wind in the bayou and to see her make her landing I went with Mr. Hart down to the Hotel and found very few persons out; the Star came in finally headed to the wind at Joe's camp and anchored safely.

Hart and myself now returned to our respective families, we had breakfast at the usual hour, after breakfast, I called all the family together and read Mass, after this we dispersed in different directions, and the cook was ordered to cook but little dinner as it was Sunday; at noon the weather darkened somewhat, and it blew still stronger; wind still N.E., that is blowing from the bay, side across into the Gulf—I had not the least apprehension of any thing like a tornado, and went from my house to Mr. Hebert, where Mrs. Bell boarded and I made light of the weather, telling them I had seen it blow as hard before this and so I had. We dined at 1 o'clock and already the rain began to come through the roof on the upper floor, and thence it found its way down into the bedrooms. To prevent the beds from being wet I bored several holes in the upper floor, and put tubs under these to catch the water, I likewise bored holes in the lower floor to let the water pass off.

Things now began to look squally: yet I had no apprehension of danger, as I had the greatest confidence in the strength of our houses and I made light of the fears of the Mille family who constantly sent to ask me if I thought there was any danger, and in jest sent them word that they had not seen the worse yet, but too true this proved: it was now about 2 p.m. from time to time I looked for the Star at anchor, and she still stood steadily; the rain descending in torrents, and it all came down in the rooms, Little Louis who was sick was placed in a bed and the teaster covered with blankets, also covering placed over him—the wind at this time increased rapidly. At three o'clock the servants came in and told me that the servants house had blown down, as this was a weak Structure, I thought nothing of it—in half an hour more I saw my Kitchen nearly doubled, blown close up to our dwelling, for the first time I began to apprehend danger, and prepared to do my best, all the servants

were ordered in the house and I told my wife that I now
saw that there was danger, but that all must keep cool,
not to be frightened for that would do no good—it was
about 4½ P.M.

The chickens in the yard were squatting in all directions, cows and calves lowing, etc. the air was darkened
and filled with Sand and water, the wind howling the like
of what I never heard. I now told wife that I expected
every moment that our house would be blown from its
blocks, but then we would be safer for the house would
then be on the ground; it came to 5 P.M. our house still
stood, I went on the gallery and to the end next to Mr.
Mille's House, at that instant I saw his house launched
forward about 5 ft. the front falling to the ground but
the back part about 4 ft. up on the back blocks, now for
us I said to myself, in about 5 seconds ours followed, but
it lay flat on the ground, One scream and all was
hushed within. I had prepared them for this, and seeing
no other damages done, the inmates stood still with
fear. I now went to the other side to see Heberts go,
but it yet stood, and it was still standing when I went
in and closed the door, My Louis was crying and he being sick as I said before thought that we were going to
leave him. He said to me, "*Pa* don't leave me behind,"
his mother and myself told him not to fear that we would
not leave him. Then a tremendous crash told me to prepare for the worse. In an instant I comprehended the
danger, and ordered every soul to get under the bedsteads
(there were three in the rooms,) as I knew the matrases
would protect them from the falling timbers for I knew
from the crash that the entire roof must have gone off;
I stood out alone on the floor, children, wife, servants
all under the beds—I now stepped to my window next
to Mille's house and looked for his home, not a piece of
it was to be seen, all had disappeared, only the Cistern
was left standing.

I now called Ceily up and opened the large family
trunk therein we put clothes for all the whites one suit,

next I put in my box of money containing some 500 or 600 Dollars I then shut it firmly I next collected a box of biscuit, and this with the trunk I placed on a bed to keep dry, now again I ordered everybody to keep quiet under the beds: at this instant another terrible crash and the whole of our upper floor was carried away, at the same time the shutters and sash were driven in and it was the utmost difficulty that I could keep the matresses on the bed under which was wife and most of the children. Now began my misfortunes, Mr. Mille at this moment came into my house from somewhere, ringing his hands, and laid down on the floor. I told him it was no way to act—to go under the bed with the others if he wanted and he did so; all this passed in the west room where were the servants and a few children I then stepped in the East room where were my wife and most of the children under the bed—the upper floor being gone the sides of the house had no supports, and the wind blowing from the N.E. it soon blew down the East Gable on the beds (two in this room) and seeing that all would be mashed under the bedsteads which now gave way I dragged and ordered all into the room of the servants and soon they were all safe again.

Seeing no farther damage doing at this moment, I now called Mr. Mille and asked him what had become of his family, he said he did not know. Stepping to the front door, and looking in the direction of the beach I saw at my front gate a lady who stayed at his house sitting in the water, for the bay water had now risen above the level of our house and was traversing into the Gulf. Seeing her there I told Mille that I would go and get her and bring her in—he said I could not, the wind was too strong. I determined to try and so soon as I quitted my house the wind pitched me towards her like a football, seeing it was to no purpose I crawled back to my house and instead of going inside I went behind the West Gable for protection from the wind, Mr. Mille following me —here on the ground I found two coils of rope that I

placed in my garret and the upper floor went off, these
ropes fell down near the corner of the gallery—I instantly suggested to Mr. Mille to tie the rope around
one of us and the one thus tied to go and get the ladies,
the other to pull in by the rope, he agreed; the storm
was now at its height, and it was about 5 P.M. I now
stooped down behind the house and commenced uncoiling
this rope to play out, just then Omer Mille came to us
from the beach, whence he came I can't tell, immediately
I gave him the end and was in the act of cutting the
rope when, Reader, down on me came the whole of the
West Gable end crushing me dreadfully the whole weight
falling principally on my breast and right leg, tearing
the Pleuria in my right breast and lacerating all the liga-
ments in my right knee—Eternal God; instantly I saw
now that nothing could save us, I looked at my leg and
cried to be taken out, directed Mr. Mille and son to raise
up the corner and my wife hearing my cries for help
came out to me—*that moment I will never forget.*

She now took command, yes she was the heroic one,
she ordered a matrass on the floor of our house for me,
therein had me dragged by the women. Our house now
in ruins and all of us on the floor, amidst bedding,
trunks armoirs etc. At this critical moment the wind
shifted E.S.E. My dear, said I, our time has come the
Gulf waters will soon cover the Island and drown us all,
No help for you all now, my arm is now powerless for
your protection, our only help must be from above. By
this time Mr. T. Mille went out to the beach and led in
his wife and placed her on the floor by my side; She had
a dreadful cut over the eye from a piece of timber I
suppose, and though in her senses she said not a word.
I now asked my wife if the gulf waters were washing
over, and looking she said they were just commencing to
cover the ground, raising up my head from Rosine's lap
who was sitting to hold it up myself laying on my back
on the matrass not able to move an inch, I looked in the
direction of the beach and there sat yet, the woman in

the water her head streaming down with blood, the waters pouring in over the beach and rushing towards our house, the time had come and I well knew it, I now called my wife and Omer Mille and requested them to say an act of Contrition for us all.

I now exhorted all to offer themselves up to God, and told my loved ones that we would all die together. Reader, no pen can describe this awful moment. My children flocked all around their Father some crying some quiet, my wife facing the gulf, the Negro women crying, old Hannah with the baby sitting close to me, Omer Mille and father also facing the beach with terror depicted on their countenances, standing on their feet, and I poor miserable worse off, than all, lay in the middle of all this motly crowd compelled to witness all this in a single moment and my utter dispair may be imagined when I knew that death was all around, and from my situation that I would be the first. Just as sure as there is another world, I then expected to be there in five minutes, were you ever as near death as that, my dearest Reader, in full health, with all those whom you loved best in this life around you in the same Situation? if not do not envy me. Yet I exhorted all to meet death as christians. the blacks I told them to remember what I often told them. To old Hannah I told her to pray, to all I cried to say acts of Contrition for death was certain.

The waters now rushed towards us with the noise of thunder, I was laying facing Heberts house, the roof was gone, but the gable end was standing, I saw his entire house whirl round and move towards the bay, and then it ran up against something and lodged, and stood still. I also saw several persons behind his Cistern dodging from the waters, all this passed like electricity—I now saw floating by our house, at my feet, the entire roof of a house, it ran up against my wife who was standing on the ground and threw her down, this was the last I saw of her, I now felt the water raise our floor and then it fell again on the ground, again the floor raised and com-

menced floating with us all on it, it ran up against the
Cistern and stood still, the waters now maddened by resistance came rushing over the floor and in an instant
we were all washed off, with every thing that was therein, as I left the floor, my poor little girl gave one scream
and jumped and caught me around the neck with both
arms and held fast, pell mell we all went from the floor
amidst pieces of the wreck and all sorts of floating
timbers.

I now rolled over and over drinking in the hated fluids
by great mouthfuls the dear child still fastened to me,
when I thought, (for reader I still could think) that I
must be near gone, I put my hands to those of my child
and broke her hold of me, God only knows what became of
the dear one, being relieved I now arose to the surface,
and in rising a few planks passing me I caught holt of
three, and in my exhausted state I saw some 3 or 4 of
my boys drowning around me just three heads and faces
visible, old Hannah too was visible, rushing forward with
the current.

A sill of a house came up to me at this moment in an
instant I laid holt of it and let go my planks—and lay
across it totally bereft of strength—as I rushed forward
I saw standing up in the marsh a *man* in whom I recognized as Mr. Mille, some 30 yards off—how he got so far
ahead of me I can't say, but sure it was he—my sill floating directly towards him, as soon as it got opposite to him
he jumped across it with me; he was standing, as near
as I can judge, in about 2 ft. of water. We now floated
towards the bay, both of us well worn out, after crossing
the bayou, our sill ran up against a drift pile, formed of
a portion of houses etc that had lodged against a small
bush, whose top I could distinguish above the water, there
was now but very little current, Mr. Mille in feeling
about observed to me that there was something solid in
which he put his hand and said he had better get on it,
without a word said, we both crawled on it, not knowing
on what we were.

Here we stayed for a few moments, and then I saw we were leaving the other drift behind and knew that we were destined for the bay: for a while all went on well enough, but I well knew what was coming, when we would be well out. It never entered my mind that we could live to cross the bay.

Schlatre now tells about the passage across the bay. It was dark the wind blowing and the waves high. He writes:

How could I expect to live, my leg broken, my side giving me intense pain so I could scarcely breathe, and my stomach full of salt water. Well, kind reader, I did live across that bay and for 5 days and nights after without food or sleep, and half naked exposed night and day to the most awful weather that ever mortal witnessed.

He and Mille were on a sort of raft made of the side of a house about 12 ft. long and 8 ft wide with a "well" an empty window frame in the middle they were blown 12 miles across the bay to the coastal marshes on the mainland.

We vomited off and on, as we drank the muddy salty water, all night, not myself as much as Mille. I told him that I feared the Sharks would cut off our legs every minute. My situation was now beyond description awful in the Extreme, I held on with the tenacity of a Terrier as the waves would pitch me about my wounded and broken knee would move back and forth like that of a bird's—the reader can imagine how I felt thus for 14 hours in these waves, yet I cheered up my companion by telling him to hold on as we were surely going on the marsh and as everything has an end we would get there if our raft did not part—and to do him justice he did hold on, for as often as I would look for him, after the passage of a wave larger than the others, I was sure to find him there, looking to see if I was washed away. I tell you this was no pleasant occupation, to see if each other were gone.

At daybreak they were in the marsh. They slept until about ten, and dozed during the day.

We slept some until 3 P.M. Where on awaking I found we were high and dry on the marsh on the most desolate looking spot that ever mortal saw, nothing but waste all around, Oh! heavens I cried what is to become of us—

Mr. Mille nearly blind from the sand of the island of the previous day blowing in his eyes which were now red as fire, and myself totally incapable of movement excepting being able to raise up on my hands about 18 inches, so that I could look around and this reader saved our lives, As we floated onto the marsh, we caught the bottom plank of a cystern some two feet wide, about 9 ft. long, and about 2½ inches thick, this we laid across the window opening and on it laid our heads where we slept to keep them above water, and Mr. Mille ever after appropriated this plank to his own use, and all my subsequent endeavors to obtain it of him for a purpose hereafter to be spoken of, were unavailing; he generally laid on this plank to keep out of the water, as for myself I had a piece of wood that I caught which served me for a pillow for 4 days after. We also caught a ceiling plank 8 inches wide and about 8 ft. long—all these things I took good care of, as I foresaw that every thing would be of use to us, if we would ever be able to get from here.

A burning thirst now began to devour us, and in our agony we longed for a piece of that ice they were using so prodigally in Plaquemine. But my mind was wide awake, though my limbs were weak; it rained almost constantly, and it soon occurred to me that we could drink the rain water, but the question was how to catch it; I put out my tongue to let the drops fall on its dry and parched surface, but soon found this would not do—Mr. Mille was now crying in agony for water, wine or Brandy, it was near Midnight by the tide, for I measured time by time by tide now, the waters had again covered

our raft, myself lying in the water on the raft, Mr. Mille
on the Cystern bottom, rain pouring down at intervals,
water we must have, and water we had to our satisfaction soon—Without saying anything to Mille I tore a
strip of my shirt about 2 ft. long and some 7 inches wide,
this I wrung out well as I could to extract the salt water,
I then took the ceiling plank and laid one end of it on the
Cystern bottom and the other on the raft to make a kind
of inclined plane, for the rain water to run down on, on
this plank I placed the rag to catch the water; as soon at
it was saturated I rung it by twisting and sucking it, into
my mouth—heavens how good that water was.

I did this several times, then I called Mr. Mille and
asked him if he wanted water, well where will you get it
said he, come said I, I will show you but mind fair play,
You will use the rag three times and myself three times,
I never can forget the expression he used when he first
began to suck that rag saturated with the rain water.
We used the rag as often as the showers would pass and
thus we had water as long as it continued to rain and it
did not cease until Thursday morning.

Schlatre saw that if they expected to be saved they must
get out of the marsh and into the bayou. He was almost
helpless and could not get Mille to do anything he continues:

It was now Tuesday morning—nearly 48 hours without a particle of food, I now gave up all hopes and laid
down, resigned ourselves to our fates—we offered up
ourselves a sacrifice for our past sins. Calling on our
maker to have pity on us the works of his hands; thus
passed the day, Mr. Mille called my attention to the flight
of birds, which he said would soon pick our bones. Seeing all hopeless now I took a piece of nail, and marked my
name in full on the side of the raft, next I pulled off my
shirts and took one portion and sticking the Ceiling plank
into the marsh I put a portion of one shirt on it for a flag,
so that in case any one passed here, they could tell who

died by the inscription; being now naked, I begged Mr. Mille to let me have his undershirt to put on, as he had pulled it off and used it as a pillow—in lieu thereof I gave him 1/3 of my ragged shirts to answer his purpose, myself keeping one third to put under my own head, the other 1/3 acting as the flag, all this being done we now laid down my arms and head bare still I lay on my breast. Whenever I wanted to change positions I called Mr. Mille to get up and turn over my broken limb as I turned my miserable body.

Now, dear Reader, you can picture to yourself if it be possible, our situation; you here behold, exposed to the inclemency of the most terrible weather, (and the worst was to come yet), two miserable creatures, half naked, starved, wounded, totally incapable of movement, in despair, 4 miles up a horrible marsh, the rain pouring down on them in torrents, liquid fires lit up the heavens from, sun down till day; the thunder rolled incessantly, the tremendous claps of which, falling on all sides of us, shook the very earth, There we lay, God in heaven, we each cried in agony that terrible night, Do in thy infinite mercy send one of thy thunderbolts in our midst, and take us to thyself Yes, in our terrible agony, on that most fearful night we called aloud for death, I was in hopes that our flag staff would attract the Electric fluid and cease our sufferings.

But brave Michael Schlatre did not give up. He determined "to do or die." He worked hard to get the raft out of the grassy marsh into moving water. Quoting the diary again:

It was 62 hours since we had tasted food. A little Grass is all that we had put into our mouths and that only on account of its sour taste. I had learned to use this weed before with the Italians who made use of it as pickels. In order to get some of this grass I went from the raft into the water, thence to the edge of the bank and in crawling my hand rested on a bunch of mussels, shell fish something similar to oysters, I pulled up some dozen; placed them on the raft and pulled off one shoe; using the heel of the Shoe as a hammer I broke them open, using one shell as a knife we scooped out the fat and ate them, thus. I broke and gave some ½ doz. to Mr. Mille and eat 8 or 10 myself. I then placed a few on the raft for farther use.

———

They were now near the bay and saw steamers and sailboats go by and could not get their attention. They had to get closer to the Gulf. He writes:

My heart gave way under the accumulation of misfortune—I begged Mr. Mille for Gods sake to let me have the Cystern bottom to swim on, assuring him on my most sacred word that in case I found assistance to return for him. You can in the mean time, said I, remain on this log. No Sir, said he, if you leave me I die, I said to him, I am worn out with labor and privation, the tide and wind against us, the bayou forks, I know not which to take, but as you please I will not force you, but die if we must, then die it shall be together, so here goes, suiting the action to the word I boarded the raft, shoved her off, directed it toward the middle of the stream and depended on Providence.

Now Reader, I thought that I had labored some on this raft, but put all my labor together and they were as nothing compared to the labor that I performed in the next two and a half hours; having been directed by the slowing descending tide. I plied my poor paddle incessantly, now prying, now paddling, now pushing, and the heavy thing moved like a snail. I well knew that life was at stake, if we did not reach the bay shore this day my strength which was going away, would be gone and then we would be left to die, and such a death—therefore, work, work, work, and after having progressed about two hundred yrds. in about an hour, the tide again came to my assistance, keeping the raft

as well as I could, on that shore whence came the wind,
I saw with delight that the raft began to advance
quicker and quicker, until finally it had no more need
of my assistance, only to keep it off of the lee shore.
In half an hour more I gave Mr. Mille's the joyful news
that at last we were in sight of the bay, about ½ mile
distant: our hearts arose in thankfulness to the Author
of our beings, for so great a favor.

On Thursday they saw another steamer come near, and
they called and called but their feeble voices could not be
heard. Finally on Friday they saw a sail boat, and waved
their ragged shirts and drawers. They were seen and a small
boat with four men rowed over to pick them up. Schlatre
concludes:

The Reader may be curious to know, how and what
was my situation at this time. Gentle Reader, a man
in good health, and with determination can, with the
aid of Providence accomplish wonders it was now exact-
ly five days since we left the Island, in that time I had
drank salt water by the gallon, lay out in the constant
rain, (cold and warm by turns) half naked, a plank
on the marsh for my bed, night and day, nothing of
consequence to eat, in addition to Pluria and ribs frac-
tured, and one knee broken, added to that I was almost
helpless for two days requiring the assistance of my poor
companion to change my position, yet I say in honesty
—that when I got aboard, had it not been for my leg,
I could just as well as not have gone to work, to help
manage the schooner, once and once only I thought my
time had come in earnest and that was on the shell bank,
lying under my small tent.

My pulse began to beat quick and strong, now said I
the fever begins, the sun was intensely warm and I
went and rolled over in the sea, then went back and
laid down under the tent. In short time I awoke and
found my pulse beat again with the regularity of a clock,

my head, was clear and collected and I felt in first rate health, just as if nothing had happened.

The Reader will perceive that Providence was with us from the first. I should have been killed under the falling house 2dly being a cripple, I should have been first to drown, 3dly death stared us in the face, in that terrible passage of the Bay 4thly death was with us for two days and nights, where our raft first lodged on the marsh, and 5thly death stared us night and day down that Bayou, and 6thly death kept us company all that fifth day after our boat passed us and 7thly death remained with us until the following Tuesday, when Mr. Mille died at the house of Mr. Brien, our kind deliverer.

Therefore I say this, a man in full health, a good constitution, a stout and courageous heart who puts his trust in the Ruler above and keeps collected in mind, and acts with judgment and decision it is difficult to lose him, no matter where placed, never despair as long as there is life and strength left, this much says one who has been sorely tried. Under all my afflictions I never despaired, but constantly cried, Mercy My Heavenly Father, but Thy will be done, not mine.

Michael Schlatre's wife, Lodoiska Desobry Schlatre (niece of Dr. Charles Clement's wife) had been washed out into the Gulf of Mexico clinging to a floating timber. An English vessel picked her up. She lived only long enough to murmur her name and address. They gave her a sailor's burial at sea.

A faded letter from her is among the Desobry family papers. It was written September 16, 1855, from her home on Bayou Jacob,* near Plaquemine. Less than a year later, just

---

*It is believed that "Bayou Jacob" at one time an important waterway before the dam was erected, was named after *Jacob* Schlatre first of this name to come to Iberville Parish.

one month past her 29th birthday, she was to die at Last Island with her seven children. The letter was addressed to Edward Desobry, her brother, then at school at Flushing Institute, Long Island N.Y. He did not learn of the Last Island tragedy, the death of his sister and his seven nephews and nieces until two months after it happened.

Mrs. Schlatre wrote amusingly of the mosquito pest at Last Island that year of 1855—so bad "that I could not sit down long enough to write you from there." She told of the "great storm" of August 29, 1855, how they had all survived, and how safe she felt at Last Island, "where at least the houses stand." She penned cheerful family gossip interspersed with news of friends who died of yellow fever which raged that year, and ended her letter with the sisterly "I shall not forget you in my daily prayers. Pray for us."

When a boy I heard my grandmother, Mrs. Charles Clement, tell about the awful "Last Island" storm, and the loss of her favorite niece, Lodoiska Desobry, (Mrs. Schlatre) along with her seven children. Grandma named one of her daughters, Lodoiska after her, later Mrs. Andrew H. Gay of St. Louis Plantation.

Today Last Island is a tiny, desolate sandbar off the coast of Terrebonne parish, east of the spot where the Atchafalaya river pours into the Gulf of Mexico. Bayou Plaquemine is again open to navigation, but the once heavy flow of summer visitors to the nearby Gulf Coast island section through that bayou waterway is now only a memory.

CHAPTER X

GENERAL GUSTAVE S. ROUSSEAU OF
MEXICAN WAR FAME

Among the prominent residents of Iberville Parish before the Civil War was Gen. Gustave Sebastian Rousseau. Gen. Rousseau was a brother of Captain Lawrence Rousseau of the American Navy who was in command of the Brazil Squadron during the Mexican War. Gen. Rousseau came of a long line of military men. His grandfather, Sieur Pierre Rousseau, was a captain in the French navy who had brought his children when very young to be reared and educated in the American Colony of Virginia.

The father of Lawrence and Gustave was Don Pedro George Rousseau, who enlisted in the American Navy from Virginia at the age of 24, and because of distinguished services, he was soon appointed to the rank of captain by the Continental Congress. In 1779 Captain Rousseau entered the Spanish service at New Orleans. This was the year that Galvez captured Baton Rouge. Galvez admired Captain Rousseau and appreciated his military and naval skill. He appointed him a Lieutenant-colonel and placed him in command of the brig GALVESTON, which was Galvez's own flagship, when the campaign against Pensacola was inaugurated. Captain Rousseau won glory at the seige of Pensacola. From 1786 to 1788 he was a commandant at Natchitoches. During this time he spent much time with Gayoso at Natchez, Mississippi. He was later made commanding general, or admiral we would call him

Upper left—Lafcadio Hearn, who borrowed from Edward Desobry of Plaquemine (lower right), the manuscript of Michael Schlatre, who had written the "Last Island" story and given it to Mr. and Mrs. Louis Desobry (lower center), his father-in-law and mother-in-law. Hearn used this material in his immortal work, "Chita".

Below—LAUREL RIDGE, a few miles below Plaquemine, remains a lovely and attractive home of the old days. It was built shortly after the Civil War by the late James Erwin Tuttle.

GENERAL GUSTAVE SEBASTIAN ROUSSEAU

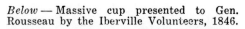

Below — Massive cup presented to Gen.
Rousseau by the Iberville Volunteers, 1846.

today, of all the warships or galleys of the Mississippi, a command which he held under all the Spanish governors from 1792 to 1803.

At one time Captain Rousseau was offered the command of Plaquemine Post that is Iberville, but he turned it down. Thus while Captain Pedro Rousseau refused to live in Iberville Parish by accepting the post of commandant there, by a strange turn of fate his son, Gen. Gustave Sebastian Rousseau, became a resident of that parish.

GENERAL GUSTAVE SEBASTIAN ROUSSEAU, born in 1806, was admitted to West Point on July 1, 1824, and was graduated therefrom on July 1, 1828. From 1830 to 1833 he was stationed at St. Louis in the Jefferson Barracks with Jefferson Davis, Sidney Johnson, Robert E. Lee, Leonidas Polk and others.

While at St. Louis General Rousseau married, on January 28, 1830, Emily Lee, who was the granddaughter of Dr. Andre Augusta Condé, of Aunis, France, he had been Post Surgeon at Fort Chartres in Illinois, and moved to St. Louis with St. Ange de Bellerive in 1765, and remained there for the rest of his life. He had married at Mobile, in 1763, Marie Ann de la Ferne, daughter of Pierre Ignance Bardet de la Ferne, a Chirurgien Major pour le Roy at Nouvelle Chartres, Mobile, Alabama. Her father, Patrick Lee, was of the family of Thomas Lee who had much correspondence with Governor O'Reilly of Louisiana in regard to trade practices, and whose letters are preserved in the archives of Seville, Spain.

In 1833 Gustave Sebastian Rousseau resigned from the Army, and went with his wife to New Orleans where they remained for some time. There he bought a slave according to the records in the courthouse. He then took up his residence on Victoria Plantation at Bayou Goula, Louisiana, which he purchased. Shortly after this he was appointed Brigadier General, Louisiana Militia. Meantime he had taken up the study of law, and was a practicing attorney in the town of Plaquemine in Iberville Parish.

Rousseau was clerk of the Plaquemine City Council from 1838 to 1841, Sheriff of the parish in 1841, and Recorder of Iberville Parish in 1853.

Gen. Rousseau re-entered the Army at the outbreak of the War with Mexico, and led the Louisiana Tigers* to the Mexican border.

He was serving as Brigadier General, Louisiana Militia, when the war started. He immediately called for volunteers to go under his command to the Mexican border. The following is the call for volunteers which appeared in the Baton Rouge Gazette on May 8, 1846:

HEADQUARTERS, 8th BRIGADE, L.M.
Plaquemine, 4th May, 1846

CIRCULAR ORDERS:

In obedience to Order No. 1, issued from Headquarters, L.M., dated New Orleans 2nd May, 1846, making requisition for volunteers to reinforce the Army under command of General Taylor, on the frontier of Texas, the Brigadier General commanding the 8th Brigade, L.M., relies with confidence upon the zeal and patriotism of the citizen soldiers under his command. He hopes volunteers will

---

*A short history of the "Louisiana Tigers," was furnished by General Allison Owen in 1944:

"The Original Louisiana Tigers, had as their emblem a tiger. Now recognized by the War Department, it is the emblem of the Washington Artillery Regiment which chose it when the Washington Artillery was organized in 1839."

"The Louisiana Tigers took part in the war with Mexico, the War Between the States, the Spanish American War, World War One and World War Two."

"Colonel Wheat's Tigers, organized at the beginning of the War Between the States, was made up of stevedores and water-front workers. They fought valiantly in the War Between the States, and disbanded when it was over with a distinguished record."

come forward and enroll themselves for a term of six months, unless sooner discharged.

On receipt of this order, the officers commanding the different Regiments composing the 8th Brigade, L.M. will forthwith open in their Regiments enrollments for volunteers, and will make returns thereof to Headquarters at Plaquemine without delay, so that the necessary measures may be taken in order that the volunteers may be organized into companies, and transported to Headquarters at New Orleans.

As it is possible that a draft will be ordered in the State of Louisiana, the commanding officers of each Regiment will forthwith forward to Brigade Headquarters at Plaquemine, a full return of their regiments, showing the name of every one, within the limits of their regiments, subject to military duty.

By order of the Brig. Gen. G. S. Rousseau, commanding 8th Brigade, L.M.

(Signed)
Adonist Petit
Acting Aid-de-camp.

Apparently General Rousseau's call for volunteers did not go unheeded, for only five days later, on May 31, 1846, the following appeared in the Daily Delta, published in New Orleans, Louisiana:

MILITARY MATTERS: When we speak of military movements now we know not where to begin or where to end. For such is the ardor—such is the excitement that pervades the city that little in the way of detail can be gathered. The influx of volunteers from the country continues to increase. Hour after hour bands of these brave spirits pass our office:

"Pride in their port, defiance in their eye,
I see the lords of human kind pass by:
Intent on high design, a thoughtful band,
By forms unfashion'd from nature's hand."

Of those that arrived yesterday, one were a company from Iberville, under the command of General G. S. Rousseau, Captain William H. Higgins, 1st Lieutenant Gustave Lauve, 2nd Lieutenants and a hundred and seven men, rank and file.

When General Rousseau returned from the Mexican War he remained at the head of the Louisiana Militia until 1855, at the same time practicing law and operating a sugar plantation. Besides this, according to the "Picayune" he held many positions of honor. But, unlike his brother, Lawrence, he did not take a very active part in the War Between the States. There are several traditional records, but no official record concerning this period of his military career. It was stated by the late Miss Regina Estavan, who was his protegee, and whom he educated to become a teacher, that he trained troops for the Confederate Army, but she was a very small child at the outbreak of the war. On the other hand it was stated by L. Allain Grace of Plaquemine, that General Rousseau had a strange influence with the Northern forces operating in North Louisiana, for he persuaded them to prevent harm from befalling the town of Plaquemine. It is, of course, possible that some of the Federal officers commanding in that district had been classmates and friends of General Rousseau at West Point, and seeing that he was not as active as he could have been, considering his military experience, they refrained from striking the heaviest blow where he lived. But this is merely a supposition; it is quite as likely that he trained troops and refused to take a more active part in the conflict. He was a man of extraordinary brilliancy, and it could be possible that he considered that secession of the Southern States was impractical and unnecessary. There were many men of the South who opposed secession, but as the war progressed they joined their neighbors and fought for the Confederacy, especially after soldiers of the North began to seize or destroy property and to commit outrages which seemed unnecessary even in the course of war.

Gen. Rousseau died at Plaquemine, Louisiana, on January 29, 1879. He was driving a gig, as usual, from his law office to his plantation, when an old Negro stopped him and begged some tobacco. As he stopped and handed the Negro the tobacco he fell forward, and died instantly.

An editorial in THE NEW ORLEANS TIMES Monday, Feb. 3, 1879.

General Gustave Sebastian Rousseau

"General Gustave S. Rousseau, an old and honored resident of the parish of Iberville, died last Wednesday.

The circumstances of his death are rather peculiar. He was on his way home from the parish of Ascension, and alone in his buggy, when death overtook him. It is supposed that his death was the result of an apoplectic fit. . . . General Rousseau graduated from West Point in the year 1828. He ranked number twenty-one in his class. He was immediately assigned as Second Lieutentant in the sixth regiment of infantry. In the year 1833 he resigned his position in the Army and commenced the practice of law. . . He volunteered for the Mexican War and held the position of Captain in the second regiment of P. E. Smith's brigade of Louisiana volunteers under Colonel Dakin, He returned to Iberville parish and resumed the profession of law. The only living graduate of West Point from Louisiana, who finished before General Rousseau, is ex-Governor Joshua Baker, whose date of graduation is 1819. Gov. Baker is at present a planter on the Teche. General Albert Sidney Johnson, who was killed at Shiloh, April 6, 1862, preceded him at West Point two years, while General Beauregard graduated ten and exGovernor Hebert twelve years later than Rousseau. General Rousseau at the time of his death was about eighty years* of age and was highly respected. He had

---

*Gen. Rousseau was not 80 but 73 when he died.

many positions of honor in his parish, which he filled with credit to himself and to the satisfaction of his constituents."

After Rousseau's death Victoria plantation was purchased by Mrs. John Hampden Randolph, who owned and lived at Nottaway Plantation between Bayou Goula and White Castle. An account in the *Louisiana Historical Quarterly* shows that the plantation was purchased from Emily Lee, widow of Gen. Rousseau, Sara Rousseau, widow of Joachim Martinez, and Octave Rousseau (son of Gen. Rousseau). Emily Lee Rousseau and her children moved to Plaquemine and lived in a house which is still standing.

CHAPTER XI

GOVERNOR HEBERT OF IBERVILLE PARISH

It seems remarkable that so many men, outstanding in Louisiana history came from Iberville Parish or made their homes there during the early days. Among them was Paul Octave Hebert who passed on to his reward in 1880, at a time when this writer was only two years old.

Paul Octave Hebert was the twelfth governor of Louisiana. He was born on December 12, 1818 on Arcadia Plantation, five miles south of Plaquemine. His father was Paul Gaston Hebert and his mother Mary Eugenia Hamilton.

Paul Hebert was descended from Louis Hebert who came to Canada with Poutrincourt in 1605. This Louis Hebert, an apothecary, was a son of Hebert, the apothecary of Catherine de Medici. There is a statue of Hebert, Poutrincourt's apothecary, in Quebec today. Most of the Hebert's in Louisiana and Canada today are his descendants.

Paul Hebert graduated from Jefferson College, St. James Parish, at the head of his class in 1836. He entered West Point in September of that year, from which he was graduated on June 1, 1840, when he was 21½ years old. He ranked first in his class every year for four years, and he was at the head of his class of 42 members when he got his commission. Among his classmates were Gen. W. S. Hancock, Gen. W. T. Sherman, Gen. George H. Thomas and Gen. Joseph Wheeler.

Young Hebert was appointed professor of engineering at West Point, the year after graduation. On August 2, 1842 he married Cora Wills Vaughn, a daughter of Thomas E. Vaughn and Henrietta Winn, owners of White Castle Plantation. Of this union five children were born.

In 1845 Hebert resigned his post at West Point and came to Louisiana. In 1847 he went to the Mexican War as a Lieutenant-Colonel and took part in several engagements—Churubusco, Chapultepec and Mexico City. He was breveted colonel for gallantry by Gen. Scott and complimented for his bravery. After the Mexican War, Col. Hebert returned to Iberville Parish to resume the life of a sugar planter. In February 1848 upon his return from the Mexican War. Col. Hebert was presented with a jewel hilted sword by the citizens of Iberville Parish. This took place at Bayou Goula. A splendid ball wound up the proceedings. The sword now is in possession of granddaughter, Mrs. G. W. Pigman of New Orleans and has this inscription:

To

Paul O. Hebert

Lieut. Col. of the 14th Reg.1 U. S. Infantry

By

The Citizens of his Native Parish Iberville

This sword is presented as a token of their regard for himself and their appreciation of his conduct and gallantry at the Battle of Contreras, Churubusco, Molino del Rey. Chapultepec, and entrance into the City of Mexico.

But he was not to live the leisurely plantation life without interruption. Governor Joseph Walker appointed Col. Paul Hebert as a delegate to the Industrial Exhibition in London which opened in May 1851. He visited Paris and while there an incident occurred which affected his future. Just after Louis Napoleon's coup d'etat Hebert attended a dinner given on the 4th of July by Americans in Paris and was asked to preside. A toast was offered to the old Republic of France and a call for the Marseillaise. The band master refused to play it, saying it was against the prefect's orders to play or sing patriotic airs. Whereupon Hebert jumped upon a chair and said, "Gentlemen, we are celebrating under the American flag—a flag of freedom which gives us the right to sing or play any airs expressive of our independence and freedom of the rights of people. I will lead—join me." In a fine voice he began the grand hymn to Liberty as the whole company joined in. The band looked on in awe and amazement. This incident was later reported in the local papers of Louisiana and added to the popularity of the future governor.

Envelope mailed from Iberville by Gov. Hebert via steamboat to New Orleans.
(Courtesy Leonard V. Huber)

In 1852 Col. Paul O. Hebert was nominated for governor against the Whig candidate Judge Louis Bordelon of St. Landry Parish. Hebert received 17,734 votes and Bordelon 15,781. Governor Hebert was one of our best governors and his activities included the following:

He encouraged the building of railroads.

He advocated a better levee system.

He promoted the public school system in the 1855 legislature and levied a one mill tax on all property to support it.

He established the Louisiana State Seminary of Learning at Alexandria which later became L.S.U.

He started the State Library.

He reorganized the State Militia.

He helped fight yellow fever in 1853.

He improved the Charity Hospital of New Orleans.

When he went into office the state was in debt $11,000 and when he went out, Louisiana had a surplus of $20,000.

He promoted education for the dumb and blind.

His first wife died on August 3, 1861. He later married Penelope Lynch, daughter of John Andrews, owner of Bellegrove. After the war Gov. Hebert became a Republican and supported Warmoth. President Grant, a friend of West Point days, appointed him Commander of Engineers in Louisiana which position he retained until his death. This occurred on August 20, 1880 in New Orleans.

Gov. Hebert was one of Louisiana's most distinguished citizens, and the Parish of Iberville is proud to claim him as its own. Many of his descendants and relatives have reached high positions in the professional and business life of the state he did so much to help develop.

Other Hebert Families

The Heberts mentioned below may have been connected with Gov. Hebert's family, although not closely. In fact, there are many Hebert families in Iberville Parish. The Hon. Alexander Hebert, whose father was a prominent physician, was born January 13, 1843. He was educated in private schools and The College of the Immaculate Conception. For sixteen years he was the district attorney of Iberville Parish.

His son, Clarence S. Hebert, served in the Confederate Army as 2nd Lieut. in the Louisiana Cavalry under Col. W. G. Vincent. He was later a Judge of the District Court. I knew him quite well and recall the high regard in which his family was held.

CHAPTER XII

OTHER EARLY PLANTERS

Col. Pierre Joseph Landry

Among the early settlers of Iberville Parish was Colonel
Pierre Joseph Landry who came from France in 1785 and
went up the river. He was probably forced to leave the old
country because of the Revolution. He was born near Nantes, Frances, in 1740, and must have
been a man of considerable wealth and distinction. Col. Lan-
dry left two notebooks, one of which is a manuscript on military tactics, written and illustrated by him. In a neat, beautiful old handwriting it gives directions for maneuvers that
are long since gone out of date. They are illustrated in odd
little figures in water color. The other notebook contains
memoranda written in France, and later his son Pierre Joseph Landry, used the same notebook to keep a diary.

This son, Pierre Joseph Landry, was born in France but
lived most of his life in Iberville Parish. Descended from these
Landrys are many prominent families of the state and they
are scattered all over Iberville and Ascension Parishes today.
There are nearly a thousand direct descendants now living.
This family has given to the state a lieutenant governor, a
member of Congress, and numerous state and parish officials.
One of his grandsons, Captain Eugene Landry, organized a
company and fought in the War with Mexico.

The son of the emigre, Pierre Joseph Landry, was a remarkable wood carver. He carved many figures which are in

existence today. He had received no artistic training and consequently his work is rather crude, but that he could do carving at all without any training is remarkable. This is particularly true when he was afflicted with arthritis or tuberculosis of the knee joint.

His carvings were one time on display at Louisiana State Museum. They were gathered together by Mr. L. Valcour Landry, now of New Orleans and for many years connected with the U. S. Customs Service. Mr. Landry's son, is Major General Robert Landry, Air Force Aide to President Truman.

In the cemetery of St. Gabriel Church on his tombstone is this epitaph:

Pierre Joseph Landry
Born at St. Malo Jan. 9, 1770
Died at St. Gabriel March, 1843
A good Republican, who is missed
by his wife and nine children,
Whose good morals were necessary.

Marionneaux Family In Iberville

The Marionneaux family came from Normandy, and settled in Iberville about 1775 or 80. Francois Charles Marionneaux married Barba Schlatre, daughter of Jacob Schlatre who held a Spanish land grant comprising Hunters Lodge Plantation.

Francois Charles Marionneaux was during his lifetime one of the largest land owners in Iberville. He held Spanish land grants comprising Myrtle Grove and Riverview plantations. State papers of Public Lands (Vol. 6) show that FRANCOIS MARIONNEAUX claimed a tract of land situated on the right bank of the river forming a second depth to his plantation. The land was bound by holdings of Dupuis and Leonard. Marionneaux proved a grant from the proper Spanish officer in 1801.

In 1818 when the Parish of Iberville applied for a charter

the application was signed by L. G. Marionneaux, Francois Marionneaux, Norbert Marionneaux, Vallerie Marionneaux, and Pierre Marionneaux.

Old church records show that at least up to 1818 there were comparatively few persons in Iberville who could read and write. In many cases, in fact in most cases, a Marionneaux signed for persons making contracts, selling property, and getting married. In 1818 Norbert Marionneaux signed for and witnessed the marriages of many couples in the Catholic Church and the priest was Father De St. Pierre.

From 1785 to 1861 there was a Marionneaux at every meeting that took place in Plaquemine, whether for schools, church matters, civic matters or otherwise.

From 1845 to 1861 the Marionneaux family were the largest or among the largest sugar producers in the parish. For instance, in 1858 Luicen Marionneaux produced 581 hogsheads; Louis Marionneaux produced 350; and Mrs. E. Robinson of Hunter's Lodge Plantation in which Marionneaux had an interest produced 240. This was a total of 1171, topped that year by Edward J. Gay who produced 1275 hogsheads. C. A. Slack produced 550.

As a boy I worked under the immediate direction of one of this family, Mr. Louis Marionneaux, during my vacation while employed at the general store of my uncle, Jacob McWilliams.

Captain Charles A. Bruslé
(Pronounced Brulay)

Among Iberville Parish's prominent citizens of eighty years ago was Captain Charles A. Bruslé of Plaquemine. He was born on February 24th, 1835, and was educated at Will's Academy at West Roxbury, Mass. He married Miss Eugenia Dardenne in 1856. He was a senator in the Louisiana State Legislature before the Civil War. When the war came on he

organized a company and was elected Captain of Company A
of the Third Louisiana Regiment, known as the Iberville
Grays. He later was aide-de-camp on the staff of Gen. Louis
Hebert. In 1878 Capt. Bruslé was elected Sheriff of Iberville
Parish and served for three terms. He was an extensive property holder and was highly esteemed by his fellow citizens.
I have many pleasant remembrances of Sheriff Bruslé. He
was fond of game, such as was then plentiful in the Iberville
section. As I may have already indicated, this writer's boyhood predilection was to become a professional hunter. The
indulging of this youthful ambition required a considerable
outlay for ammunition, shot, powder and shells. The excess
from my gamebag, beyond requirements at grandmother's
home, partridges, doves and snipe, always found a ready and
fair-price market at the Bruslé home. Dozens of times did I
"rein up" my horse at the big impressive looking Plaquemine
mansion and never do I remember a rejection of the proffered
string of birds.

In this connection I might say the Sheriff's home, in the late
eighties, was one of the handsomest and best kept in the town.
It was across the street from the residence of Charles H. Dickinson. My merchandising efforts, however, did not stop at
profits from the chase but went on to other things. I sold
plenty of fresh butter, and later acquired agencies for various
newly developed home specialty gagdets. Always the Bruslé
home was a buyer as were many of my Plaquemine friends.
Soon my boyish efforts bore fruit and it was possible to buy
with my own money a much desired "safety" bicycle, the then
new fad, replacing and discarding the old "bike" with a moun-
tainous high wheel in front and small trailer one in the rear—
a device that frequently brought grief because of "headers" to
the street. I was once even thrown into an unbending iron
rail, as the big front wheel balked at the near side of a railroad track crossing.

The Wilberts

The late Anton Wilbert was the founder of the now very large Wilbert interests in Iberville. Mr. Wilbert, a quiet unassuming business man whom I remember well, died in 1887, leaving his lumber business, now very profitable, to the management of his six, highly capable sons, Messrs. John, Peter, Charles, Joseph, Fred and George Wilbert.

The story of the House of Wilbert, now owners of great plantations and sugar mills, capitalists and bankers with wide interests besides lumber, is another typical American saga of successful business men. They were men who worked hard, "kept their feet on the ground," made a strong impression on their times while today their descendants very ably carry on the business which came down from pioneer Anton.

The Schwings

Cypress shingles were the premier roofing of Louisiana homes. Nearly all South Louisiana buildings except the slate covered buildings of the Vieux Carré, heart of New Orleans, were once shingle-roofed. There was always a large demand for cypress shingles. Another highly successful Plaquemine saw mill firm was the Schwing Lumber and Shingle Co., Ltd. The bright and aggressive young Edward B. Schwing got into the lumber business in my youth. After the death, recently, of the highly respected Mr. Ned Schwing of Plaquemine, the mill and other big Schwing interests, have been continued in operation under the capable direction of son Calvin K. and W. B. Middleton, husband of the former Miss Maria Schwing.

Above—John Andrews, builder of Belle Grove and his first wife Penelope Lynch Andrews. From portraits in possession of Mrs. George Pigman.

Below—Typical plantation home, corner Coliseum and Felicity Streets, New Orleans, where John Andrews died.

Chapter XIII

MISCELLANIES

Transportation on the River

This writer well remembers the horse-drawn or man-pulled *bateaux* and small towboats that, in my plantation days were still very laboriously passing upstream in front of Retreat plantation, just as they had been doing for a hundred years. How these rough looking river men in little groups of two or three, with long towropes attached to straps on their shoulders could keep the little "keel boat" vessels moving upstream—how they could stand the terrific effort of climbing along an uneven and often muddy shore, and, at the same time, pull on the big heavy towropes, I never could understand. The man on the boat doing the steering had an easy job compared to the poor towline fellows who were literally beasts of burden. Occasionally a boat passed up the river that had the help of a little wiry horse scrambling along the slippery river bank with a man driver.

At Plaquemine a small steam vessel, known as "the ferry", was in use to transport people and small freight to the opposite shore, the boat was not big enough to carry vehicles. Skiffs, rowed usually by two men—no outboard motors in those days—were the only ferry accommodations we had in our immediate section. On the bayous, Indian canoes, "pi-

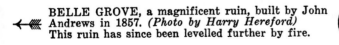
BELLE GROVE, a magnificent ruin, built by John Andrews in 1857. *(Photo by Harry Hereford)* This ruin has since been levelled further by fire.

rogues" and skiffs still rendered important service. The gasoline engine had not yet appeared and steam operation was quite out of the question, except for larger vessels.

I lived in Iberville at a time when there were palatial steamboats on the Mississippi and when "packet boats" were still plentiful on the river. I recall especially the great Steamboat, J. M. White. She was undoubtedly one of the finest that ever plied the waters of the Mississippi.

Steamboat traffic was booming in the eighties, and I well remember the big St. Louis "Anchor Line" boats with the great ANCHOR trade mark hung between the smoke stacks, passing with flags flying and bands of music playing on the deck. A great sight indeed. The trip to St. Louis on those palatial boats was long popular. Then there were the many packets plying between New Orleans, Natchez and "The Bends."

Back in the grand old days of steamboating, floating palaces rushing by at close intervals, the timbre and melodiousness of steamboat whistles was often a matter of interested conversation. Many persons could tell the different steamboats by their whistles. It was said that the whistle of the great packet, Edward J. Gay, was the most melodious on the river. When that famous steamer sank in 1890 the whistle was one of the first things salvaged.

When a planter's family was preparing to go to New Orleans by steamboat a colored retainer would be stationed on the levee front landing to listen for the boat whistle, generally heard and recognized as to name while the boat was many miles away. The Negro would then send word to the family so they could get into the waiting carriage and drive to the river. In the meantime the "spotter" would start waving a large cloth or flag to get the pilot's attention, thus bringing the boat in for a landing. It was always an exciting moment as the big boat dropped its stage plank and the "rousters" came ashore to tie up the boat, preparatory to taking on passengers and what freight there might be. The "mud clerk" or mate would come ashore to help escort the ladies down the plank. Far up above the scene, on the upper deck, would stand the captain watching anxiously to see that nothing went wrong, and hoping that his boat would not run into stray stumps "sawyers" and floaters, the cause of the sinking of so many boats.

When we were planning a trip to New Orleans the effort would be to so arrange matters that we could travel on the fast moving "White," and thus enjoy its deluxe accommodations and excellent food. This boat had a lovely-sounding, five-tone whistle and her feather-crowned chimneys were about eighty feet tall.

As I recall it the filigree work in the main saloon was outstandingly beautiful and impressive. The most skilled artisans of Europe and America had contributed to the decorations and the furniture. The furniture, imported from France, was of heavy walnut with an inlay of contrasting lighter wood, forming the boat's initials within a holly wreath. All chinaware, designed especially for the White, had her picture handpainted and burned in. The silverware—specially made—was the finest money could buy. Fine Irish linen napkins had the boat's initials worked by hand. The skylights were beautiful stained glass. And I can see now with memory's eye the beautiful silver cups swinging gaily on the side of the massive cooler.

The staterooms were, as described by Ray Samuel in a recent issue of "Dixie" (Times-Picayune States), exceptionally large and comfortable. To this youthful country bumpkin the appointments and furnishings appeared magnificent. There were wide promenade decks outside the staterooms, and 400 people could be accommodated comfortably on these. Inside the long cabin were the great ponderous candelabra swinging on gilded iron rings.

Near the stern the White had a nursery for the children and up on the "texas" was a unique feature, a richly furnished

"Freedman's Bureau" for well-to-do Negroes. Writing of the "texas" reminds me that as a small boy, when I got on board, it was always my desire to get up there as soon as possible, and into the pilot house just above. The captain was always kindly disposed towards us, for we were plantation owners and shippers of produce to New Orleans, and he allowed us special courtesies and privileges. On one occasion having ingratiated myself into the favor of the pilot, this friendly riverman allowed me to help turn the big steering wheel. My effort as a steersman was not particularly sucessful, as, becoming a little confused, I threw the wheel too far to the left and the boat started turning round instead of keeping the straight ahead course down the river. The pilot laughed, but quickly "took over" to get her back on her course. It was always a memorable experience to take a trip to New Orleans on the great J. M. White, pride of the able and much-loved Captain John Tobin.

The river from Baton Rouge to New Orleans was known as the "Lower Coast" and from Baton Rouge to St. Francisville and Natchez as the "Upper Coast." In later years it was my pleasure to meet some of the steamboat captains who were the personalities of the day, the well known Captain Cannon and Mrs. Blanche Leathers, wife of Bowling Leathers, master and pilot of the famous T. P. Leathers. She came by her command in an entirely natural way, as for years prior to Leathers' death, this remarkable wife had travelled with her husband on the boat. Mrs. Leathers was the daughter of the late James Douglas of Tensas Parish, at one time said to be one of the largest cotton planters in the South.

Mrs. Leathers was master and pilot of the great stern wheeler Natchez, and in 1897 once brought her boat into New Orleans with 500 passengers and slightly more than 4,000 bales of cotton—the largest cargo of its kind ever to reach the Crescent City, until the Henry Frank broke the record with 8,000 bales. Anyone who met Mrs. Leathers could not fail to be impressed by her vivid personality, her commanding presence and her emphatic manner of expressing herself.

Traffic on the Father of Waters is said to be heavier today than it ever was, but the old-time steamboat romance is gone. Dwellers on the Mississippi now see nothing but great tow-boats, tankers, and power boats. With a water shortage facing many of our large cities, and a general lowering of the nation's water level it is well to keep in mind that the Mississippi River — the nation's largest and the world's longest — is one of the great natural assets of the Middle South. It serves as the nation's largest inland waterway system of transportation, and, as a source of an almost unlimited supply of water for industrial and consumer use it is unexcelled.

With the drainage basin containing in excess of 1.2 million square miles and extending from the western reaches of Montana and Canada to the west central sections of Pennylvania and southern New York, the Mississippi River offers the largest potential source of water on the North American continent. The annual mean flow of the Mississippi River through the confines of Iberville Parish is at a rate in the neighborhood of about 200 billion gallons per day—enough water to supply every person in the United States with about 1400 gallons of water per day—a figure far above the total per capita usage of the nation.

As the February, 1952 "Middle South News," tells us, the Mississippi is *not* a vast theoretical source of water wrought with complexities—but a practical reservoir which is being tapped by industries as well as cities for industrial and drinking water with very simple treatment and at an extremely modest cost. The outstanding example of the usefulness of the Mississippi as a water source is the City of New Orleans which obtains its water from the river at an average rate of 101 million gallons daily. Water is pumped into large filtering reservoirs, treated and then pumped to consumers.

Another effective example of the Mississippi River as an

industrial water source is the great Esso Standard Oil Company's refinery at Baton Rouge, Louisiana, only fifteen miles above Plaquemine. This one industrial plant consumes more water than the entire city of Cleveland, Ohio. Water for the plant is almost exclusively supplied by the Mississippi river. As times goes on, this factor of abundant water is bound to make itself known in a rather compelling way as far as the Middle South area is concerned.

Louisiana pioneers like Joseph Erwin saw the Mississippi River as a great transportation artery, one which would immensely facilitate the moving of plantation crops to market. Erwin, and other pioneering geniuses, looked out upon alluvial lands unexcelled in richness, but awaiting development; they saw virgin acreage with immense potentialities for the production of wealth in growing cotton and sugar.

What they did not and could not see was that, along the banks and in the lower reaches of the great river, there was to be extensive and successful oil drilling operations on their Louisiana plantations which would later bring a wealth of Black Gold to make Southern Louisiana a big oil producing region and the near-by Crescent City the "Oil Capital" of the South.

Our pioneers, quite understandably, could not have visualized the finding of "Yellow Magic," a substance which now gives this area prominence as the home of the second greatest sulphur producing deposits in the world. Sulphur is a truly magic element, one to which early man attributed miraculous qualities and which today is producing miracles for industry and agriculture. The American farmer, whether cotton planter, grain grower, orchardist, poultry raiser or truck gardener, has come to realize that of all the earth's elements, sulphur is one of the most useful to him, with new uses being found yearly.

More than one-third of all sulphur mined is used in the manufacture of fertilizer and returns to the soil to aid agriculture. In the early 1800's farmers found that the only accessible source of phosphorus, vital to all growing plants, was to be obtained from animal bones, which were finely ground and spread on the fields. But this bone meal was scarce and did not decompose rapidly enough. Agricultural chemists finally discovered that a mineral—phosphate rock—would provide an ideal susbtitute, and, when treated with sulphuric acid, would produce a high-quality superphosphate. Phosphate rock fortunately was abundant and proved to be relatively inexpensive. Today superphosphates made from this rock are the most widely used agricultural nutrients.

Our cotton crop, as we of the South know, is one of our greatest sources of wealth. Millions of people are dependent upon King Cotton for their livelihood. At present sulphur is playing an ever-greater part in lowering the cost of producing American cotton.

How happy it would have made our pioneering planters if they could have visualized other possibilities in addition to the plantation development they had in mind. The cutting-out of the great forests in the rear for needed lumber and fuel at first caused no apprehension to plantation dwellers, but later there came a fear that in some sections the unused or under-used cut-over lands would become a problem. Now reforestation and tree farming is restoring the woodlands, very opportunely then came the pulpwood industry with its unbelievably large flow of bags, boxes, paper, textiles and plastics to an awaiting market. All of this is the result of the great pulpwood production which now comes from the fast growing Middle South forests.

It is now widely acknowledged that the plantation country possesses a remarkable combination of economic advantages—varied agricultural and mineral raw materials, dependable low cost power and natural gas, excellent transportation, mild climate and friendly people, constantly expanding markets, and *last, but not least, the great Mississippi River with its almost unlimited supply of water.*

SUGAR CANE IN IBERVILLE

For one hundred years Louisiana produced more sugar than any state in the union. It is still the largest cane sugar producing state, but beet sugar production greatly exceeds that of cane. Iberville Parish is one of the largest sugar producing sections of the state. History tells us that the Jesuit Fathers brought sugar cane production to Louisiana. Their plantation where they grew their cane is now that part of New Orleans extending from Common Street to about Jackson Avenue along the river. It was Etienne de Boré, however, who first made sugar in commercial quantities at the uptown plantation location now covered in part by beautiful Audubon Park. Its cultivation soon spread to the parishes. Joseph Erwin was one of the early sugar planters.

John Dymond, editor of the *Louisiana Sugar Planter*, wrote in 1906:

> The fine lands of the parish of Iberville have made it one of the most noted centers of sugar production in Louisiana for over a hundred years. Some of the best known plantations in the state were located in Iberville, including those of Edward J. Gay, Dr. J. P. R. Stone, August Levert, the Barrows, Craigheads, Murrells, Urquharts, Randolphs, Tuttles, Supples, Wares, Ventress and many others.

> The lands of Iberville parish lie comparatively high, above tidewater level; hence their drainage is good. While that portion of the parish lying on the east bank is excellent in every respect, that lying on the west bank is regarded as rather superior in quality and accessibility —it being penetrated by the noted Bayou Plaquemine, one of the leading navigable streams of the state.

As an evidence of the excellent drainages of these lands a visitor to that section was carried by Hon. Edward J. Gay, a short time prior to 1905, four miles to the rear on the St. Louis Plantation. There he saw a large peach orchard established, containing a great drainage canal ten feet deep and *dry to the bottom.*

Many years before this the parish of Iberville suffered largely by crevasses, during the high water seasons, but since the organization of the Atchafalaya Levee District and the gradual but constant enlargement of all the levees in the district, the parish has escaped overflow with all the rest. The sugar production about 25,000 tons per annum in 1906 brings into the parish about two million dollars for this one crop.

In 1905 there were 29 large capacity sugar mills in operation in Iberville. These took the place of possibly more than 100 mills required in former days to "grind" the cane crop. But sugar was not Iberville's only crop. At the turn of the century the cotton section of Iberville Parish extended from the settlement known as Grosse Tete to the town of Maringouin, a distance of about ten miles. There was to be found some of the finest and largest cotton plantations in the state.

To those of us who remember the tall, loaded-with-sugar Blue Ribbon cane of the old days, prior to the coming of the mosaic blight, which nearly ruined the sugar industry of our state from 1920 to 1930, the cane of today seems a somewhat weedy looking substitute. Far be it from me to deprecate the manner in which the great and loved-by-all sugar industry of Louisiana bravely and intelligently overcame the handicap of diseased conditions by bringing in new varieties of cane because the cane is not as edible as formerly. But, as I look at the bamboo-like disease-resistant cane of today—the result of changed conditions—my thoughts go back longingly to the beautiful Ribbon Cane of yesteryear. With a large "barrel," about one and a half inches in diameter on the average, it was tender and easy to chew.

My purpose is to take the uninitiated back to the days when the stalks of cane were peeled of their heavy covering and cut up into small sections for chewing. We ate this sweet juicy cane by squeezing the juice out with our teeth and spitting out the "bagasse." Today we do not see the raw cane being consumed by hundreds of individuals in the eager way that was an almost universal custom come "grinding time."

An examination of the Iberville Parish map of 1883, made by Charles Dickinson, at the time he was parish surveyor, shows the somewhat discomforting and surprising fact that many names of wealthy and highly-connected planters of only a half century ago are no longer found in Iberville. For instance, around the turn of the century Austin Woolfolk owned both the *Center* and *Sunny Side* plantations. He was said to be one of the largest sugar producers in Louisiana. Only 75 years ago John Hampden Randolph, a scion of the great Virginia family, owned the big *Nottaway* plantation with its magnificent baronial home. The Coles owned *Rebecca,* the Du Fossats owned *Celeste,* and the Stephensons, *Claiborne.* Samuel Gourrier owned *York;* John A. Dardenne, *Crescent;* Dr. Roman Schlater, *Star;* Col. George B. Wailes, *Texas;* and Dr. J. P. R. Stone owned *Evergreen.* Dr. Charles Clement owned *Retreat,* and Charles H. Dickinson, *Live Oaks.* Many other names great in the old days, and prominent in the building of Iberville, are no longer on the rolls of the parish.

Among the more recent large-scale sugar planters, those who were known far and wide as a part of this remarkable and at one time highly profitable industry—men who, under pressure of government control (planting, production and manufacture) passed out of the picture, leaving the battle to present day operators—we find such names as Gen. Allen Jumel, owner of *Point Clear;* James Robertson, *Hunter's Lodge;* Michael Schlater, *Enterprise;* W. W. and James A. Ventress, *Granada Alhambra;* George B. Reuss, *Allemania,*

Retreat, Germania and *Cuba;* James A. Ware, *Belle Grove* and *Celeste.*

A partial list covering a few of the great sugar-plantation men of yesteryear—men whose names were known and looked upon a few years ago as permanent parts of the life of Iberville Parish — includes: David Urquhart and Gen. Adolph Meyer owners and operators of the *Cora* and *Anandale* plantation; M. Liddell Randolph, *Blythewood;* D. Batt Barrow, *Tanglewild;* Charles D. Craighead who owned *Tennessee;* David N. Barrow and B. C. LeBlanc, *Star Pecan;* and Jacob McWilliams and Charles N. Roth who only a half a century ago owned and operated *Myrtle Grove* and *Medora.* "Times change" and in no great business has this been more exemplified than in the change which has come in the production of the great staple, sugar, in the Parish of Iberville.

EARLY PROTESTANT CHURCH

The first Presbyterian church in Louisiana outside of New Orleans was organized at Plaquemine about 1828. The first minister was David Dunmore Chesnut of Milton, Penn., who was graduated from Washington College at Washington, Penn., in 1827. (Washington College was later combined with Jefferson College in 1865 to form Washington and Jefferson College. Some of the early students were Stephen Foster and William H. McGuffey of the McGuffey readers).

Mr. Chesnut evidently came to Iberville at the invitation of Joseph Erwin and other Presbyterians. He married Catherine Wilson, Erwin's granddaughter, whose father, Nicholas, had brothers and sisters living in Washington, Penn. Mr. Chesnut was ordained as minister and was in charge of the Church at Plaquemine as well as Ascension and E. Baton Rouge. According to the alumni records of Washington and Jefferson College he served as minister from 1829 until 1837 when he died. Whether activities of the church ceased upon the death of this minister I do not know. Reverend D. D. Chesnut was a writer and editor and made an impression upon the history and people of Iberville that is deserving of mention. In 1833 he established and owned the second newspaper in Iberville Parish — *The Condenser* with M. Miller as the editor.

The only record book of the present Church extant shows that the Presbyterian Church at Plaquemine was organized or re-organized on August 5, 1843 by Bishops Warren and Woodbridge. This must have been a Methodist group as there are no bishops in the Presbyterian Church, and the reference is to the building itself as three Protestant groups used the same meeting house—Methodist, Episcopalian and Presbyterian. A permanent Church was erected in 1858.

The Clement and Dickinson families as well as Erwins along with many of the Protestant faith, attended the above church. It was located at the corner of Court and Seminary Streets, across the street from the home of the "pillar" of this particular church, Mr. Jacob McWilliams, son-in-law of Dr. Charles Clement. "Uncle Mac"—as every one called him— had his coachman or "yardman" look after the church, the handsome little edifice being always well cared for. I remember very well the several times when Dr. B. M. Palmer, famous Presbyterian minister from New Orleans, was the guest preacher and incidentally a guest at Uncle Mac's home. We youngsters were somewhat awed but never afraid of the kindly, bearded man who was one of the great orators of the time.

The little church was well attended in those days of the eighties and early nineties. The parsonage on the side street in the rear of the church was a comfortable home for the preacher. There were occasional old-fashioned "revivals" held at this church, I remember the great emotional and religious interest stirred up on such occasions, and the conversion of prominent citizens who came forward to the altar rail in answer to the revivalist's plea. This particular building was demolished about 1943.

A CIVIL WAR LETTER

Threatened as we are with a third World War and as our boys are going again to training camps, it is interesting to read a letter written by Dr. Charles Clement's youngest son, Alfred Henry, 90 years ago when a raw recruit in the Confederate army.

When the war between the states was declared the young man and his older brother Charles, were students at Princeton University. They immediately left for Louisiana. Upon arriving home my father-to-be and his brother enlisted at once in Fenner's Battery, Louisiana Field Artillery, Confederate States of America, under Col. Joseph Breaux. They were assigned to Camp Lewis near Carrollton for training. The following letter was one of several written by Alfred Clement from Camp Lewis to his sister Lodoiska Clement, who later became the wife of Andrew H. Gay. Mr. Gay, at that time, was serving as a Confederate soldier but in a different unit.

Camp Lewis,
March 31, 1862

My dear sister:

I seize upon a few moments of leisure to answer your kind letter. Believe me that nothing but my arduous duties has prevented me from replying long before this.

Please send 2 or 3 pairs of thin cotton socks. I find that one can walk better in light socks. If you have an opportunity send my pen. I have to do all the Company writing. The business of each day is to call the roll of the Company at 5½ a.m. Immediately after this I call at each tent and learn the number of sick men. I then write out a report which I take to the Adjutant's office. I then return to quarters and superintend the cleaning up. As soon as this is done I attend the school of the officers. I then get breakfast. At a quarter to nine I march my guards to the Col.'s tent where their arms and uniforms are inspected. At half past nine I go with the Company upon Company Drill. This lasts an hour and a half. Between eleven and four o'clock I have no regular duties, further than to see that those men detailed to special duties do not neglect them. At 4 o'clock I go with the Company upon Battalion Drill. This occupies one hour and three quarters. At six o'clock we go upon dress parade. We get through at seven. I am then compelled to sit up until 9 o'clock in order to call the roll. I must then wait until the Bugler calls "lights out" before I lie down. I have the most irksome position in the Company, still I like it, for it keeps me employed.

Give my love to all again.

Your affectionate brother,
Alfred H. Clement

After the war was over Alfred Clement took over the management of his father's Retreat Plantation and continued as a sugar planter until his death in 1880.

Mott Rev. Antᵉ Blane
Archbishop of & at New Orleans

1852

Envelope mailed from Iberville before stamps came into use.
(Courtesy Leonard V. Huber)

1896 — (From left) W. E. Clement, Charles H. Dickinson, Alfred H. Clement, Edward J. Gay. Closely related and at one time residents of Iberville Parish.

The locks at Plaquemine which for fifty years connected the bayou with the Mississippi River. Now abandoned and no longer in use. Replaced by modern and larger locks at a nearby location.

THE TRADE WIND HOTEL

This was the hotel at Last Island which was destroyed by the great storm of August, 1856. It must have been one of the finest, if not the finest, resort hotel in the United States. The hotel was built by Hall and Hildreth, the owners of the St. Charles Hotel in New Orleans. (This picture is made from a print loaned by J. Wesley Cooper and used in his book "A Treasure of Louisiana Plantation Homes," published by the Southern Historical Publications, Inc., Natchez, Miss., 1961.)

THE UNSOLVED DISAPPEARANCE OF CHARLES ASH MIX
OF IBERVILLE

Charles Ash Mix, son of Ferrand Mix and Ann Ash of Philadelphia, was a ship owner who settled in Plaquemine with his wife, Celeste Chopoton of Detroit. His daughter Caroline Mix, married Lucien Marionneaux. Mix spent his time between his son-in-law's Plantation Myrtle Grove, and England, to which country he frequently sailed on one of his merchant ships of which he owned three. In 1852 he told his friends that he was going to tour the west, and would be gone for some time. He left on one of his ships and never returned. A world-wide search was made for him and his ship—but no trace was ever found.

In 1880 his succession was opened, and money which he had inherited from his mother was paid to his widow, it was marked "Ship Money."

When Livingston purchased Louisiana from France in 1803, approximately $5,000,000 was held out to pay for ships which had been taken by France in Napoleon's time from American owners. The Ash family were ship owners, and Ann Ash Mix, who died in 1873 at 94, got her portion of it. This is in the records at the Court House at Plaquemine.

IN SLAVERY TIMES

In June of 1857 the Police Jury of Iberville Parish passed favorably on the petition of five prominent planters that the fines which they had paid for failing to observe the law which required that there must be a white man overseer or other white workers for every thirty working slaves be remitted.

THE PLAQUEMINE CLUB

In 1900 there was established at Plaquemine one of the few social clubs in Louisiana. If we do not count the Elks Clubs

I do not know of any other social club in Louisiana outside of the city of New Orleans in existence at that time.

The Plaquemine Club was an aristocratic body composed of leading sugar planters, merchants, and professional men of Iberville Parish. Its club rooms were in the Roth and McWilliams block of brick buildings near the People's Bank Building. The rooms were well lighted, elegantly furnished and decorated with costly tapestries. J. S. Mather was the Secretary-Treasurer.

THE WHITE CASTLE OPERA HOUSE

White Castle about fifty years ago boasted an opera house seating 350 persons. It had two dressing rooms for the actors, as well as drop scenery, properties and stage paraphernalia.

A BIT OF IBERVILLE HISTORY

Iberville Parish historically is one of the oldest sections of Louisiana. Sieur de Iberville, after whom the parish is named, went up the Mississippi River in 1699 disembarking about ten miles below what is now the town of Plaquemine.* A large group of Bayou Goula Indians welcomed him with a grand pow-wow. Father Du Ru, a Jesuit missionary, remained behind to establish a church and school for the Indians.

The great explorer Iberville was the first white man to navigate Bayou Plaquemine. In its primeval state this big

---

*Plaquemine, now the largest town and the Parish Seat of Iberville is on the West Bank of the Mississippi River about fifteen miles below Baton Rouge. It is reached in about two hours, or less, by driving up the Baton Rouge air-line highway from New Orleans, turning off at the point marked Donaldsonville Ferry, and, after crossing the river, continuing on an almost straight, fine, concrete road. Or one can drive to Baton Rouge and crossing the ferry to Port Allen, go south on a good road to Plaquemine. By going a few miles further one can cross on the river bridge instead of the ferry.

Bayou, next to the Atchafalaya River, was the largest outlet
for the flood waters of the Mississippi River. The bayou was
in early times the route to the Attakapas Country—the south-
western part of Louisiana, inhabited, before the white man

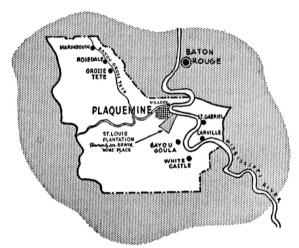

Map of Iberville Parish.

came, by the man-eating Attakapas Indians. The first white
settlers of that section were the Acadians, and they reached it
by way of the Mississippi River and Bayou Plaquemine.

Longfellow in his "Evangeline" tells how the forlorn maid
came with a group in a flatboat down the Ohio and the Mississippi, then through Bayou Plaquemine until they got to
Bayou Teche in the Attakapas region, now known as the
Evangeline Country.

He writes:

"They, too, swerved from their course; and, entering
Bayou Plaquemine,
Soon were lost in a maze of sluggish and devious
waters,
Which, like a network of steel, extended in every di-
rection."

A century ago there occurred an extensive "cave-in" at the point where Bayou Plaquemine joins the Mississippi. According to the New Orleans Picayune of January 6, 1852 the "General Council" of New Orleans was undertaking an "examination of the Bayou situation," this was done at the urging of a Mr. Payne. It was said the Mississippi "might flow through the breach" and "by changing its course do great injury to New Orleans." This gives an idea of the one-time size of Bayou Plaquemine.

The overflow from the Mississippi continued until, due to the almost complete "chocking up" of Grand River, the Plaquemine waterways route to the sea, it was necessary to close off the bayou by means of a dyke of large proportions. This damming up of the big Bayou was done a year after the close of the Civil War. In the "eighties," when the water in the bayou was at times very low, the big empty gap in the Plaquemine terrain gave—as I recall it—a sort of "Grand Canyon" appearance to the old bayou bed, or so it seemed to the uninitiated.

The building of the high lift locks in the nineties opened the Plaquemine waterway to use again, and now large barges and boats can navigate the bayou to and from the Mississippi River.

Saint Gabriel on the left bank of the Mississippi is the oldest settlement in the parish and the first church edifice was built there in 1761. However, the Church was established in 1760 since the first records show that date. The last entry in the records of this early Catholic church was made in February 1807. About 1765 a few settlers located around Bayou Goula and what is now Plaquemine. In 1769 there were only 376 men, women and children in the parish, not counting the Indians. These settlers were mostly Acadians. It is interesting to know that early church records with births, marriages and deaths going back to the 17th century were brought down from Canada by the Acadians and deposited in the St. Gabriel Church. In 1897 high water threatened the church and the Acadian records were brought to New Orleans and placed in the record vaults of the Cathedral. Manchac or what the French called "Iberville River" was the boundary line between Spanish and English-speaking territory, and the important part of Iberville Parish was then on the east bank of the Mississippi River. Bayou Manchac was once a useful short cut from the Mississippi to the Amite River. This Iberville Parish Bayou, was for years the international boundary line between Great Britain and the territory of Spain.

Old maps show that when Bayou Manchac ran into the Amite River which in turn emptied into Lake Maurepas (and this was connected with Lake Pontchartrain) that all the land south of Bayou Manchac was surrounded by navigable waters and formed an island. This was known as the Isle d'Orleans. When Jefferson sent a delegation to purchase Louisiana, what he really wanted was this island on which was located the City of New Orleans. But Napoleon was willing to sell all of Louisiana, and so instead of buying just the island, Jefferson's commissioners headed by Livingston, bought the whole of Louisiana for about fifteen million dollars or four cents an acre. Jefferson had been willing to pay this price for Isle d'Orleans alone.

In 1807, the year Joseph Erwin, still troubled over the Dickinson-Jackson tragedy, and the untimely death of his son-in-law, came to Iberville Parish, there occurred on the banks of Bayou Manchac, dividing line between Iberville and East Baton Rouge, the duel between Governor W. C. C. Claiborne and Daniel Clark. It came about over what seems a trivial matter. Clark, Member of Congress from Louisiana, in December 1806 made a statement in the U. S. House of Representatives in which he said, according to the Louisiana Gazette, "that the militia of the Territory had been neglected, and had seen a black corps preferred to them." The governor wrote on May 23, 1807, that he had seen this statement in the Orleans Gazette and he wanted a retraction from Mr. Clark. Daniel Clark acknowledged the letter on the 24th, but refused to retract or explain. The actual statement made by Congressman Clark as printed in the Annals of Congress was milder, and did not mention a "black corps." Claiborne then demanded satisfaction on the field of honor. His second was John W. Gurley, and Clark's second was Richard R. Keene. For some reason the duel was fought in Iberville Parish. The Louisiana Gazette of June 12, 1807 carried this squib:

> "A duel was fought June 8th 1807 near Manchac Fort between Gov. Claiborne and Daniel Clark, Esq. At first fire the Governor received Mr. Clark's ball through his right thigh. His Excellency has reached town and is out of danger."*

Along in 1826 when the overflows caused it to be troublesome the Bayou Manchac was dammed up, and the river connection to Lake Pontchartrain and the Gulf Coast closed. Many times the matter of reopening this outlet has been broached, but nothing was ever done.

During the Spanish domination the settlements above New Orleans were known as the German Coast in St. Charles Parish and lower St. John Parish; the Acadian Coast on both sides of the Mississippi in St. James and Ascension Parishes; the Iberville Coast already described; and the Pointe Coupee Coast on the West Bank. At each of these more or less loosely defined political divisions was a post in charge of a commandant who administered the laws, heard complaints and acted as judge in lawsuits and in the settlement of community property. In fact, he was a dictator, subject only to the orders of his superiors.

---

*From "Duelling In Old New Orleans" by Stuart O. Landry.

CHAPTER XIV

BELLE GROVE—GLORY OF THE PLANTATION PAST

In lower Iberville Parish two miles from White Castle is the ruin of what was once the queen of Louisiana mansions. The Ladies Home Journal said of it many years ago: "In all the Southland there is no mansion so grand, more magnificent and imposing. Belle Grove is now a noble ruin." Before the fire of March 15th, 1952, even the ruin was magnificent, no doubt the most impressive in the entire Mississippi Valley. The walls are still standing although all the wood work is burned away.

At one time the Mississippi River was a brief mile distant, but now is only one hundred yards away from the dead mansion. There were spacious gardens and a grand avenue of oaks but the seventeen acres of magnificent gardens and trees have disappeared into the river.

On the former 6000-acre estate of John Andrews, sugar baron, the shell of the 75-room mansion is only a few miles from beautifully maintained "Nottaway," ante-bellum home of the wealthy Virginia planter, John Hampden Randolph. Both houses were built in the same lush period, 1857.

Andrews, also from Virginia, came to Louisiana in 1850. After making a fortune in sugar to add to his already immense wealth he commissioned the able James Gallier, and his architect son of New Orelans, to build this "Greek Revival" mansion. It obviously however, did not conform to some of the characteristics of the Louisiana Classic plantation house.*

Mrs. George W. Pigmant† of New Orleans, the former Dorothy Hebert, whose mother was born in this house, recalls that her great-grandmother died at age of 32, leaving five daughters who were belles of the parish. The wedding of Emily Andrews to Edward Schiff of Paris, France, is still famous in Louisiana's social annals. It was indeed an elegant and elaborate affair. There were fifty house-guests who stayed a week and five hundred additional guests who came just for the wedding, all with their maids and valets who arrived by steamboat. Imbert, the famous New Orleans chef and caterer, came with his entire staff a week in advance to prepare his daubes glaces, his pyramids of nougat, and his incomparable salads and bouillons, and remained throughout the entire season of fetes.

The great Greek porticos of Belle Grove were hung with a thousand lights which shone far out into the river, dancing cloths were laid over the lower floors and the chambers were all festooned with flowers. The feast was so bounteous that the very boatmen on the Mississippi, who brought "the dear five hundred up the river to Belle Grove landing came in for their share." writes one chronicler.

Andrews was ruined by the War. His great fortune swept away he sold Belle Grove to Henry Ware shortly after the close of the conflict between the states. After the death of this second owner in 1880 the home passed to his son, James A. Ware. Belle Grove was then known far and wide for the magnificence of its appointments, its more than $500,000.00

---

*Another famous New Orleans architect, Henry Howard, in 1872, claimed he built Belle Grove.

†Mrs. Pigman says: "After the war and sale of Belle Grove in 1868 my great-grandfather stored his furnishings from the house in a warehouse in New Orleans. They were burned and among them were tapestried curtains woven in France for the windows that had cost him $5000."

worth of furnishings and art objects gathered in Europe by Mrs. Eliza Stone Ware. The splendor of the entertainments which often extended into weeks, and the glamour of its special affairs made invitations to Belle Grove much sought after. There was a private race track and James Ware maintained a racing stable. Big crowds were attracted to the improvised Clement "speedway," or mile-long trotting track in front of nearby Retreat Plantation, whenever Ware entered into competition races with others from Iberville Parish. At the death of James A. Ware, his son, John Stone Ware, continued the racing tradition, adding another private race track to the one his father had already built.

The third Ware owner operated the big establishment until the early nineteen twenties. At that time, due probably to the mosaic disease which attacked the sugar cane and crop failures, Mr. Ware found it expedient to cease operating Belle Grove, notwithstanding its tremendously interesting past and the glory of by-gone years.

Many of us who are familiar with the pattern of the old-time Louisiana homes marvel at the unusual yet beautifully proportioned Greek Revival architecture of Belle Grove. Its difference from the Mississippi river classic plantation mansions did not terminate with its outward appearance. There was, according to Iberville authorities, an innovation in the way of a very large dumbwaiter to the butlers' pantry above. Instead of the big cisterns used elsewhere there was a system of storing water overhead in big copper tanks.

Effort after effort was made to save and restore Belle Grove, the stricken beauty of the house having appealed to quite a few wealthy people. But some years ago it was estimated that the cost of repairs and restoration would run over a million dollars. Above all the house was threatened by the inexorable river, the ever-reaching power of which already had taken most of the oaks in front of the property.

Now that fire has claimed the old mansion instead of the river, Belle Grove is with the ghosts of the past. Perhaps like the Phoenix, in a hundred years from now in a happier and fairer time, another mansion will be built along the Mississippi that will rival Belle Grove in the splendor of a new and better day.

CHAPTER XV

SOME PERTINENT THOUGHTS
"All Goes Back to the Land"

As I come to the end of this pleasantly absorbing task I want to leave with my readers a few thoughts that occur to me as I look back over the years in an attempt to glean from the history of Iberville Parish and her stalwart sons the reasons for economic ups and downs and the depressions, the rise of socialism and the "welfare state" as opposed to the pioneering spirit of individualism which made our nation great. From this microcosm—Iberville—come pertinent truths that may help us toward a safer, more pleasant and freer society.

Upon all sides we hear what social science is doing for the world today. Aided and abetted by politicians with vote-getting theories of price control and production control, their creation, the welfare state, offers health protection and security for all and so on. England is put forward as an exemplar of the accomplishment of scientific social planning, but social science has failed in its objectives and lags far behind the tremendous advance in the physical sciences—a *technological advance* which has brought great progress in human well-being. Yet like ambition it has over-stept itself, so much so as to have produced, among other things, the frightening atomic bomb, endangering the continuance of our civilization.

While not referring particularly to plantation land, Winston Churchill long ago said: "All goes back to the land. Everything we eat, wear, or use comes from the land."

How these observations about social phenomena and forces

concern Iberville Parish particularly I want to point out. This great section had made exceptional progress in wealth, culture and modern-day improvements during the past century. Among Louisiana Parishes it stands in the front rank. Yet—according to experts—there is room for improvement in land use, agriculture, horticulture, and cattle raising.

In October of 1945 a very complete and informative survey of Iberville Parish Resources and Facilities was completed and published in attractive book form. This was gotten out by the Iberville Parish Planning Board, composed of representative Ibervillians, in cooperation with the State of Louisiana Department of Public Works, Planning Division. The book is available at many libraries and is recommended reading for those interested in the Parish. Its closing recommendations were as follows:

1. Development of industries that can make use of raw materials and surplus crop production, with the view of establishing a more balanced economy.
2. Better land use through improved drainage, crop rotation, range and woodland management and reforestation.
3. Use of natural facilities in development of recreational sites for use of inhabitants and to attract tourists and vacationers.
4. Improvement of living conditions in both rural and urban areas, with particular emphasis on better sanitation.
5. Improved transportation facilities.

CATTLE INDUSTRY GROWTH AMAZING

In view of the pressing world need for more food, especially more meat, it is pleasing to see the growing tendency in Iberville and other parishes of the plantation country towards greater diversification, the turning in part from agriculture to stockraising. From this and other developments a considerable amount of partially drained, unused or under-used land, may soon be brought up to standard and widely utilized for the grazing of meat animals. The land use situation in Louisiana —it might be said—is typical of the entire South, where there are still great areas of undeveloped natural resources. It is not unusual to find only about 30% of the land in a parish, or county, under cultivation. Large tracts are sometimes held out of use for speculative purposes, awaiting a market. Here indeed is what might be called a "New Frontier" for our awakened social sciences and the modernly equipped "pioneers" and land-use experts of the future.

The truth of the matter is that farming in Louisiana and elsewhere, even in this electrical and mechanical age, has too long been a somewhat back-breaking, sweaty business. For farmers there is no eight hour day or forty hour week with double pay for overtime. All kinds of hazards such as weather and insect pests beset him, and unless the farmer grows some staple like sugar, cotton, corn, or wheat there is no certainty that even a good harvest will bring a monetary reward.

For the growers of the above staples there is government aid. Whether our economy can stand the continued strain of "parity" for the producers of these staples is open to doubt. Unless one has a genuine love of growing things and a feel for nature's wonderful unfoldings, farming is for many people a rather monotonous existence under present conditions—one in which life becomes a sort of treadmill.

It is my thought that giving the farmer a real stake in the land through a deeply fundamental and badly needed change in taxation methods, and the "scientific approach" now in the making, as opposed to the socialistic idea of "land redistribution", would make for a far better social and political system. It is noteworthy that the "land reform" and full use of our natural resources idea now being advocated by some modern economists calls for enlightened private development rather than by government redistribution and "levelling down" methods. These last have failed in the past and cannot but continue to fail in the future because of an underlying and inherent defect in such methods. Something has to be done but we must go forward instead of backward.

Unless then we can, through scientific land-use taxation methods, plus such innovations as "tree-crop agriculture," fish culture, horticulture, hydroponics and stock raising, accompanied by use of improved automatic machinery and labor saving processes, make farming more attractive, food, meat, wool, cotton, lumber and products of the farm will continue to go up in price, because the young people will continue to leave the farm and seek employment with the manufacturing and other industries of the cities. As in other times and other civilizations, they are attracted by high weekly wages and to those places where amusement and diversions are available.

On the other hand, the law of compensation inevitably works out in that when leaving the farm or small hamlet, our young men and women give up much that is sweet, pure and beautiful and morally uplifting. We who have lived on the farm know what this means to youth especially, and we will never concede that this unhealthy drift is inevitable, and that it cannot be overcome. The question is what to do and how. The tide must be turned. Science, belatedly, is preparing to call the signals which will indicate how we can get people back to the land. That happy consummation is, as I have said, at last in the making. Science, helpfully for all, is now moving rapidly towards letting our people know that high housing and food costs and the great and always worsening meat shortage, a long-time problem and one which up to this time no person, or group of persons seemed capable of solving, are brought about by an entirely unnecessary and correctible economic disequilibrium between our natural resources and available man-power.

With reference to the old-time spirit of freedom of enterprise which made the country great, it must be emphasized that the Founding Fathers were not hemmed in as we are today. They did their work in a New World of easy accessibility to land, and particularly in an atmosphere of what might well be called Responsible Individualism in the production of food, clothing and living necessities. Their incentives, choices, values and ethical judgments were distinctly and uncompromisingly individualistic. In the admirable words of Thomas Davidson: "That which is not free is not responsible, that which is not responsible is not moral." This means that free choice is an absolute prerequisite of morality.

"Honest Abe" Lincoln said many years ago, "you can always trust the people to do the right thing, providing they first have the right information." Let us take heart that this newly developed scientific orientation may be, to the sociological world, as important as the great "germ-theory" discovery of Pasteur was to the medical. Let us hope the change comes before we enter the era which may end in the grim world depicted in George Orwell's "Nineteen Eighty-four," when knowledge of all facts which do not serve the interests of the ruling party are consigned to limbo.

As a result of this new and very vital approach, society will be able to release and use, automatically and naturally, much human energy now pent up, dangerously frustrated, unused or wasted. Unused and under-used land, natural and human resources of all kinds can be put to work on an incentive basis and without the threatened centralized, stifling, bureaucratic, regimentation. Individual "self-starters," or those with venture capital, will, as confiscating taxation recedes, again surge forward to take advantage of the freedom and opportunity to produce goods and create wealth. With the help of this advance in science the huge government debt can and will be liquidated.

With the bringing to fruition of the results of the much

discussed and widely written of "Input-Output Economics" scientific study, and the new "Theory of Values in Social Science," we should be able to get back to safe ground. When we put our own economic house in order then we will be far more ready for world leadership, for healthful and happy living, the dependable antidote to unrest and insecurity. Thus only can we hope to escape further spiritual and material retrogression and degradation.

Referring to the often unrecognized flaw in our American economic system, which endangers the entire structure, Prof. W. G. O'Donnell of Pittsburg University, said recently in a leading article in the "American Journal of Economics and Sociology," "a theoretical system cannot rise above its framework of reference, and philosophical foundations, on merely internal modifications and refinements." This able analyst, teacher, and writer says that, if we are to avoid the costly consequences of "present incongruity, tensions and disorders of a neurotic modern society of individuals frustrated in their collective aspiration," there must be a follow-through based on the "scientific approach." The rock-bound guide to all this, however, will be the deep-down fundamentals of the American Constitution, and the long-ago but intuitively indicated values, the relation of individuals to each other, to the land and to the state. It is late, but never too late to bring about a desperately needed tax change and economic reorientation.

We are told that in the new approach to this great and long unsolved problem of values and ethics it is no longer fashionable for scientists to "shrug shoulders" at its mention. Men like John Dewey, F. S. C. Northrop, Durkheim as well as Sombart, Pareto, Max Weber, Pound and Kelsen have manifested increasing interest. In fact the great and highly respected Dewey has been one of the foremost leaders in the movement.

It is said that we must go "from the static to the dynamic," from facts to interpretation, from operations to consequences.

O'Donnell has told us that "it may be that real liberty is not only a matter of opportunity among immediately available opportunities, but a matter of providing valuable alternatives, and the ways and means to intelligent choice and selection." As our forefathers knew, the purpose of economics or any other science, is to serve the "art of creative living." In the words of Ruskin this means the long overlooked fact that "there is no wealth but life."

To sum up, the "responsible individualism" of business — men and pioneers, strong men like Joseph Erwin and Samuel Clement and other great plantation builders surmounting tremendous obstacles, is what is desperately needed today. With the right statistical and economic information, this individualism will prevail and will bring prosperity and peace such as the world has never known.

As the research and consolidation work in sociology now under way begins to show results, Responsible Individualism, and the dignity of man may again become the militant faith of our people so that they will successfully challenge the advocates of collectivism and the *irresponsibility* of the "welfare state." Truly we are entering upon great times. The proper values and human relationships in the social and economic sciences will bring a revival of the old-time pioneering spirit. Thus only can we hope to defeat the socialistic, collectivistic, and civilization-destroying forces that now menace us, and make possible for every one, continuing prosperity, liberty and pursuit of happiness.

Lastly, this tribute to the pioneers of Louisiana and the plantation barons of other days and the hope expressed here for the future, might well be closed with a quotation from Daniel Webster, one of history's great men, a thinker and patriot, who enunciated these words of wisdom before the Civil War, at a time when the lamp of newly found economic freedom and Responsible Individualism guided our feet. The

incentive system of the Founding Fathers, embodied for the
first time anywhere in our Constitution, belonged, as it should
to everybody. Our business men, as some claim, did not make
the system—*the truth is the incentive system invented them.*
Have we stopped a little short of the goal that rightfully belongs to us? With the future greatness of our country just
beginning, Webster said:

> And there is open to us, also, a noble pursuit to which
> the spirit of the times strongly invites us. Our proper
> business is improvement. Let us cultivate the resources
> of our land, building up its institutions, promote all its
> great interests, and see whether we also, in our day and
> generation, may not perform something to be remem-
> bered.

FURTHER REFLECTIONS—1961

It seems to me that the great problem of the world today is
land reform. Governments seize upon this idea because of
its appeal to the masses. Lenin won the Russian Revolution
by promising the peasants land. Castro did the same thing in
Cuba. But these dictators, having achieved power by false
promises and shedding crocodile tears, then proceeded to take
over the land for the government, thereby strengthening their
dictatorships and increasing their power.

That there is a need for land reform in Cuba, Brazil, Latin
American countries, Asia, indeed, in North America and Europe, cannot be gainsaid. That there is some appreciation of
this fundamental problem is shown by this quotation from the
California *Analyst*.

"There is a peaceful revolution going on, almost unnoticed
in the little Caribbean island of Jamaica, one of Cuba's
neighbors, which bids fair to point the way to democratic and
effective land reform. First one parish after another is
adopting a modified form of placing all the local taxes on the
value of land, and exempting improvements, orchards and
crops from taxes."

THE STORM AT LAST ISLAND AS IT GATHERED IN FORCE

Last Island, the swank summer resort for the people of New Orleans and southern Louisiana, was destroyed by a terrible hurricane on August 10th, 1856. We have given Michael Schlatre's account of the storm in another place. And, of course, Lafcadio Hearn is "Chita" has told in magnificent prose this story of the tragedy of Last Island. (From an illustration from Frank Leslie's of August the 30th, 1856, in the collection of Leonard V. Huber).

THE DESTRUCTION OF LAST ISLAND

The wind blowing from the Gulf piled up the waters which overwhelmed the hotel and the houses on the island. Many were washed away and drowned. (From Frank Leslie's of August the 30th, 1856, in the collection of Leonard V. Huber).

It is too bad that Castro did not use this plan in Cuba.

The *Analyst* goes on to say: "Experience proves that wherever the land bears a tax anywhere resembling its true value, absentee-ownership and speculation just does not pay."

This has happened in the California irrigation districts, in Australia, New Zealand and Denmark. In Denmark this method of taxation has reduced farm tenancy from nearly 50% of the agricultural production to less than 5%.

The last half of the twentieth century finds in America enormous numbers of people who have been forced by our land-gamble, price-inflation system of land tenure into city areas, much as happened in ancient Rome. That accounts basically for our social wrongs, moral decline, unemployment the "Welfare State" and centralization of governmental controls.

At present Latin America is more disturbed and troubled than ever. Russell Frazer wrote recently in the Los Angeles *Times*:

> There is a new play opening this year. It is on a world stage. You will have an orchestra seat. However, you will not like it!
>
> The drama is called "Latin America on the March."
>
> A rather stuffy title, perhaps, but it means that the dispossessed and disinherited of the earth down there are waking up.
>
> Castro did it. We could have headed him off when he started out . . . Instead of moving toward democracy, Castro veered in the opposite direction: communism and tyranny.
>
> President Kennedy's economic and political scouts have given him the facts, and they are gloomy. But if Americans are to understand this drama, we had better know a few of them . . . :
>
> 1. If communism in five countries is to be scotched, the power of the feudal overlords, who hold vast tracts of land and pay virtually no taxes, must be broken . . .

2. If the feudal overlords pay their just share of taxes, U. S. assistance would not be necessary. . . .

And what does this mean to us, especially the Kennedy administration: Fortunately, the President is facing up to it. He is insisting that tax and land reform is a condition of U.S. aid. This is a long step forward. Indeed, if he rigorously adheres to it, the battle for freedom in Latin America may be won.

If the curtain comes down on Act 1, however, without it, watch for an explosion in Act II!

And it looks as if at least one state in the troubled country of Brazil is taking steps calculated to solve the problem. An article in *Labor* (national organ of the railroad brotherhoods), Feb. 11, 1961 said:

"Signs multiply of a growing recognition that wiser tax methods could help remedy economic and social troubles. One recent sign is a *New York Times* report that Brazil's richest state, Sao Paulo, has made a start toward solving 'one of Latin America's most explosive problems—the need for land reform.'

"The report says Carvalho Pinto, conservative governor of the state, has asked its legislature to approve a program which includes 'progressively higher taxes on unworked and unforested lands.' This tax reform 'is expected to encourage cultivation and reforestation of big private landholdings.'

"Back of this tax move," the report adds, "is a situation that's typical of most Latin American countries." It points out that Brazil does not lack land, but most of it is held in big estates. Of the 500 million acres of agricultural land in Brazil, only 66 million acres are cultivated, even poorly. Much of the rest, as a result of neglect, is eroded, burned over, and badly needs reforestation to save it and restore it to productivity.

"Eighty per cent of the farm population does not own

any land," the report says. "Two per cent of the land-owners hold 50 per cent of the land."

That situation has been causing social unrest and *play-ing into the hands of the communists*, the report points out. The tax reform and other land reforms proposed by the conservative governor, it explains, are designed to *force the big landlords to sell some of their land to small farmers, and also to encourage better use of the land which the landlords retain.*" (Italics mine)

Yes, the Communists are smart. In Latin America they stress the land question—land monopoly by the great land owners, injustice toward the dispossessed. They know the natural longing of human beings for land, so they cry, "Down with the great landlords, action — any kind of action." They know the rising, seething, feelings of the masses about in-equality in wealth, and they craftily ascribe that to the land situation. The fateful result of their work we see developing in every direction.

The world is aflame with communist agitators and orators, stirring, as in China, vast hordes of people to wild, fanatical, even blood-thirsty, hatred of the land-owners. We see confis-cation, action a la Castro and a powerful appeal to the emo-tions—and the mobs love it.

President Kennedy's aid-proposal for Latin America coupled with land reform and scientific land-value taxation is in keeping with fundamentals stressed by the great Saint Thomas Aquinas. Here we have a hopeful approach to the problem of checkmating the communist appeal to the landless masses. While unemployment and the need for "free-market" access to land in the United States has not reached the critical situation we see to the south of us, it is only a matter of time when the same maladjustment will cause a terrific explosion here.

Our welfare-state troubles, and the rising mob spirit (as shown at San Francisco) is directly related to the failure to right the one deeply fundamental injustice now evident in our own backyard.

Raised as I was in the years of easy access to land and the accompanying peace that was ours (preceding the two World Wars), I was horrified as a youngster of twenty years when the Spanish-American War became imminent. I said to myself: "That cannot be, war is a thing of the barbarous past." Since then speculation in land has caused prices to soar and hot and cold wars have torn nations apart. "Rebarbarization" and moral decline have proceeded at an ever accelerating pace.

I have written extensively elsewhere on the land problem and since I have dilated on this subject here, it is fitting that I quote from a brochure of mine, "A Common-Sense Answer to the Violence Problem."

The key to the "land value taxation" proposal is to *gradually* remove taxes from man-made products and, again, gradually put them on the land. The tax jungle we are lost in is an affront to reason, an obstacle to production and consumption. Income taxes deter and penalize all who work. Purchase taxes distort production, raise prices and restrict consumption.

It is in this manner that we will find a common-sense answer to the highly dangerous Cuban situation as well as in other countries south of us. With land-utilization conditions as they are throughout Latin America, the "Violence" problem is bound to multiply progressively. Communism in Russia came into being as a direct result of highly concentrated ownership of land. The refusal of the Grand Dukes and great land owners to accept "land-value taxation" or to face the problem intelligently (and with justice to all) brought on the Communistic cataclysm from which the world now suffers.

The proposed method of land-value taxation means *no threat* to private ownership. Rather it will bring a restoration of natural, healty growth in thousands of communities

where development has been stopped or stunted due to tremendously inflated "asking-prices" for unused, or under-used,
land.

To avoid political domination and favoritism, "Local Land
Utilization Clinics" will be formed. As in the case of the draft
boards they would, on a fair-to-all, *free-market basis*, study
and determine land (site) values and the gradual application
and collection of ground-rent for community purposes. Mem-
bership on such Incentive Taxation Clinic Boards would in-
clude representatives of capital, labor, land owners and consumers.

Emphasis is laid upon the "Violence" idea because our
mistake—as in previous civilizations—has been in failing to
recognize that social organization, as related to land-use, is a
manifestation of Cosmic Energy. As we enter the Atomic age
it becomes suicidal for us not to adjust to these new, but old-
as-time, ultra-powerful requirements of Nature. Only in this
way can the individual achieve full freedom.

Some badly informed writers have been endeavoring to cast
aspersions on President Kennedy's "Latin America, Alliance
For Progress." Far from being against the "interest of free
enterprise" and a "grave infringement of private property,"
the proposed Land-and-Taxation-Reform program would seem
to be the only way to save the countries to the south of us. The
communistic, land-confiscation, carrot-held-out-to-the-donkey
plan proved successful in Cuba because of a basic land-use
maladjustment. A *glaring injustice*, which appears all
through the countries to the south of us, favors the communist cause.

My thought is the *Castro* fiasco may yet prove to be a *bless-
ing in disguise*. It may even be that, with success of Land and
Taxation Reform in Latin America, its good effects will filter
through to the United States. As E. C. Harwood, Director,
American Institute for Economic Research, recently said:

"The outcome of the American crisis of the 1960's apparently will determine the future course of Western civilization. It may yet be considered the most significant development of the past two centuries —— equal in importance to the crisis of the 1770's when the turning was toward life and progress, rather than toward retrogression and extinction."

The "counterrevolution" against our U.S.A. 1776, forward move is in progress *here* and throughout the world. It is clearly recognized as communism; but Fascism, various Socialist governments, the New Deal, and the welfare state all have grown from the same roots, the festering need for *basic* "Land and Taxation Reform" as now envisioned in the Alliance for Progress. Many of the great land owners are accepting this program as a way of not only saving their holdings but going on to far better things. Our *near* future will not be joyous, and the laurels of victory will not quickly be pressed upon our brows. But we can in all sincerity say this: ours may well be the *decisive voice* — the final increment of weight that shifts the balance, and brings our civilization to the course that leads to survival.

In writing this 1961 addenda to my Final Thought of ten years ago, I must apologize to my readers for bearing down so heavily on land reform. This same idea was enthusiastically advocated and written about long ago by no less a personage than the great Winston Churchill. I am forced to express my ideas about world problems because, as Heine says, "Great ideas compel us to go out into the arena and fight for them." And I echo the saying of Madame de Staël, "The search for Truth is the noblest occupation of man, its publication a duty."

"Man is at the crossroads." Instead of the "unlimited destruction" that everyone seems to fear, we can achieve unlimited well being—if we support President Kennedy in this truly basic, tax-and-land-reform proposal, as mentioned in the preceding quotation from Fraser. Only thus can peace and prosperity be achieved in Latin America, and, indeed, all over the world.

Saint Thomas Aquinas long ago told us, "Justice is far more important than charity." Instead of heeding that advice, nations have tried to substitute the Welfare State, resulting in communistic land confiscation and tyranny in large areas instead of *basic justice as regards God-given land.*

I close with a quotation from Walt Whitman—a sentiment which greatly intrigued me as a youth during the idyllic plantation life days. From "Leaves of Grass":

"This is what you shall do, love the earth, and sun, and animals, despise riches, give alms to everyone who asks, stand up for the stupid and crazy, devote your income and labor to others, hate tyrants, argue not concerning God, have patience and indulgence toward other people, take off your hat to nothing known or unknown, or to any man or number of men; go freely with powerful uneducated persons, and with the young, and mothers of families, read these leaves (his own works) in the open air every season of every year of your life; reexamine all you have been told at school or church, or in any book, and dismiss whatever insults your own soul."

AFTERWORD

For the second edition of
"Plantation Life on the Mississippi"
By
Charles H. Dickinson

The author has asked me to say a final word for the new edition of his delightful book now being re-issued because of popular demand.

This comes about because of my connection with the Clement family and the association of my family with his in the Iberville country for a period of over one hundred years.

In the decade since the appearance of "Plantation Life on the Mississippi" many changes have occurred in the affairs of the world and its thinking, and I will comment on these later. But, first, a more personal allusion.

My father, the great-grandson of Charles Dickinson of the famous Jackson-Dickinson duel—we were both named after him—died in 1954. Two of his boyhood friends, Edward J. Gay, at one time U. S. Senator from Louisiana, and Alfred H. Clement, the author's brother, have since this book appeared in 1952—gone to the "Great Beyond."

These three with the author attended school together, hunted, swam the Mississippi River, and enjoyed that era of rugged individualism when the region was emerging from the aftermath of the War-Between-the-States. All this, of course, was before my time. As adults the four Ibervillians scattered, but always maintained close contact and affection for each other.

My father, Charles H. Dickinson, in early life moved his family to California. There he lived a busy, rewarding life. Active in real estate and other businesses in and around Los Angeles, he retired at the end of World War II. The memory of Louisiana and his dear friends there always remained deep in his heart.

It was my great fortune to return to the home of my ancestors in Iberville Parish recently. Accompanied by my wife Doris we went to New Orleans where we met Will Clement, and with him took the well-remembered trip to Plaquemine. There we were met by Andrew Price Gay, the present-day master of historic St. Louis Plantation, the 5000-acre estate purchased by Grandpa Erwin in 1807.*

We then drove down the "river road" to *Retreat Plantation*, boyhood home of the author, William Clement. Rambling through the grounds we saw the crumbling brick-foundation of the once lovely old plantation home destroyed by fire years ago. Outlines of the once extensive gardens and orchards could still be seen. To the rear of the property there were broken foundations of the sugar mill.

Of the plantation cottages, called "quarters," for the colored workers, only one remained where once lived a carpenter, "Uncle Aaron." It was occupied until recently by his daughter, a much-loved domestic of the Clement family.

Returning to Plaquemine we visited the cemetery where rest the hallowed remains of many of the Dickinson, Clement and Gay families. Before the establishment of this cemetery burials were made on the plantations. On the St. Louis

---

*Andrew Price Gay is now putting some of this land into the Gay Subdivision, a high class residential development. The town of Plaquemine is growing and this suburban development is meeting with success. Joseph Erwin is remembered by having a street named after him.

Plantation I saw the small private graveyard where are entombed Joseph Erwin and seven of his immediate family—his wife, John Wilson, David D. Chesnut, and others. A large tree stands like a lonely sentinel guarding the resting place of these Iberville pioneers.

Our party then repaired to the Gay mansion on the St. Louis Plantation, built 125 years ago, where Andrew Gay and his wife, Nancy, entertained us at a luncheon reminiscent of the olden days of southern hospitality.

That afternoon we drove thirty miles to Live Oaks Plantation on Bayou Grosse Tete near the town of Rosedale. The drive along the banks of the bayou was inspiring as it retains much of the scenery and charm of primitive days. While gasoline boats are occasionally seen, the canoe and the skiff are still the picturesque water craft of the bayou.

It is difficult to describe my emotion on reaching the Live Oaks mansion. This is indeed the home of my ancestors. Built in 1830 by my great-grandfather it has been given loving care throughout the years (See Chapter IV). The latest owners, Mr. and Mrs. Lee Merrill, were most kind and showed us through the house and over the grounds. Truly a memorable experience for me.

Andrew Gay couldn't make the trip to Live Oaks, and turned us over to a good friend, Charles Edward Postell, banker of Plaquemine and member of a distinguished Iberville Parish family. We came back by a different route via Port Allen on the Mississippi River opposite Baton Rouge. From there I had a fine view of Louisiana's State Capitol, which towers high above the surrounding country. It was built by the famous Huey Long and he lies buried in a beautiful green spot at the foot of "steps of the states."

Reaching Plaquemine Mr. Postell invited us to his lovely home where relaxation and bountiful refreshments awaited.

Now that I am back in California I have had time to think about my trip and to reflect on the perils of our own time.

First, I want to say that I remember my father's intense interest in the writing of "Plantation Life on the Mississippi" and how happy and proud he was to assist in some measure in its preparation by sending information, family mementos, records and photographs.

He and I both felt the book was important, not only as history, but that perhaps it meant something more than simply recording proud family names and lineage. We recognized that these ancestors were the pioneers, the rugged individualists who opened up the land. These people built up the country in the first place, and then re-built it after the disastrous War-Between-the-States, until today we have the tremendous industrial and agricultural complex of Louisiana and the middle south.

But more important, they established a philosophy of life that is being carried on by their descendants wherever they may go—a love of land and the proper use of it, a ruggedly individualistic philosophy—yet a humanitarian and progressive one. They loved the wonderful old plantation estates along the Mississippi with the great, fertile fields and the moss-hung oaks.

There was strength to be derived from the heritage of swimming, hunting and fishing and the emphasis on individual initiative these pursuits developed in the young people that those of us who were not as fortunate in our boyhoods in city streets and less-free environment can still take hope from. The boys from the plantation and river environment went from there to greater things—to leadership in industry and to leadership in thinking—to presenting in their writings studies of the multifold problems with which a more complex civilization seems so plagued.

The descendants of the plantation people have not only lived up to the ideals of their ancestors, but have exerted wide influence and inspired others. This is an influence that emphasizes, not just the carefree and leisurely life of plantation days, but the necessity of vision and hard work required to build a country and a culture. We need today the strength of the old culture, so often celebrated as the "pioneer spirit." We could gain an insight into our own lives and the determination to resolve new situations which have new faces but which are only old problems in a new guise.

Today is the Fourth of July as I finish these remarks, and there comes to mind my father's stories of the old-time celebrations of the Glorious Fourth at Plaquemine with oratory, parades and fireworks. These occasions reflected a deep source of joy in being an American. Little children, sitting by their parents' sides before flag-draped band stands, learned something of history and the frontier spirit which fought its way across the continent to create a great nation.

We need a re-birth of patriotism.

APPENDIX

THE ERWIN FAMILY

Motto: LOCK SICK—"Be True"

Another motto of the Erwin Family: HAUD ULLUS LABENTUM
VENTIS—"Deterred by no Light Winds."
According to John Hugh McDowell:

"Irving or Irvine is contracted from *Erivine* which comes from an
ancient Celo-Sytlich word ERIN-VIENE or ERIN-FIENE, which signifies
'a true or brave Westland man.' Erwin in old Gaelic and Welsh means
west. (Ireland today is called Erin being west of Albion.) The earliest
inhabitants of Britain were Celts. Of these there were two branches

Gaelic { Irish
         Highlanders of Scotland
Cymric { Welsh
         Brittainy
         Ancient Gauls"

The Ervine Clan of Scotland are the ancestors of the American Irvines,
Irvings, Irwins, Erwins, Ervings, and those of similar spelling*

The ancient family of Erevines is mentioned at a very early date in
the history of Scotland, a chief of this name was Abathane of Dull, a position of importance.

According to Scottish history, the Abathane of Dull married a daugh-
ter of King Malcolm II, A. D. 1004. The Abathane of Dull was Crynin
Ervine, as spelled in a record in the British Museum, and his wife was
Beatrix. Crynin Ervine and Beatrix of Scotland were the parents of
Duncan who married Sybilla. This was the Duncan murdered by his cousin,
Macbeth. Later on, Malcolm III, son of King Duncan and Sybilla, attacked
with his army the murderer of his father and he, Duncan's son, in turn
caused the death of Macbeth. King Duncan, son of Beatrix and Crynin
Ervine, through his grandson, King David, was the ancestor of all the
Scottish kings.

A branch of this Erevine family, headed by its chief, Irvine of *Bon-*

---

*This and the following paragraphs are taken with omission and changes from
Annie E. Miller's "Our Family Circle."

shaw, in Dumfrieshire, early acquired that estate, and to this day Bonshaw is owned by a member of the clan.

Robert Bruce, fleeing from King Edward, came to Bonshaw, and made William De Irwyn, his armour-bearer and secretary. He proved so faithful, that when Robert Bruce became King of Scotland he granted *William de Irwyn*, (1323) by charter under the great seal the royal forest of *Drum*, Aberdeenshire, and erected it into a free barony the next year.

For political or religious reasons numerous members of the Erinveine clan of Scotland, (The name of these early Scotch Erevines was variously spelled Ervine, Irwin, Erwin, Irvin, Irwyne, and later Irvine,) left their ancestral home of Bonshaw, Drum and other estates, and settled in Ulster, Ireland.

About 1730 and later many of the Scotch-Irish Irwins, Erwins, Irvings, etc., crossed the ocean and located mainly in Pennsylvania, Virginia, and North Carolina, their descendants later settling in different parts of the country. It is claimed that six Irwin (or Erwin) relations came over on the same ship, some settled in Bucks Co., Penn., others in other states. Their names were: William, Arthur, John, Hugh, Nathaniel, and Alexander. Nathaniel, after living in Mecklenburg, Co., moved to Coddle Creek and Rocky River, near Concord. Col. Robert Erwin of Lancaster County, Pa. (b.1738) was the son of William Erwin, this might have been the Robert Erwin who was the father of Joseph who came to North Carolina in 1758.
(Note)

Besides President Theodore Roosevelt, whose mother was a Bulloch and descended from the Irvines, it is said that the Scotch Erevine Clan had as descendants in the U. S. Pres. Andrew Jackson; Pres. Benjamin Harrison; Washington Irving, the author; Gov. Francis of Missouri; Gov. Zeb Vance of North Carolina; the two Taylor brothers, who were governors of Tennessee; Gen. Robert Irwin of Revolutionary War fame; and many other distinguished men of the past, as well as many who are prominent at the present time.

JOSEPH ERWIN GENEALOGY

Robert Erwin married Martha ———— (Martha Erwin, Joseph's mother, furnished food and other supplies to the Continental Army. North Carolina Archives). Their son, Joseph Erwin, married Lavinia Thompson, Jan. 14, 1782, the daughter of Robert Thompson and Letitia (Robert Thompson, a son of John Thompson, a Presbyterian minister, was killed at the Battle of Alamance in 1771). Joseph Erwin, born 1761, Guilford Co., N. C., died April 14th, 1829 in Iberville Parish, La., married Lavinia Thompson, born Jan. 28, 1763 in North Carolina and died Feb. 13, 1836 in

APPENDIX 221

Iberville Parish. (She had first married James McCamey.) Their children were:

I. John   V. Eliza
II. Jane   VI. Nancy
III. Leodocia VII. Joseph
IV. Thompson VIII. Isaac

See *North Carolina State Department of Archives and History.* "The North Carolina Revolutionary Army Accounts," Vol. I, page 39, folio 2, shows payment to Joseph Erwin as member of Revolutionary Army forces. Vol. 6, Page 40, shows Hillsboro, treasurer, paid him as member.

I

JOHN ERWIN

John Erwin, born December 20, 1783 in North Carolina, died February 25, 1828 in Iberville Parish, married Margaret Rivers, a native of Greenville Co., Virginia whose parents brought her to Tennessee as a girl. She was descended from Col. John Flood of Jameston, Virginia who came from England in 1610. She died on May 12, 1830. Their children were:

1. Joseph died young.
2. Eliza married (1) James M. Cummings, (2) Benj. F. Holmes.
3. Margaret married Fred M. Kent of East Baton Rouge.
4. Leodocia died young.
5. Martha married Isadore Larguier of East Baton Rouge.
6. Thomas Rivers Erwin went to Texas in 1832 where he married in 1836, Mrs. Harriet Cox of Brazoria Co. He then moved to California and then to Louisiana. He had two children, Thomas R. who did not marry, and Harriet who married P. Eugene Freeman. They had three daughters.
7. Lavinia died December 14, 1844, she married (1) Warren Aborn, (2) John Perico.

II

JANE ERWIN

Jane Erwin, born June 25, 1787, died July 28, 1821, first married Charles Dickinson, their child was:

Charles Dickinson, married Maria A. Turner, they had three children.
1. Ann Jane
2. Mary Augusta, 1841, 1872, (wife of Andrew H. Gay.)
3. Charles Henry

Jane Erwin after death of her first husband married John B. Craighead. Their children were:

1. Joseph Erwin Craighead who married Phoebe White, he died Nov. 1847) and had Robert, Thomas B., Charles D., Jane, William J. and John B., Jr.

2. Thomas B. Craighead.

III

LEODOCIA ERWIN

Leodocia Erwin, born November 2, 1789, died August 1, 1852, married William Blount Robertson, son of Gen. James Robertson founder of Nashville. Their children were:

1. Charles D. Robertson

2. William B., Jr.

3. James E.

4. Tennessee married Charles W. Combs

5. Lavinia married Augustus Talbot

6. Edward W.

For a complete list of the descendants of Leodocia Erwin Robertson, see Appendix B. No. 9, Page 550 "Gen. James Robertson, Father of Tennessee" by Thomas Edwin Matthews.

IV

THOMPSON

Thompson Erwin died young November 27, 1791.

V

ELIZA ERWIN

Eliza Erwin, born December 20, 1793 in North Carolina, died July 3, 1834 in Iberville Parish, she married Nicholas Wilson October 22, 1813 at Nashville. Nicholas Wilson was born April 5, 1786 in Colerain, Ireland and died October 17, 1825 in Iberville Parish, La., Their children were:

1. Catherine, born Aug. 20, 1813, died Feb. 9, 1882, she first married D. D. Chesnut, they had three children: Amelia who married Simon O. Landry, Eliza who married F. A. Kent and Catherine, who married Dr. Albers. Her second husband was Lorin Very.

2. Lavinia, born March 28, 1815, married first David Barrow, who died shortly after his marriage, their child David Barrow, Jr. married Lucretia Pilcher. Their children were: David, III, who married Ella Mimms, Ann Lavinia who married B. C. LeBlanc and Nellie who married Joseph Gore. The widow of David Barrow later married William E. Edwards, their children were: Eliza who married Seay, Greek Scholar and Prof. of L. S. U. at Pineville; Belle perished on Steamboat "Fashion"; Jennie married Bemiss of N. O., their children were Bessie (Mrs. John Carlson of Seattle, Wash.) Mattie and Belle; Maria married James Wilson, died in Paris, France; Ida married Alfred H. Clement and their children were, Alfred H. and William E.; other children of Lavinia were Whithal, Nicholas, Henry and William.

3. Caroline, born July 13, 1825, first married Charles H. Sheafe then Simms of Baltimore.

4. John, born Dec. 1822, married but no children.

5. Joseph Erwin, born March 16, 1817, died 1885, went to Texas 1840, married Theresa A. McGreal on April 1, 1842 at Brazoria, she died 1910. Their children were:

   a. Erwin Nicholas,* died 1888, married Ella McGrew, their children were: Lucille who married Dr. S. M. Lister (Houston), Joseph Erwin* who had two daughters, John McGrew* who had two children and Ashley Fly, who has four sons.

   b. Eugene Joseph,* died 1921, married Anna Della Sweeney, who died 1904, their children were: Eugene Jr., Louis Janin,* who married Dec. 19, 1900, Josephine Wesiger; Willie D.,* died 1927, married Mildred Wortham in 1908, their children were, Eugene,* who had a daughter, and Helen who married Poris A. Smith of Bay City, Texas who had a son; Mary Alice died young; Terese married 1909 Flint McGregor, their daughter married Jesse B. Gilmer of El Paso on Dec. 1934, they have a daughter and live at Amarillo, Texas; Rosea married Effie Bromfield of Lubbock, Texas.

   c. Carrie E. died in 1934.

   d Lavinia E. died 1902, married Dr. John C. Ashcom, had no children.

   e. Louis Janin

   f. Alice died 1878, married S. M. Field, had no children.

   g. Kate married Dr. A. W. Fly of Galveston, no children.

   h. Walter L.,* died 1918, married had one daughter.

6. Alexander born Dec. 6, 1818, married Josephine Baronheit.

*Lawyers.

VI

NANCY ERWIN

Ann (Nancy) Erwin, born Aug. 10, 1796, died Feb. 12, 1837, she married Col. Andrew Hynes, March 2, 1817. Their children were:

1. Margaret, who died March 1848, she married Andrew Ewing, their child was Andrew Ewing.
2. Mary Jane, married Phocian R. McCreary.
3. Lavinia who married Edward J. Gay of St. Louis, Mo., owner of St. Louis Plantation, Iberville Parish, La., their children were:
   a. Nancy, married Andrew Price.
   b. John, married Nana Connor.
   c. Andrew, who first married Mary Augustus Dickinson, their children were: Anna; Andrew H.; Lavinia; and Mamie Sue. After her death he married Lodoiska Clement, their children were Edward J. born May 5, 1878; and Charles and Henrietta, who died in infancy.
4. William R.

VII

JOSEPH ERWIN

Born July 25, 1798. Died about 1835.

VIII

ISAAC ERWIN

Isaac Erwin, born Jan. 17, 1800, died 1872, married first Mary Nichols of Nashville Aug. 9, 1821, she died Sept. 9, 1832. (Mary Nichols was the daughter of Capt. John Nichols, a friend of Joseph Erwin). Their children were:

1. Jane Nichols
2. John Nichols
3. Joseph Henry
4. William B.
5. Thomas G.

He then married Carmelite Picou of Iberville. From this union ten children were born, one of whom, Leudivine (died Feb. 5, 1935), married Stephen Garrett, they had two children, Mrs. Cammie Henry and Stephen Garrett.

t

APPENDIX 225

CLEMENT GENEALOGY

Charles Clement, born August 24, 1745, married Sarah Titus, born
February 2, 1753. Their children were:

I. Henry Clement, born December 14, 1773.

II. Amy Clement, September 28, 1775.

III. Jonathan Clement, born February 18, 1778.

IV. Samuel Clement, born January 4, 1781.

V. Sarah Clement, born December 14, 1783.

VI. Amy Clement, born April 26, 1786.

VII. Joanna, born January 17, 1789.

VIII. Charles Clement, born October 19, 1793.

IX. Charles Clement, born November 22, 1797, married Henrietta
Desobry, born December 23, 1804. Their children were:

1. Mary Fort Clement, born May 2, 1828, married Gervais Schlater
on October 29, 1846, their children were:

a. Mary Pamela Schlater, born July 31, 1847, married James
H. Grover on August 1, 1867.

b. Henrietta Clementine Schlater, born November 26, 1848, married Richard T. Semmes in 1870.

c. Henry Clement Schlater, born November 16, 1851.

d. Edwin Schlater, born October 16, 1853.

2. Henrietta Clement, born February 19, 1830.

3. Sarah Clement, born March 2, 1832.

4. Minerva Clement, born May 5, 1833, married Jacob McWilliams
July 23, 1856.

5. Charles Clement, born April 27, 1835.

6. Maria Dickinson Clement, born October 30, 1836, married George
L. Bright, May 15, 1856. Their children were:

a. Mary Ozilton Bright, born April 30, 1857, died June 11,
1950. She married Lucas E. Moore.

b. Henrietta Clementine Bright, born July 9, 1858, married
Chester John Inches Dec. 3, 1884

c. George Clement Bright, born September 22, 1862.

d. Ella M. Bright, born January 8, 1864, married James T.
Wood.

7. Alfred Henry Clement, born August 23, 1838, married Ida Edwards. Their children were:

226 APPENDIX

a. William Edwards Clement, born Oct. 17, 1878.

b. Alfred H. Clement, Jr., born Sept. 3, 1877.

8. Laura Clement, born October 28, 1840, married Henry Carlton Miller, their children were:

a. Henrietta Augusta Miller, born July 6, 1867.

b. Laura Maria Miller, born October 8, 1868.

c. Charles Clement Miller, born July 11, 1870.

d. Ethel Axton Miller, born April 12, 1880.

9. Lodoiska Clement, born April 12, 1843, married Andrew H. Gay, their children were:

a. Edward J. Gay, born May 5, 1878.

b. Henrietta Clement Gay, born Oct. 31, 1879, died August 21, 1882.

c. Charles Clement Gay, born Sept. 11, 1881, died Dec. 18, 1882.

THE WILSON FAMILY

The Wilson family is an old Scotch-Irish Presbyterian family. They came to America after the Erwins and settled in Pennsylvania. President Wilson was probably connected with this family since his branch came from a nearby county in Ireland, County Tyrone, and lived about twenty miles from Coleraine. They settled in Ohio not far from Washington, Pennsylvania.

Marcus Wilson came to America from Coleraine, County of Londonderry, Ireland. He had five children. On June 26, 1786 he and his family including the wife of John, the eldest son, and their infant son Nicholas came to America. Alexander settled in Philadelphia. James went to Washington, Pa., where he died 1828 aged 70 years. John and family (with his father) remained three years in Philadelphia. In 1789 they went to Washington, Pa. John was a cabinet maker. He was elected Justice of the Peace Feb. 1, 1799 and held this office until old age. He was 85 years old when he died. He had 12 children. They married well and their children and children's children were often prominent and well-to-do. Many of his descendants are listed in Who's Who in America. Among them are Richard Harding Davis and Rebecca Harding Davis.

John's wife—Catherine Cunningham Wilson—lived to be nearly 90 years old. She was a remarkable old lady and impressed the family and friends with her piety, her dutifulness, her character and ability. She was a poet. She was the mother of twelve and at the time of her death her grand children numbered 73, her great grand children 112 and her great-great-grandchildren 5. These latter were Nicholas' descendants, one of whom was the father of Stuart O. Landry.

Marcus Wilson was born 1721 in Ireland, died 1812. He married Martha Campbell in Ireland. Their children were:

1. Alexander

2. Isaac

3. James

4. Marcus

5. John who was born 1762 in Coleraine, Ireland, died March 16, 1847 at Washington, Pa. He married in Coleraine, Ireland, Catherine Cunningham, born 1769 in Coleraine, died Dec. 15, 1857, Washington, Pa. She was the daughter of Christopher Cunningham (born 1731, died 1773) and Mary Henderson (born 1732, died 1786).

   Her sister married the Episcopal Bishop of North Ireland. John and Catherine's children were:

   a. Nicholas, born April 5, 1786 in Coleraine, Ireland, died Oct. 17, 1825, Iberville Parish, married Eliza Erwin Oct. 22, 1812 at Nashville, Eliza was born Dec. 20, 1793 in North Carolina and died Jan. 1834 in Iberville Parish.

   b. Mary
   c. Martha
   d. Margaret
   e. Jane
   f. Marcus
   g. Ann
   h. John K.
   i. Catherine
   j. Alexander
   k. James
   l. Eleanor

DICKINSON GENEALOGY

Rebecca Thomas, born 1662 was the widow of Solomon Thomas and the daughter of Dr. Thomas Wynne and his wife Martha Brittall, who died in 1670. Dr. Wynne was the personal physician of William Penn, and Speaker of the First Assembly of Pennsylvania. He was born in North Wales in 1627 and came to Pennsylvania with William Penn in the good ship "Welcome" in 1682. Dr. Wynne died March 17, 1692.

John Dickinson, married Rebecca (Thomas) Wynne Sept. 16, 1692. His will was probated April 29, 1718. These Dickinsons lived in Talbot Co., moved to Dorchester Co., Md. Their children were:

   I. John

   II. Charles

   III. Sidney

   IV. Mary Kersey

I

JOHN

John, born 1693 (John's son, John Dickinson of Talbot Co., Md., born 1732, died 1808 was an American Statesman and Member of Pennsylvania Assembly, the Continental Congress and Federal Constitutional Convention. He wrote many pamphlets in the cause of freedom and was called "The Penman of the Revolution." He was a private and later a Brig. Gen. in Revolutionary War. See Article in Enc. Brit.)

II

CHARLES

Charles, born 1695, married Sophia Richardson,* July 8, 1725. His will probated Nov. 4, 1779. Charles was prominent—a justice of the Co. 12 years. Later part of Dorchester Co., was made into Caroline Co., and a member of the Committee of Correspondence. Charles and Sophia's children were:

1. Henry† of Caroline Co., Md. died about Nov. 1789, married Elizabeth Walker about 1775, who died about 1786. She was the daughter of Rev. Philip Walker. Dickinson married the 2nd time in 1787, Debora Perry. Henry was elected Lt. Col. of the East Battalion that fought in the Revolution. He became an Episcopalian. He was active in the cause of the Freedom of Maryland. Held several offices of honor. Henry and Elizabeth's children were:

    A. Charles of Caroline Co. (born 1778, died May 30, 1806) married Jane Erwin of Nashville, Tenn. (born June 27, 1787, died July 28, 1821). Jane married (2) James B. Craighead of Nashville. Charles and Jane's child was:

        a. Charles Henry Dickinson, born March 9, 1806, died July 5, 1846, married April 17, 1828, Anna Maria Turner born Oct. 14, 1814, died Jan. 1886. Charles and Anna Maria had three children, Anna Jane, Mary A., and a son Charles H. Dickinson, born 1846 died 1898. This Civil War veteran, Dickinson, in 1869 married Charlotte Elizabeth Devall, a plantation owning family of the Port Allen, Louisiana section. Their children were Mary Gay, Anna Jane, Frances Taber, Charles Henry, Cora Lee, Augusta L., Bessie Devall,

---

*Sophia Richardson was the daughter of Daniel Richardson who married Elizabeth Welsh (his will dated April 7, 1722). Daniel was the son of Wm. Richardson and Elizabeth (1st Talbot) Ewen (will probated May 28, 1698). (For Richardson genealogy see Warfields "Founders of Anne Arundal and Howard Counties Maryland"; H. D. Richardson's "Sidelights on Maryland History"; "History of Caroline Co., Md."; wills, deeds of Maryland, etc.)

†A provision of Col. Henry Dickinson's will "I also give the said Charles my Coat of Arms."

Andrew Gay, Minerva McWilliams, David Devall and Edith
Kent Dickinson.
After Charles Dickinson's death, Jane Erwin married J. B.
Craighead, their children were: Joseph Erwin Craighead,
Thos. B. Craighead.

B. Philip
C. Elizabeth
D. Rebecca who married Thos. Daffin.

(Charles and Sophia's children were also):

2. John
3. Sydney (girl)
4. Margrete

References for Dickinson Genealogy: Deed books and Will books of
Maryland; Maryland Historical Society; Pa. Historical Society; Tenn.
Historical Society; History of Caroline Co., Md.; W. H. Watson's History
of the Dickinson Family.

MARRIAGE CONTRACT BETWEEN HENRIETTA DESOBRY
AND DR. CHARLES CLEMENT

Record of Conveyances — Book K — Sept. 1823 - Jan. 1826 No. 660
Parish of Iberville

Be it known that on this thirtieth day of June in the year of Our Lord
one thousand eight hundred and twenty six that before me John Dutton,
Parish Judge in and for the Parish of Iberville, personally came and appeared Dr. Charles Clement of the said Parish, native of Washington,
Duchess County, and State of New York of the one part, he being of the
age and majority, and Henrietta Desobry, also of the said Parish, native
of Baracoa, Cuba, minor daughter of Felix Desobry deceased and Francoise
Abelard, the said Henrietta duly authorized herein by her mother for that
purpose here present of the other part, which parties taking into view their
intention of entering into and joining in marriage have made and entered
into the following articles agreement.

Article First:— The said Henrietta Desobry brings in marriage a
negro girl named Francoise, aged about ?

Article Second:— The said Francoise Abelard declared Widow of
Felix Desobry deceased declared that she makes a donation pure and
simple and irrevocable inter vivos in favour of marriage to her said
Daughter Henrietta Desobry, who accepts same with assistance of her
curator ad hoc Louis Desobry, the aforesaid negro girl Francoise.

Article Third:— It is agreed by and between the parties that the
amount of the property of the future husband is four thousand dollars, con-

sisting in a slave name William, and in sundry sums of money now in his possession or due to him by mortgages and other titles.

Article Fourth:— The future husband declares that in case the said future wife should survive him without issue born of said marriage, and gains at his decease shall not amount to the sum of four thousand dollars, that the future wife shall take and enjoy out of the property that may remain between them at his decease, one half thereof for her own use and benefit forever.

Article Fifth:— There shall exist no legal ortant mortgage on the property of the future husband or on the property to be acquired during said marriage.

Whereof an act this:—

Thus done and passed in my office in presence of J. A. Haase, and Robert Loyd witnesses who have signed with the parties and me the said judge.

Charles Clement	Robert Loyd
Henrietta Desobry	J. A. Haase
Louise Desobry	John Dutton, Judge.

9 781565 544369

Printed in the United States
869400002B